OXFORD TEXTBOOKS IN LINGUISTICS

Series editors
Keith Brown, Eve V. Clark, April McMahon, Jim Miller, and Lesley Milroy

Pragmatics

OXFORD TEXTBOOKS IN LINGUISTICS

Pragmatics

Yan Huang

OXFORD
UNIVERSITY PRESS

OXFORD

UNIVERSITY PRESS

Great Clarendon Street, Oxford OX2 6DP

Oxford University Press is a department of the University of Oxford.
It furthers the University's objective of excellence in research, scholarship,
and education by publishing worldwide in

Oxford New York

Auckland Cape Town Dar es Salaam Hong Kong Karachi
Kuala Lumpur Madrid Melbourne Mexico City Nairobi
New Delhi Shanghai Taipei Toronto

With offices in

Argentina Austria Brazil Chile Czech Republic France Greece
Guatemala Hungary Italy Japan Poland Portugal Singapore
South Korea Switzerland Thailand Turkey Ukraine Vietnam

Oxford is a registered trade mark of Oxford University Press
in the UK and in certain other countries

Published in the United States
by Oxford University Press Inc., New York

© Yan Huang 2007

British Library Cataloguing in Publication Data
Data available

Library of Congress Cataloging in Publication Data
Data available

Typeset by SPI Publisher Services, Pondicherry, India
Printed in Great Britain by the
MPG Books Group, Bodmin and King's Lynn

ISBN 978–0–19–929837–2 (Hbk.)   978–0–19–924368–6 (Pbk.)

7 9 10 8 6

Contents

Symbols and abbreviations

Symbols

~	negation
+>	conversationally implicates
~ +>	does not conversationally implicate
+>>	conventionally implicates
~ +>>	does not conventionally implicate
>>	presupposes
~ >>	does not presuppose
‖-	entails
~ ‖-	does not entail
< >	Q- or Horn-scale
[ ]	I-scale
{ }	M-scale
K	speaker knows that
*	example sentence that follows is syntactically ill-formed or semantically anomalous
?	the example utterance that follows is pragmatically anomalous

Abbreviations

ACC	accusative case
ADDR	addressee pronoun
AFF	affirmative
AGR	agreement
ART	article
ASP	aspect
AUX	auxiliary

CAUS	causative
CL	classifier
CLI	clitic
CMP	comparative
CNJ	conjunctive
COMP	complementizer
CTR	contrastive
DAT	dative
DECL	declarative
DEF	definite
DEM	demonstrative
DIR	directional
DUL	dual
DUR	durative
EMPH	emphatic
ERG	ergative
EVD	evidential
F	feminine gender
FOC	focus
FUT	future
GEN	genitive
GER	generic
HON	honorific
IMPF	imperfective
IMPV	imperative
INDEF	indefinite
INDIC	indicative
INF	infinitive
INS	instrumental
IRR	irrealis
LF	Logical Form
LOC	locative
LOG	logophor/logophoric
M	masculine gender
MOD	modality
N	neuter gender
NEG	negative
NOM	nominative/nominalizer

NP	noun phrase
OBJ	object
OBV	obviative
PASS	passive
PAST	past tense
PERF	perfective
PF	Phonological Form
PL	plural
POSS	possessive
PRES	present tense
PREP	preposition
PROG	progressive
PRON	pronoun
PROX	proximate
PRT	particle
PURP	purposive
Q	question marker
REAL	realis
REFL	reflexive
REL	relative marker
SBJV	subjunctive
SBOR	subordinator
SEQ	sequential
SG	singular
SIM	simultaneous
SUBJ	subject
TNS	tense
TOP	topic
1	first person
2	second person
3	third person

The abbreviations used in the glosses of the original sources are retained, except for those that have been altered for the sake of uniformity. For abbreviations that are non-conventional and/or language-specific, consult the original examples.

For my daughter, Elizabeth; my wife, Lihua Li; and my parents

from Hurford and Heasley 1983: 23). What (1.25) basically says is that a proposition, being the most abstract of the three notions, can be expressed by different sentences. A given sentence, being the next most abstract of the three notions, can itself be instantiated by different utterances, which are the least abstract of the three notions.

(1.25)   Relationship between sentence, utterance, and proposition

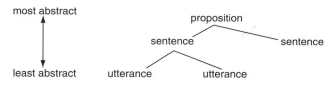

1.3.2. Context

We move next to **context**. Context is one of those notions which is used very widely in the linguistics literature, but to which it is difficult to give a precise definition. From a relatively theory-neutral point of view, however, context may in a broader sense be defined as referring to any relevant features of the dynamic setting or environment in which a linguistic unit is systematically used. Furthermore, context can be seen as composed of three different sources—a view known as the 'geographic' division of context (Ariel 1990). In the first place, there is the physical context, which refers to the physical setting of the utterance. For example, the interpretation of (1.26) depends on the knowledge computable from the physical context of the utterance, that is, the spatio-temporal location of the utterance.

(1.26)   *He*'s not the chief executive; *he* is. *He*'s the managing director.

The second type is the linguistic context, which refers to the surrounding utterances in the same discourse. What has been mentioned in the previous discourse, for instance, plays a crucial role in understanding the elliptical construction used by Mary in (1.27).

(1.27)   John: Who gave the waiter a large tip?
          Mary: Helen.

Thirdly and finally, we have the general knowledge context.[4] The information derivable from this type of context explains why (1.28a) is pragmatically well-formed but (1.28b) is pragmatically anomalous. This is because, given our real-world knowledge, we know that whereas there is a Forbidden City in Beijing, there is no such a tourist attraction in Paris.

(1.28)   a. I went to Beijing last month. The Forbidden City was magnificent.
         b. ?I went to Paris last month. The Forbidden City was magnificent.

Clearly, what is involved here is a set of background assumptions shared by the speaker and the addressee. Stalnaker (1974) called this **common ground**. The notion of common ground has been further developed by Clark (1996), who distinguished communal from personal common ground. The former refers to the set of background assumptions shared by members of a community, and the latter to the body of background knowledge two members of a community share from their past experience of each other (see also Roberts 2004 for a survey of the dynamic treatment of context in a number of formal semantic theories including Discourse Representation Theory (DRT), Dynamic Montague Grammar, and File Change Semantics).

1.3.3. Truth value, truth condition, entailment

Finally, we come to the three central notions of truth value, truth condition, and entailment.

Truth value and truth condition

The notion of **truth value** is associated with that of proposition, and the notion of **truth condition** is linked to that of sentence.

As already mentioned, a proposition may be true or false. But the truth or falsity of a proposition may vary from utterance occasion to utterance occasion. For example, the proposition expressed by the sentence *The book is on the desk*, when uttered as a statement, is true in a situation where the book is indeed on the desk, but is false in another situation where the book is not on the desk. However, on a particular occasion, a proposition has a definite truth value,

---

[4] Other terms include background, common-sense, encyclopaedic knowledge, and real-world knowledge context.

that is, it is either true or false. It is true if and only if it corresponds to some state of affairs that obtains on that occasion, and it is false if and only if it does not. This is known variously as the 'corresponding', 'realistic', or 'simple' theory of truth (e.g., Bradley and Swartz 1979).

On the other hand, while a sentence, outside particular uses, does not have a truth value, it does have truth conditions. What, then, are truth conditions? They are the conditions that the world must meet for the sentence to be true. A classic example, which originated with the logician Alfred Tarski, is given in (1.29).

(1.29)   *Snow is white* is true if and only if snow is white.

What (1.29) tells us is under what conditions the English sentence *Snow is white* may be used to make a true statement about the external world. Or, put slightly differently, it tells us what condition must hold for the world, for the proposition expressed by the English sentence *Snow is white* to be true.

Abstracting away from (1.29), we obtain the basic Tarskian formula for a theory of truth in (1.30).

(1.30)   *S* is true if and only if *p*,

where *S* is the name of a sentence in a language, and *p* is the set of conditions under which that sentence is true.

Let us now look at an illustration of how the notion of truth condition can contribute to sentence-meaning. Consider (1.31).

(1.31)   a. Only John$_1$ voted for John$_1$.
      b. Only John$_1$ voted for himself$_1$.

Assuming that John was not the only person who voted, the question that arises is whether (1.31a) and (1.31b) share the same truth conditions. The answer is negative. This is because for (1.31a) to be true, John must have received only one vote, namely, the vote from himself, but there is no such truth condition for (1.31b). For (1.31b) to be true, John could have received all the votes including the one from himself (e.g., Huang 2000a: 242). Therefore, the meanings of (1.31a) and (1.31b) are different simply because the truth conditions for (1.31a) and (1.31b) are different.

On the other hand, there are aspects of meaning that cannot be accounted for in terms of truth conditions. A simple example illustrating this point is given in (1.32) below.

(1.32)   a. We want peace and they want war.
         b. We want peace but they want war.

(1.32a) and (1.32b) share the exactly same truth conditions. However, the use of *but* in (1.32b) conveys a contrast between the information contained in the first conjunct and that contained in the second conjunct. Clearly, the meaning expressed by the use of *but* (standardly called a **conventional implicature**, about which more in Chapter 2), is not captured by the notion of truth condition.

Entailment

Next, the semantic relation of **entailment** can be defined in terms of truth as follows.

(1.33)   A proposition (or sentence expressing a proposition) p entails a proposition (or sentence expressing a proposition) q if and only if the truth of p guarantees the truth of q.[5]

What (1.33) basically says is this: for p to entail q, whenever p is true, q is also true. By way of illustration, let us take a few examples.

(1.34)   a. The guerrillas killed the American ambassador.
         b. The American ambassador died.

In this pair of sentences, (1.34a) entails (1.34b). This is because if it is true that the guerrillas killed a certain American ambassador, then it follows ineluctably that the American ambassador died. The same story holds for (1.35).

(1.35)   a. There's a horse on the grassland.
         b. There's an animal on the grassland.

Whenever there is some entity that is a horse, then it is necessarily the case that this is also an animal, and hence (1.35a) entails (1.35b). Finally (1.36).

(1.36)   a. All of the company's employees got a pay rise.
         b. Some of the company's employees got a pay rise.

---

[5] Notice that a few authors, such as Saeed (2003) and Cruse (2004), adopted a narrower definition for entailment. One such definition is as follows (Saeed 2003: 98): 'A sentence p entails a sentence q when the truth of the first (p) guarantees the truth of the second (q), and the falsity of the second (q) guarantees the falsity of the first (p).'

Again in this pair, (1.36a) entails (1.36b). The reason is that if it is true that all of the company's employees got a pay rise, then there is no way to avoid the conclusion that it is also true that some of the company's employees got a pay rise.

Now try Exercise 2 on pp. 18–19.

Note finally that one of the most important properties of an entailment is that it is not **defeasible**, that is, an entailment cannot disappear in any linguistic or non-linguistic context. This is why it must be seen as semantic in nature. In fact, a number of other semantic relations such as equivalence and contradiction can also be defined in terms of entailment.

1.4. Organization of the book

The remainder of this book is divided into two parts. Part I covers those topics that are standardly included in a pragmatics textbook. Within this part, Chapter 2 is concerned with classical and neo-Gricean pragmatic theories of conversational and conventional implicature. The focus of Chapter 3 is on presupposition. Chapter 4 is devoted to speech act theory, concentrating on the classic work by Austin and Searle. Chapter 5 provides a descriptive analysis of various types of deixis.

Part II deals with topics which represent new ground in pragmatics, but which are under-represented in any of the existing pragmatics coursebooks. In particular, it focuses on various interfaces between pragmatics and other (core) areas of inquiry. Chapter 6 discusses the pragmatics–cognition interface, concentrating on Sperber and Wilson's relevance theory. The interface between pragmatics and semantics is the topic of Chapter 7. Finally, Chapter 8 examines the interaction and division of labour between pragmatics and syntax, focusing on anaphora and binding.

Key concepts

pragmatics
syntax
semantics

Part I

Central topics in pragmatics

This part covers those topics that are standardly included in a pragmatics textbook. Chapter 2 is concerned with classical and neo-Gricean pragmatic theories of implicature. The focus of Chapter 3 is on presupposition. Chapter 4 is devoted to speech act theory, concentrating on the classic work by Austin and Searle. Chapter 5 provides an in-depth descriptive analysis of various types of deixis.

2

Implicature

The notion of **implicature** (both **conversational** and **conventional**) was originated by the Oxford philosopher H. P. Grice.[1] The central ideas were introduced by him in the William James lectures delivered at Harvard in 1967 and were partially collected and published in Grice (1989). In these lectures, Grice presented a panorama of his thinking on meaning and communication—what he called his 'tottering steps' (Grice 1989: 4) towards a systematic, philosophically inspired pragmatic theory of language use, which has since come to be known as Gricean pragmatic theory. Since its inception, the Gricean paradigm has revolutionized pragmatic theorizing and to date remains one of the cornerstones of contemporary thinking in linguistic pragmatics and the philosophy of language.

This chapter is organized as follows. Section 2.1 discusses the classical Gricean theory of conversational implicature. In Section 2.2, I present two neo-Gricean pragmatic theories of conversational implicature.

[1] Though some proto-Gricean ideas can be traced back at least to the fourth-century rhetoricians Servius and Donatus, later to be reiterated by the nineteenth-century English philosophers John Stuart Mill and Augustus De Morgan (Horn 1988, 2004). See Chapman (2005) on the life and work of Grice.

Finally, Section 2.3 examines the notion of conventional implicature, comparing and contrasting it with conversational implicature.

2.1. Classical Gricean theory of conversational implicature

On a general Gricean account of meaning and communication, there are two theories: a theory of **meaning$_{n[on]n[atural]}$** and a theory of conversational implicature. In his theory of meaning$_{nn}$, Grice (1957, 1969, 1989) emphasized the conceptual relation between natural meaning in the external world and non-natural, linguistic meaning of utterances.[2] He developed a reductive analysis of meaning$_{nn}$ in terms of the speaker's intentions.

(2.1)   Grice's theory of meaning$_{nn}$

S means$_{nn}$ p by 'uttering' U to A if and only if S intends:
- (i)   A to think p,
- (ii) A to recognize that S intends (i), and
- (iii) A's recognition of S's intending (i) to be the primary reason for A thinking p.

where S stands for the speaker, A for the audience, U for the utterance, and p for proposition (see also Levinson 2000: 13).

Defined thus, the essence of meaning$_{nn}$ is that it is communication which is intended to be recognized as having been intended. In other words, meaning$_{nn}$ or speaker-meaning is a matter of expressing and recognizing intention (but see Gauker 2003 for a dissenting view). What is of theoretical interest here is that as pointed out by Levinson (2000: 13), 'meaning$_{nn}$

---

[2] According to Grice (1957, 1969, 1989), in the case of natural meaning, x means that p entails p. This explains why (ii) is semantically anomalous.

Grice (1989: 213)
- (i)   Those spots meant measles.
- (ii) *Those spots meant measles, but he hadn't got measles.

By comparison, in the case of non-natural meaning or meaning$_{nn}$, x means that p does not entail p. Now contrast (iii) and (iv) with (i) and (ii) above.

(Grice 1989: 214)
- (iii) Those three rings on the bell (of the bus) mean that the bus is full.
- (iv) Those three rings on the bell (of the bus) mean that the bus is full. But it isn't in fact full—the conductor has made a mistake.

(or something of the sort) draws an outer boundary on the communicational effects that a theory of communication is responsible for'.

2.1.1. The co-operative principle and the maxims of conversation

In his theory of **conversational implicature**, Grice (1961, 1975, 1978, 1989) suggested that there is an underlying principle that determines the way in which language is used with maximum efficiency and effectively to achieve rational interaction in communication. He called this overarching dictum the **co-operative principle** and subdivided it into nine **maxims of conversation** classified into four categories: Quality, Quantity, Relation and Manner. The names of the four categories are taken from the German philosopher Immanuel Kant (Grice 1989: 26). The co-operative principle and its component maxims ensure that in an exchange of conversation, the right amount of information is provided and that the interaction is conducted in a truthful, relevant and perspicuous manner.

(2.2) Grice's theory of conversational implicature
  a. The co-operative principle
     Make your conversational contribution such as is required, at the stage at which it occurs, by the accepted purpose or direction of the talk exchange in which you are engaged.
  b. The maxims of conversation
     Quality: Try to make your contribution one that is true.
        (i) Do not say what you believe to be false.
        (ii) Do not say that for which you lack adequate evidence.
     Quantity:
        (i) Make your contribution as informative as is required (for the current purposes of the exchange).
        (ii) Do not make your contribution more informative than is required.
     Relation: Be relevant.
     Manner: Be perspicuous.
        (i) Avoid obscurity of expression.
        (ii) Avoid ambiguity.
        (iii) Be brief (avoid unnecessary prolixity).
        (iv) Be orderly.

The Gricean co-operative principle and its attendant maxims in (2.2) can be simplified in (2.3) (Huang 2000a: 206).

(2.3)   Grice's theory of conversational implicature (simplified)
   a. The co-operative principle
      Be co-operative.
   b. The maxims of conversation
      Quality: Be truthful.
         (i) Don't say what is false.
         (ii) Don't say what lacks evidence.
      Quantity:
         (i) Don't say less than is required.
         (ii) Don't say more than is required.
      Relation: Be relevant.
      Manner: Be perspicuous.
         (i) Avoid obscurity.
         (ii) Avoid ambiguity.
         (iii) Be brief.
         (iv) Be orderly.

2.1.2. Relationship between the speaker and the maxims

What can a speaker do with regard to the maxims? In the first place, he or she can straightforwardly observe the maxims. Second, he or she can violate a maxim. For example, he or she may breach the first submaxim of Quality by telling a deliberate lie.[3] Third, he or she can opt out of a maxim. This can be demonstrated by a speaker's use of hedges in conversation.

(2.4)   Opting out hedges in English
   a. Quality:
      As far as I know,
      I'm not sure if this is true, but...
      I may be wrong, but...
   b. Quantity:
      As you probably already know,
      I can't say any more,
      I probably don't need to say this, but...

---

[3] There are, of course, circumstances under which the speaker is not expected to follow the maxims. In a court of law, for example, witnesses are often not required to volunteer information, thereby violating the maxim of Quantity.

   c. Relation:
      Oh, by the way,
      I'm not sure if this is relevant, but...
      I don't want to change the subject, but...
   d. Manner:
      I'm not sure if this is clear, but...
      I don't know if this makes sense, but...
      This may be a bit tedious, but...

There is thus evidence that speakers are not only aware of the maxims, but they are trying to follow them. Fourthly, a speaker can ostentatiously **flout** or **exploit** a maxim, to be illustrated shortly (see also Grice 1989: 30).

> At this point, have a go at Exercises 1 and 2 on p. 59.

2.1.3. Conversational implicature$_O$ versus conversational implicature$_F$

Assuming that the co-operative principle and its associated maxims are normally adhered to by both the speaker and the addressee in a conversational interaction, Grice suggested that a conversational implicature— roughly, a set of non-logical inferences which contains conveyed messages which are meant without being part of what is said in the strict sense[4]—can arise from either strictly **observing** or ostentatiously **flouting** the maxims. Let us call conversational implicatures that are engendered by way of directly observing the maxims **conversational implicatures$_O$**. As an illustration, consider (2.5)–(2.8) (I use '+>' to stand for 'conversationally implicates').

(2.5) Quality:
      Tim Berners-Lee invented the World Wide Web in 1989.
      +> The speaker believes that Tim Berners-Lee invented the World Wide Web in 1989, and has adequate evidence that he did

---

[4] See also Horn's (2004: 3) more recent definition of conversational implicature as 'a component of speaker meaning that constitutes an aspect of what is meant in a speaker's utterance without being part of what is said'.

(2.6)   Quantity:
       John has six credit cards.
       +> John has at most six credit cards
(2.7)   Relation:
       John: What's the time?
       Mary: The museum hasn't opened yet.
       +> It's at least before whenever the museum normally opens
(2.8)   Manner:
       John went to a McDonald's and bought two hamburgers.
       +>John first went to a McDonald's and then bought two hamburgers[5]

Given the second submaxim of Quality, when a speaker makes an assertion, he or she conversationally implies that he or she believes it, hence the relevant conversational implicature in (2.5). The submaxim can also account for '**Moore's paradox**', so called by Wittgenstein (1953: 190). The paradox is concerned with the question why an utterance such as (2.9) is pragmatically anomalous. The answer is straightforward: (2.9) is a violation of the epistemic commitment of what a speaker asserts (Levinson 1983: 105, see also Grice 1989: 42, Austin 1962, Gazdar 1979, Atlas 1993, Bach 2004).

(2.9)   ?Tim Berners-Lee invented the World Wide Web in 1989,
       but I don't believe he did.

(2.6) exemplifies the fulfilment of the first submaxim of Quantity. Since the speaker has used a semantically weaker expression (i.e., the cardinal number six), where a semantically stronger one of equal brevity (e.g., the cardinal number seven) is available, he or she would contradict the first submaxim of Quantity if the semantically stronger expression held. Consequently, he or she believes that the semantically stronger statement does not hold. Furthermore, he or she has not done anything to stop the addressee from thinking that he or she thinks so; therefore he or she conversationally implicates that John has at most six credit cards,[6] although

---

[5] Of course, (2.8) can also conversationally implicate (i) below.

(i)   John went to a McDonald's in order to buy two hamburgers

[6] Fretheim (1992) argued that the 'at most' interpretation of a cardinal number in Norwegian can be conversationally implicated only if the cardinal number is contextually salient. This is signalled by certain intonational patterns of the language. Otherwise, the meaning of the cardinal number is 'exactly *n*'. One anonymous referee of this book believes that the same holds for English.

truth-conditionally, the utterance in (2.6) is not incompatible with the possibility that he in fact has, for example, seven credit cards.

The conversational implicature arising in (2.7) results from the observation of the maxim of Relation. If this maxim is to be satisfied, Mary's utterance has to be taken as relevant. Since John has asked a question, Mary should be providing an answer. Assuming that in saying what she has uttered, Mary is co-operatively answering John's question, we can infer that while Mary is not in a position to provide a straightforward answer, nevertheless she thinks that the museum's not being open yet might help John to get a partial answer, such as the one indicated above.

Finally, the conversational implicature in (2.8) is derived from following the fourth submaxim of Manner. By this submaxim, the speaker is expected to arrange the events in the order in which they took place, and the addressee is expected to draw inferences in such a way. (2.8) is also an instance of **iconicity**: the ordering of the linguistic elements iconically reflects that of the events.

Secondly and more interestingly, conversational implicatures can be generated by way of the speaker's deliberately flouting the maxims. Let us call conversational implicatures thus induced **conversational implicatures$_F$**.

As mentioned above, the maxims of conversation, as proposed by Grice, may be overtly and blatantly breached. Faced with such a conspicuous flouting by the speaker, the addressee then has two options. One is to think that the co-operative principle has been abandoned as well. But he or she may—and characteristically does—choose a second option. He or she may assume that despite the speaker's apparent failure of co-operation, he or she is still observing the co-operative principle, and reasons roughly thus. If the speaker is still co-operative, and if he or she is exploiting a maxim in such a way that I should recognize the infringement, then he or she is doing so in order to convey some extra message, which is in keeping with the co-operative principle at some deeper level. Moreover, he or she knows that I am able to compute what that message is. A few examples will suffice to illustrate conversational implicatures$_F$.

(2.10)   Quality:
        Chomsky is a great sociolinguist.
        +> Chomsky is no sociolinguist at all
(2.11)   Quantity:
        War is war.
        +> e.g., Terrible things always happen in war. That's its nature, and it's no use lamenting that particular tragedy

(2.12)   Relation:
         John: Susan can be such a cow sometimes!
         Mary: Oh, what a lovely day today!
         +> e.g., One shouldn't speak ill of people behind their back
(2.13)   Manner:
         a. John smiled.
         b. The corners of John's lips turned slightly upward.
         +> John did not exactly smile

Any student of linguistics knows that (2.10) is patently false, thereby clearly and openly flouting the maxim of Quality. However, in order to preserve the assumption of co-operation, the addressee must assume that the speaker is trying to convey something rather different from what he or she has actually said, that is, the ironic reading which is opposite to the literal meaning of the sentence. A similar analysis can be made for other types of 'figure of speech' such as metaphor, litotes, and hyperbole (but see Sperber and Wilson 1986 for a dissenting view).

(2.11) is a tautology, and as such, is superficially uninformative. Confronted with this blatant breaking of the maxim of Quantity, the addressee assumes that the speaker is actually co-operative and has to work out why he or she has made such an apparently uninformative utterance. The only way to do this is to interpret it as in fact highly informative. This explains the creating of the conversational implicature along the lines I have indicated.[7]

[7] According to Wierzbicka (1987, 1991), (2.11) cannot be used straightforwardly in French, German, Russian, Polish, Japanese, and Korean. On the basis of this observation, she claimed that tautological constructions like (2.11) are language-specific, and therefore cannot be universally accounted for in terms of the Gricean maxim of Quantity. But one of the anonymous referees has pointed out to me that tautological examples of the type illustrated by (2.11) are in fact possible in French, as in (i) and (ii).

  (i)   La guerre, c'est la guerre.
        'War is war.'
 (ii)   À la guerre comme à la guerre.
        'War is war.'

Another anonymous referee has noted that the same holds for Russian. He or she has provided the following example, taken from a Russian grammar book.

(iii)   delo delom a ljubov' ljubov'ju.
        'Business is business and love is love.'

See also Fraser (1988) and Ward and Hirschberg (1991).

What does Mary's response have to do with John's bad-mouthing Susan in (2.12), since it initially appears to infringe the maxim of Relation? Clearly, if the assumption that Mary is still co-operative is to be maintained, we have to interpret her response as highly relevant at some non-superficial level. One of the possible ways to do so is to read it as conversationally implicating Mary's disapproval of John's bad-mouthing people behind their backs.

The use of the prolix sentence (2.13b), where the simple sentence (2.13a) is available and would normally have been used, deviates sharply from the third submaxim of Manner. But on the assumption that the speaker is co-operative, the conversational implicature is essentially that the speaker is not in a position to use the term 'smile' here, or that it is less than smile that he or she wants to communicate.

We thus have the first Gricean dichotomy between conversational implicature$_O$ and conversational implicature$_F$, namely, the distinction between those conversational implicatures that are generated from a simple assumption that the speaker is observing both the maxims and the co-operative principles, and those that are engendered in more complex ways on the basis of the speaker flouting a maxim but nevertheless following the co-operative principle. Grice's major achievement here was in providing a unified analysis of both types.

> See whether you can tackle Exercises 3, 4, and 5 on pp. 59–60 now.

2.1.4. Generalized versus particularized conversational implicature

A second Gricean dichotomy, independent of the first, is between those conversational implicatures which arise without requiring any particular contextual conditions and those which do require such conditions. Grice called the first kind **generalized conversational implicatures**, as in (2.14), and the second kind **particularized conversational implicatures**, as in (2.15).

(2.14)   Most of John's friends believe in marriage.
          +> Not all of John's friends believe in marriage
(2.15)   John: Where's Peter?
          Mary: The light in his office is on.
          +> Peter is in his office

The implicature in (2.14) has a very general currency. Any utterance of the form 'Most x are Y' will have the default interpretation 'Not all x are Y'. This interpretation will go through without needing any particular contexts (see Ariel 2004 for further, detailed discussion of *most*). By contrast, the implicature in (2.15) depends crucially on its linguistic context. Mary's reply points to the possible connection between the light in Peter's office and his location, namely, if the light in Peter's office is on, he may be in his office. Without such a specific context, we will not have the implicature under consideration in (2.15). The theoretical importance of this Gricean dichotomy has recently been subject to heated debates. Hirschberg (1991: 42–4), Welker (1994: 21–3) and Carston (2002), for example, doubted whether such a distinction can be maintained. On the other hand, Levinson (2000) put forward a rigorous defence of it (see also Grice 1975, 1981, 1989: 37–8 for further discussion).

> Take a look at Exercise 6 on p. 60.

2.1.5. Properties of conversational implicature

Conversational implicatures are characterized by a number of distinctive properties (Grice 1975, 1989, Sadock 1978, Levinson, 1983, 2000, Huang 1991, 1994: 4–5, 2000a: 206–7, 2003). In the first place, there is **defeasibility** or **cancellability**: conversational implicatures can simply disappear in certain linguistic or non-linguistic contexts. How? They are cancelled if they are inconsistent with (i) semantic entailments, (ii) background assumptions, (iii) contexts, and/or (iv) priority conversational implicatures.[8] Let me take them one by one. (I shall postpone the discussion of (iv) until Section 2.2.3.)

First, conversational implicatures evaporate in the face of inconsistency with semantic entailments, as the utterances in (2.17) show. (I use '~+>' to signify 'does not conversationally implicate'.)

(2.16) His wife is often complaining.
        +> His wife is not always complaining

---

[8] In addition, Q-implicatures can also be cancelled by metalinguistic negation. I shall discuss this in Section 2.2.2.

(2.17) a. His wife is often, in fact/indeed always, complaining.
    b. His wife is often, and perhaps/maybe/possibly/even always, complaining.
    c. His wife is not only often but always complaining.
    d. His wife is often, or perhaps/maybe/possibly/even always, complaining.
    e. His wife is often, if not always, complaining.
    ∼ +> His wife is not always complaining

All the utterances in (2.17) have the potential conversational implicature indicated in (2.16). However, all the sentences in (2.17) bear the semantic entailment that his wife is always complaining due to the use of phrases such as *in fact always*. Consequently, the potential conversational implicature is defeated by the inconsistent entailment.

Next, conversational implicatures are suspended if they are not in keeping with background or ontological assumptions, often referred to as real-world knowledge. This is the case with (2.19).

(2.18) John and Mary bought an apartment near the Louvre in Paris.
    +> John and Mary bought an apartment near the Louvre in Paris together, not one each
(2.19) The Americans and the Russians tested an atom bomb in 1962.
    ∼ +> The Americans and the Russians tested an atom bomb in 1962 together, not one each

Given our knowledge about history, it was impossible for the USA and the USSR to test an atom bomb together in 1962, because they were enemies at that time, thus the disappearance of the potential 'togetherness' conversational implicature.

Third, conversational implicatures are annulled when they run contrary to what the immediate linguistic context of utterance tells us. Imagine the following exchange in a music shop.

(2.20) John: This CD is eight euros, and I haven't got any money on me.
    Mary: Don't worry, I've got eight euros.
    ∼ +> Mary has got only eight euros

Here, given the immediate linguistic context of utterance, Mary's response does not produce the usual conversational implicature that she has got only eight euros. This is because all the information needed here is whether or not Mary has enough money for John to buy the CD rather than the exact amount of money she might in fact have.[9]

---

[9] Note that the following joke is based on defeasibility of conversational implicatures (Leech 1983: 91).

A second property exhibited by conversational implicatures is **non-detachability**: any linguistic expression with the same semantic content tends to carry the same conversational implicature. (A principled exception is those conversational implicatures that arise via the maxim of Manner, about which later.) This is because conversational implicatures are attached to the semantic content, rather than the linguistic form, of what is said. Therefore, they cannot be detached from an utterance simply by replacing the relevant linguistic expressions with their synonyms. This is illustrated in (2.21), which indicates that the use of any linguistic expression that is synonymous with *almost* will trigger the same conversational implicature.

(2.21)   The film almost/nearly won/came close to winning an Oscar.
　　　　+> The film did not quite win an Oscar

The third property, **calculability**, means that conversational implicatures can transparently be derived via the co-operative principle and its component maxims. The fourth, **non-conventionality**, means that conversational implicatures, though dependent on the saying of what is coded, are non-coded in nature (Grice 1989: 39, Bach 1994a: 140). In other words, they rely on the saying of what is said but they are not part of what is said. They are associated with speaker or utterance but not proposition or sentence. Fifthly, according to the principle of **reinforceability**, conversational implicatures can be made explicit without producing too much of a sense of redundancy. This is because conversational implicatures are not part of the conventional import of an utterance. For example, the conversational implicature in (2.22) is made explicit in (2.23). But (2.23) is not felt to be semantically redundant.

(2.22)   The soup is warm.
　　　　+> The soup is not hot
(2.23)   The soup is warm, but not hot.

Finally, we have **universality**: conversational implicatures tend to be universal, being motivated rather than arbitrary. Examples (2.24)–(2.28) from different languages all assert that some young people like pop music, and conversationally imply that not all young people like pop music. Example

Steven: Wilfrid is meeting a woman for dinner tonight.
Susan: Does his wife know about it?
Steven: Of *course* she does. The woman he is meeting *is* his wife.

(2.29) from Malagasy asserts that some young people like famous songs, and conversationally implicates that not all young people like famous songs. All this shows that if a language has 'all' and 'some', the use of the semantically weaker 'some' will universally carry the conversational implicature 'not all'.

(2.24) (Arabic)
        Ba'ag   al-Shababal-yafian   al-musiqa   al-Harkia.
        some   young people like-PL   the-music   the-pop
        'Some young people like pop music.'

(2.25) (Catalan)
        A   alguns   joves   els   agrada   la   música   pop.
        to   some   young people   to them   like   the   music   pop
        'Some young people like pop music.'

(2.26) (Chinese)
        yixie   nianqing   ren   xihuan   liuxing   yinyue.
        some   young   people   like   pop   music
        'Some young people like pop music.'

(2.27) (Modern Greek)
        Se   merikus   neus   aresi   i   pop   musiki.
        to   some   young people is pleasing   the   pop   music
        'Some young people like pop music.'

(2.28) (Kashmiri)
        kanh-kanh   noujawan   chu   pop   musiki   pasabd karan.
        some   young people be-3SG   pop   music   like
        'Some young people like pop music.'

(2.29) (Malagasy)
        Misy   tanora   tia   ny   hira   malaza.
        exist   young   like   the   song   famous
        'Some young people like famous songs.'[10, 11]

---

[10] The best-known apparent counterexample to the universality claim for conversational implicatures is provided by Keenan (1976) (see also Sarangi and Slembrouck 1992, Rundquist 1992, Haviland 1997, Marmaridou 2000: 241). In this work, Keenan claimed that the Malagasy-speaking culture of Madagascar is a speech community in which Grice's co-operative principle, and in particular his first submaxim of Quantity, are not adhered to; e.g., in talking to her son, a Malagasy mother would use the following sentence to refer to her husband/the boy's father:

Mbola mator y ve ny olana?
'Is the person still asleep?'
+> the person in question is not the speaker's husband/the boy's father

You may now be ready to tackle Exercise 7 on p. 60.

2.2. Two neo-Gricean pragmatic theories of conversational implicature

Since its inception, Grice's classical theory of conversational implicature has revolutionized pragmatic theorizing, generating a large number of reinterpretations, revisions, and reconstructions. For example, the whole Gricean mechanism of the co-operative principle and its constituent maxims has been subject to various attempts at reduction. Early attempts include Harnish (1976), in which Grice's maxims of Quality and Quantity are collapsed into a single maxim: make the strongest relevant claim justifiable by your evidence. Kasher (1976) argued that the entire Gricean machinery can be seen as following some sort of 'most effective, least effort'

This led Keenan to conclude that Grice's theory is culture-specific rather than universal. However, as pointed out by Brown and Levinson (1987: 288–9) and Horn (1988), if we examine the case more closely, we will find that it is not just in conformity with Grice's first submaxim of Quantity, it actually requires the existence of this submaxim for it to be interpreted. As Keenan herself was aware, Grice's first submaxim of Quantity does generally hold for the Malagasy-speaking culture, as is attested by (2.29). (This was confirmed to me by Larry Horn, personal communication, who checked this fact with Keenan after her paper was published.) What Keenan showed was that in the Malagasy culture, the first submaxim of Quantity may be overridden by some sociolinguistic principle such as the one of avoiding guilt. It is because of a particular Malagasy taboo on exact identification that the mother would avoid using a more informative term such as 'your father' to refer to her husband. If the first submaxim of Quantity did not work at some deeper level, the boy would fail to recognize the intended referent. This is therefore a case of 'no deviation from the norm without a reason'. The deviation here is the Malagasy taboo on exact identification, but the norm is the rsal first submaxim of Quantity (see also Huang 2004b).

onversational implicatures may be **indeterminate**. Here is inson (1983: 118):

d

ing, or/and

rationality principle. More recently, Welker (1994) has tried to make use of a superpragmatic principle, which requires the speaker to produce an utterance that brings the common ground closer to the conversational goals and is better than any other utterance the speaker could have provided. However, of all the reductionist models, the most influential are the two-principled Hornian and the three-principled Levinsonian neo-Gricean pragmatic theories, to which I shall now turn.[12]

2.2.1. The Hornian system

Horn (1984, 1989, 2004) suggested a bipartite model. On Horn's view, all of Grice's maxims (except the maxim of Quality) can be replaced with two fundamental and antithetical principles: the **Q[uantity]-principle** and the **R[elation]-principle**.

---

[12] Another influential reductionist model is, of course, Sperber and Wilson's (1986) relevance theory, which will be discussed in detail in Chapter 6. In a quite contrary spirit to the reductionist approach, Leech (1983) proposed that the Gricean maxims be proliferated. In particular, he argued that a politeness principle should be added to the Gricean mechanism, and that it should be taken as co-ordinate in nature to Grice's co-operative principle (see also Leech 2003). However, a number of arguments can be mounted against such an expansionist analysis. First, if we are allowed to invent a maxim for every regularity that is actually observed in language use, not only will we have an indefinite number of maxims, but pragmatic theory will be too unconstrained to be falsified. Secondly, the distribution of politeness (who has to be polite to whom) is socially controlled. By contrast, language usage principles of the Gricean sort are of a quite different status. The co-operative principle defines an 'unmarked' or socially neutral (indeed asocial) presumptive framework for communication, the essential assumption being 'no deviation from rational efficiency without a reason'. Politeness considerations are, however, just such principled reasons for deviation. Therefore, linguistic politeness is implicated in the classical way, with maximum theoretical parsimony, from the co-operative principle. Thirdly, the assumption of co-operative behaviour is hard to undermine: tokens of apparent unco-operative behaviour tend to get interpreted as in fact co-operative at a 'deeper' level. Now, if politeness principles had maxim-like status, we would expect the same robustness: it should be hard to be impolite. But this is clearly counterintuitive (Brown and Levinson 1987: 4–5). To these, we can add that the expansionist approach is also inconsistent with the spirit of 'Occam's razor' (see Chapter 1), namely, the doctrine that theoretical entities are not to be multiplied beyond necessity (see also Huang 2004b).

(2.30)   Horn's Q- and R-principles
   a. The Q-principle
       Make your contribution sufficient;
       Say as much as you can (given the R-principle).
   b. The R-principle
       Make your contribution necessary;
       Say no more than you must (given the Q-principle).

In terms of information structure, Horn's Q-principle, which collects Grice's Quantity$_{-1}$, Manner$_{-1}$, and Manner$_{-2}$ maxims, is a lower-bounding pragmatic principle which may be (and characteristically is) exploited to engender upper-bounding conversational implicatures: a speaker, in saying '... p ...', conversationally implicates that (for all he or she knows) '... at most p ...'. The *locus classicus* here is those conversational implicatures that arise from a prototype **Q-** or **Horn-scale**. Prototype Q- or Horn-scales are defined in (2.31) (Horn 1972, Ducrot 1972, Grice 1975, Gazdar 1979, Atlas and Levinson 1981, Levinson 1987a, 1987b, 2000; see also Hawkins 1991, Matsumoto 1995).

(2.31)   Prototype Q- or Horn-scales
       For $<S, W>$ to form a Q- or Horn-scale,
          (i) A(S) entails A(W) for some arbitrary sentence frame A;
         (ii) S and W are equally lexicalized, of the same word class, and from the same register; and
        (iii) S and W are 'about' the same semantic relation, or from the same semantic field,

where S stands for 'semantically strong expression' and W stands for 'semantically weak expression'. Some examples of Q- or Horn-scales are given in (2.32). (I use '$< >$' to represent a Q- or Horn-scale.)

(2.32)   a. <all, some>
         b. <hot, warm>
         c. <excellent, good>
         d. <the, a>
         e. <beautiful, pretty, attractive>

By way of illustration, take, for example, (2.32a). Here, *all* is semantically stronger than *some*, because it entails *some*, but not vice versa; *all* and *some* are relatively equally lexicalized; and both are quantifiers, that is, both are from the same semantic field. The same story can be told of (2.32b)–(2.32e).

Next, consider (2.33).

(2.33)   a. *<iff, if>
      b. *<regret, know>
      c. *<(p because q), (p and q)>

Do (2.33a)–(2.33c) form Q- or Horn-scales? The answer is no. Given (2.31ii), (2.33a) is ruled out as a genuine Q- or Horn-scale. This is because in English there is no unitary lexeme which standardly means the same as *if and only if*. In other words, *iff* (which is in a special register) and *if* are not lexicalized to the same degree. Recently, Levinson (2000: 79) has further pointed out that the equal lexicalization condition is particularly relevant to the stronger lexical expression in a Q- or Horn-scale. Next, by (2.31iii), (2.33b) is excluded. The reason is that *regret* and *know* are about different semantic relations. For any two or more lexical expressions to constitute a Q- or Horn-scale, they must be about the same semantic relation, and neither/none is allowed to introduce additional semantic fields. More or less the same can also be said about the pseudo Q- or Horn-scale (2.33c) (see also Huang 2004b).

An example of Q-implicatures is given below.

(2.34)   <excellent, good>
      The company is providing a good digital TV service for this area.
      +> The company is not providing an excellent digital TV service for this area

On the other hand, the countervailing R-principle, which subsumes Grice's Quantity$_{-2}$, Relation, Manner$_{-3}$, and Manner$_{-4}$ maxims, is an upper-bounding pragmatic law which may be (and systematically is) exploited to invite low-bounding conversational implicatures: a speaker, in saying '...p...', conversationally implicates that (for all he or she knows) '... more than p...' (see also Atlas and Levinson 1981). This is illustrated in (2.35), adapted from Grice (1989: 38).

(2.35)   John broke a finger yesterday.
      +> The finger was one of John's

Viewing the Q- and R-principles as mere instantiations of Zipfian economy (Zipf 1949), Horn explicitly identified the Q-principle ('a hearer-oriented economy for the maximization of informational content') with Zipf's Auditor's Economy (the Force of Diversification) and the R-principle ('a speaker-oriented economy for the minimization of linguistic form') with

Zipf's Speaker's Economy (the Force of Unification). Furthermore, Horn argued, quoting Martinet (1962: 139) as support, that the whole Gricean mechanism for pragmatic inference can be largely derived from the dialectic interaction (in the classical Hegelian sense) between the Q- and R-principles in the following way.[13]

(2.36)   Horn's division of pragmatic labour
         The use of a marked (relatively complex and/or prolix) expression when a corresponding unmarked (simpler, less 'effortful') alternate expression is available tends to be interpreted as conveying a marked message (one which the unmarked alternative would not or could not have conveyed).

In effect, what (2.36) basically says is this: the R-principle generally takes precedence until the use of a contrastive linguistic form induces a Q-implicature to the non-applicability of the pertinent R-implicature (see also Huang 1991, 1994, 2000a, 2003, 2004b, 2006b).

2.2.2. The Levinsonian system

Horn's proposal to reduce Grice's maxims to the Q- and R-principles was called into question by Levinson (1987a, 1987b, 1991, 2000). In Levinson's view, Horn failed to draw a distinction between what Levinson called semantic minimization ('semantically general expressions are preferred to semantically specific ones') and expression minimization (' "shorter" expressions are preferred to "longer" ones').[14] Consequently, inconsistency

---

[13] It has been argued that the two counterbalancing forces at work are actually the ones which enjoin volubility and taciturnity, respectively. See Green (1995) for discussion of volubility.

[14] There is, of course, a strong tendency for the two distinct minimizations (or economies) to be conflated. This general correlation, in fact, follows directly from the Zipfian theory of economy. Zipf's Principle of Economic Versatility stipulates a direct correlation between a lexical item's semantic versatility and its frequency of use ('the more semantically general, the more use'); his Law of Abbreviation postulates an inverse relation between a lexical item's frequency of use and its length ('the more use, the shorter'). Taken jointly, the prediction is 'the more semantically general, the shorter' (Zipf 1949, Horn 1984, Haiman 1985a, 1985b, Levinson 1987a, Huang 1994). Considered from a slightly different perspective, the general correlation between semantic minimization and expression minimization may be seen as an instance of iconicity.

arises with Horn's use of the Q- and R-principles. For example, in Horn's division of pragmatic labour (2.36), the Q-principle seems to operate primarily in terms of units of speech production, whereas elsewhere, in Q- or Horn-scales (2.31), for instance, it seems to operate primarily in terms of semantic informativeness.

Considerations along these lines led Levinson to argue for a clear separation between pragmatic principles governing an utterance's surface form and pragmatic principles governing its informational content. He proposed that the original Gricean programme (the maxim of Quality apart) be reduced to three neo-Gricean pragmatic principles: what he dubbed the **Q[uantity]-**, **I[nformativeness]-**, and **M[anner]-principles**. Each of the three principles has two sides: a speaker's maxim, which specifies what the principle enjoins the speaker to say, and a recipient's corollary, which dictates what it allows the addressee to infer. Let me take them one by one.

(2.37)   Levinson's Q-principle
The Q-principle
Speaker's maxim:
Do not provide a statement that is informationally weaker than your knowledge of the world allows, unless providing a stronger statement would contravene the I-principle.
Recipient's corollary:
Take it that the speaker made the strongest statement consistent with what he knows, and therefore that:
(i) if the speaker asserted A(W), where A is a sentence frame and W an informationally weaker expression than S, and the contrastive expressions <S, W> form a Horn-scale (in the prototype case, such that A(S) entails A(W)), then one can infer that the speaker knows that the stronger statement A(S) (with S substituted for W) would be false (or K~ (A(S)));
(ii) if the speaker asserted A(W) and A(W) fails to entail an embedded sentence Q, which a stronger statement A(S) would entail, and <S, W> form a contrast set, then one can infer the speaker does not know whether Q obtains or not (i.e. ~K(Q) or equally {P (Q), P~(Q)}).

The Q-principle can be simplified as follows (e.g. Levinson 2000, Huang 2004b).

(2.38)   The Q-principle (simplified)
Speaker: Do not say less than is required (bearing the I-principle in mind).
Addressee: What is not said is not the case.

The basic idea of the metalinguistic Q-principle is that the use of an expression (especially a semantically weaker one) in a set of contrastive semantic alternates (such as a Q- or Horn-scale) Q-implicates the negation of the interpretation associated with the use of another expression (especially a semantically stronger one) in the same set. In other words, as mentioned above, the effect of this inference strategy is to give rise to an upper-bounding conversational implicature: a speaker, in saying '...p...', conversationally implicates that (for all he or she knows) '...at most p...'. Seen the other way round, from the absence of an informationally stronger expression, one infers that the interpretation associated with the use of that expression does not hold. Hence, the Q-principle is essentially negative in nature.

Three types of Q-implicature can then be identified: (i) **Q-scalar** implicatures, (ii) **Q-clausal** implicatures, and (iii) **Q-alternate** implicatures. Q-scalar implicatures are derived from prototype Horn-scales. They are schematized in (2.39) and illustrated in (2.40), in addition to e.g., (2.6), (2.14), (2.16), (2.22), and (2.34). (The '$\sim$' is for negation.) (See also Chierchia 2004, who attempted to reduce Q-scalar implicatures partially to grammar.)

(2.39)   Q-scalar : <x, y>
         y +>Q-scalar $\sim$ x
(2.40)   <identical, similar>
         The two impressionist paintings are similar.
         +> The two impressionist paintings are not identical

Next, Q-clausal implicatures are inferences of epistemic uncertainty. Like Q-scalar implicatures, Q-clausal implicatures also rest on a set of contrastive semantic alternates, but in this case, of a constructional kind. Wherever there is a construction Y(p), where p is not entailed by Y(p), and there is an alternative construction X(p) semantically similar and of roughly equal brevity to Y(p) except that X(p) does entail p, then the use of the semantically weaker Y(p) Q-implicates that the speaker does not know whether p obtains or not (Grice 1989: 8, Gazdar 1979: 59–62, Levinson 2000: 108–11, but see Atlas 1993 for a different view). Q-clausal implicatures are schematized in (2.41) and exemplified in (2.42)–(2.45).

(2.41)   Q-clausal: <X(p), Y(p)>
         Y(p) +>Q-clausal p, $\sim p$
(2.42)   (Disjunction)
         <(p and q), (p or q)>

Mary is a vegetarian or an environmentalist.

+> Mary is perhaps a vegetarian, or perhaps not a vegetarian; perhaps an environmentalist, or perhaps not an environmentalist

In (2.42), while (p and q) entails its constituent sentences, (p or q) does not. This has the consequence that if the semantically weaker (p or q) is used, then the speaker Q-implies that he or she does not know whether it is p or not, and whether it is q or not, hence the implicatures specified above.

(2.43) (Conditional)
        <(since p then q), (if p then q)>
        If John wants to access the internet from home, he should buy a dial-up modem.
        +> John may want to access the internet from home, or he may not want to; he perhaps should buy a dial-up modem, or he perhaps should not

The same is true of (2.43). Here, (if p then q) is the non-entailing counterpart to (since p then q). Therefore the use of it will generate the Q-clausal implicature of epistemic uncertainty.

(2.44) (Modal)
        <necessarily p, possibly p>
        It's possible that Buddhism is the world's oldest living religion.
        +> It's possible that Buddhism is the world's oldest living religion, and it's possible that Buddhism isn't the world's oldest living religion

In (2.44), *necessarily p* is semantically stronger than *possibly p*. If the speaker avoids using it and instead opts for the semantically weaker *possibly p*, then he or she intends to Q-implicate that he or she does not know whether p obtains or not.

(2.45) (Verbal doublet)
        <(know that p), (believe that p)>
        Mary believes that Nigel has visited Kafka's house on Golden Lane in Prague.
        +> Nigel may have visited Kafka's house on Golden Lane in Prague, he may not have

Finally in (2.45), (know that p) entails p but (believe that p) does not. By the same reasoning, the use of the latter will carry the Q-clausal implicature that the speaker does not know whether p is the case or not.

We move finally to Q-alternate implicatures, which come from a non-entailment semantic (contrast) set (Harnish 1976, Horn 1989, Hirschberg

1991, van Kuppevelt 1996, Levinson 2000). Roughly, we have two subtypes here. In the first, the lexical expressions in the set are informationally ranked, as in (2.46). Let us call Q-implicatures deriving from such a set **Q-ordered alternate** implicatures. By contrast, in the second subtype, the lexical expressions in the set are of equal semantic strength, as in (2.48). Let us term Q-implicatures thus induced **Q-unordered alternate** implicatures.

(2.46)   <succeed, try>
         In 1888, van Gogh tried to set up an artist's studio at Arles.
         +> In 1888, van Gogh did not succeed in setting up an artist's studio at Arles

In (2.46), *succeed* is semantically stronger than *try*, but it does not entail *try*, as is attested by (2.47). Therefore, *succeed* and *try* form a semantic contrast set, but the set is non-entailing. However, as in the case of Q-implicatures arising from a Q- or Horn-scale, the use of the semantically weaker *try* in (2.46) gives rise to a similar Q-implicature, which we have called Q-ordered alternate implicature.

(2.47)   John succeeded without even trying.
(2.48)   <boil, grill, stir-fry, ... >
         Stir-fry the bean sprouts, please,
         +> Please don't, for example, boil the bean spouts as well

Finally, the lexical expressions in (2.48) are of equal semantic strength, hence forming an unordered semantic set. In cases like this, the use of any lexical expression in the set will engender a weak Q-implicature that in the meantime, the speaker is not in a position to use any other lexical expressions in this set.

> Now try to do Exercises 8, 9, and 10 on pp. 60–1.

One of the interesting features of Q-implicatures is that they can normally be cancelled by **metalinguistic negation**—a term introduced by Horn (1985) following Ducrot (1972). Metalinguistic negation is a device for rejecting a previous utterance on any grounds whatever including its morphosyntactic form, its phonetic realization, its style or register, and/or the implicatures it potentially engenders (Horn 1985, 1988, 1989: 363; see also Burton-Roberts 1989). It is characterized by a number of distinctive properties. In the first place, it consists of a negative sentence followed by a rectifying clause. Secondly, it is a rejoinder to a previous utterance, to aspects of which it objects. Thirdly, taken descriptively, it constitutes a truth-conditional contradiction. In the fourth place, when spoken, it tends to occur with a special, so-called contradiction intonation contour. Fifthly, it does not allow the use of negative polarity items like *any*. Sixthly, it does not permit negative incorporation. In the seventh place, its interpretation is frequently the outcome of a reanalysis. Finally, it is essentially an instantiation of quotation, mention, or representational use (Horn 1985, 1989, Levinson 2000: 211–12, Carston 2002: 295).

This non-truth-functional use of negation can be distinguished from standard, descriptive, truth-functional propositional negation. Consider (2.49).

(2.49)   a. Xiaoming was not born in Peking, he was born in Shanghai.
         b. Xiaoming was not born in Peking, he was born in Beijing.

(2.49a) represents the ordinary, truth-functional negation: what is negated is its truth-conditional semantic content. By contrast in (2.49b) we have metalinguistic negation. What is objected to is not its descriptive content (otherwise the two sentences would constitute a logical contradiction), but rather some property of the representation falling within the scope of negation. In (2.49b), the aspect that is objected to by the metalinguistic negation is the old-fashioned Wade phonetic spelling of Beijing, the capital of China.

Here are three more examples of metalinguistic negation.

(2.50)   I didn't have nine euroes left, I had nine euros left.
(2.51)   They don't grow tom[a:touz] there, they grow tom[eiDouz] there.
(2.52)   Susan didn't marry three times, she married four times.

What is metalinguistically negated in (2.50) is the morphological, plural spelling form of *euro* in the previous utterance; what is rejected in (2.51) is a phonetic aspect of *tomatoes*; and finally what is objected to in (2.52) is the potential Q-implicature of the previous utterance, namely, Susan married at most three times.

See whether you are now ready to do Exercise 11 on pp. 61–2.

Returning to Q-implicatures, the use of metalinguistic negation can cancel the Q-implicated upper bounds, as in (2.53), on a par with the cancellation of Q-implicatures by inconsistent semantic entailments, as in (2.54) (see also Huang 1991, 1994, 2000a, 2003, 2004b, 2006b).

(2.53) a. His wife isn't often complaining, she's always complaining.
        b. Mary isn't a vegetarian or an environmentalist—she's both.
        c. It isn't possible John will become a great archaeologist—it's certain he will.

(2.54) a. His wife is often complaining, in fact she's always complaining.
        b. Mary is a vegetarian or an environmentalist—perhaps she's both.
        c. Not only is it possible John will become a great archaeologist—it's certain he will.

Next, there is Levinson's (2000) I-principle.

(2.55) Levinson's I-principle
        Speaker's maxim: the maxim of minimization
        'Say as little as necessary', that is, produce the minimal linguistic information sufficient to achieve your communicational ends (bearing the Q-principle in mind).
        Recipient's corollary: the rule of enrichment
        Amplify the informational content of the speaker's utterance, by finding the most specific interpretation, up to what you judge to be the speaker's m-intended point, unless the speaker has broken the maxim of minimization by using a marked or prolix expression.
        Specifically:
         (i) Assume the richest temporal, causal and referential connections between described situations or events, consistent with what is taken for granted.
        (ii) Assume that stereotypical relations obtain between referents or events, unless this is inconsistent with (i).
        (iii) Avoid interpretations that multiply entities referred to (assume referential parsimony); specifically, prefer coreferential readings of reduced NPs (pronouns or zeros).
        (iv) Assume the existence or actuality of what a sentence is about if that is consistent with what is taken for granted.

Setting aside its four instantiations, the I-principle can be simplified as follows (Levinson 2000, Huang 2004b).

(2.56) The I-principle
        Speaker: Do not say more than is required (bearing the Q-principle in mind).
        Addressee: What is generally said is stereotypically and specifically exemplified.

Mirroring the effects of the Q-principle, the central tenet of the I-principle is that the use of a semantically general expression I-implicates a semantically specific interpretation. In other words, as remarked above, the working of this inferential mechanism is to induce a lower-bounding conversational implicature: a speaker, in saying '...p...', conversationally implicates that (for all he or she knows) '...more than p...'. More accurately, the conversational implicature engendered by the I-principle is one that accords ·best with the most stereotypical and explanatory expectation given our knowledge about the world. Schematically (I use '[ ]' to represent an I-scale.):

(2.57)   I-scale: [x, y]
      y + >I x

Some cases of I-implicature are given below.

(2.58)   Conjunction buttressing
     p and q +> p and then q
             +> p therefore q
             +> p in order to cause q
     John pressed the spring and the drawer opened.
     +> John pressed the spring and then the drawer opened
     +> John pressed the spring and thereby caused the drawer to open
     +> John pressed the spring in order to make the drawer open

(2.59)   Conditional perfection
     if p then q +> iff p then q
     If you give me a free Beethoven, I'll buy five Mozarts.
     +> If and only if you give me a free Beethoven will I buy five Mozarts

(2.60)   Membership categorization
     The toddler cried. The daddy gave her a cuddle.
     +> The daddy was the father of the crying toddler

(2.61)   Mirror maxim
     John and Mary bought a BMW.
     +> John and Mary bought a BMW together, not one each

(2.62)   Frame-based inference
     Mary pushed the cart to the checkout.
     +> Mary pushed the cart full of groceries to the supermarket
     checkout in order to pay for them, and so on

(2.63)   Bridging cross-reference
     John toured the Old Town Square in Prague. The Hus monument is magnificent.
     +> There is a Hus monument in the Old Town Square in Prague

(2.64)   Inference to stereotype
Have you met our new nurse?
+> Have you met our new female nurse

(2.65)   Indirect speech act
Have you got a watch?
+> If you have got a watch and know the time, please tell me what it is

(2.66)   Definite reference
It's a Song vase and on the base of the vessel are four Chinese characters.
+> It's a Song vase$_1$ and on the base of the vase$_1$ are four Chinese characters

(2.67)   Lexical narrowing
John doesn't drink.
+> John doesn't drink alcohol

(2.68)   Negative raising
John didn't think that the government had used too much stick and too little carrot.
+> John thought that the government had not used too much stick and too little carrot

(2.69)   Negative strengthening
Maria doesn't like the English weather.
+> Maria positively dislikes the English weather

(2.70)   Noun–noun compound
a. the government's drugs campaign
+> the government's campaign against drugs
b. the government's safe-sex campaign
+> the government's campaign for safe sex

(2.71)   Specialization of spatial term
a. The nail is in the wood.
+> The nail is buried in the wood
b. The spoon is in the cup
+> The spoon has its bowl-part in the cup

(2.72)   Interpretation of possessive construction
a. John's father
+> the one to whom he is son
b. John's office
+> the one he works in
c. John's class
+> the one he attends
d. Newton's ideas
+> the ones originated from Newton
e. Halley's comet
+> the one named after Halley

(2.73) Coreferential interpretation

John said that he had a reviving espresso after lunch.

+> John$_1$ said that John$_1$ had a reviving espresso after lunch

(2.74) Proper name narrowing

Have you been to Shakespeare's birthplace?

+> Have you been to the birthplace of William Shakespeare, the English dramatist and poet?

(2.75) Adjective interpretation

a. a brown cow

+> most of its body surface is brown

b. a brown book

+> most of its cover is brown

c. a brown newspaper

+> all its pages are brown

d. a brown crystal

+> both its inside and outside are brown

e. a brown paperbag

+> the whole paperbag is brown

f. a brown house

+> only the outside of the house is brown

g. a brown eye

+> only the iris is brown

(2.76) Systematic ambiguity

a. The whole nursery burnt down.

+> The buildings of the whole nursery burnt down

b. The whole nursery went on a country outing.

+> The staff and children of the whole nursery went on a country outing

The class of I-implicatures is heterogeneous, but the implicatures in (2.58)–(2.76) above share a number of properties. First, they are more specific than the utterances that engender them. For example, in (2.58), from the use of the semantically general *and*, we get the semantically more specific interpretation 'and then', etc. In (2.67), the speaker uses the semantically general *drink*, and the addressee infers it as 'drink alcohol', which is semantically more specific. In (2.75), from *a brown newspaper*, we obtain the semantically more specific interpretation that 'all the pages of the newspaper are brown'. The same can be said of all the other examples. Second, unlike Q-implicatures, I-implicatures are positive in nature. Third, they are characteristically guided by stereotypical assumptions. This is true, for instance, of (2.62), (2.64), and (2.70). Fourth, they are generally non-metalinguistic, in the sense that they make no reference to something that might have been said but was not (Levinson 2000: 119). Finally, they normally cannot be cancelled by metalinguistic negation (Horn 1989), as shown by (2.77)[15] (see also Huang 1991, 1994, 2000a, 2003, 2004b, 2006b).

(2.77)   a. John didn't break a finger yesterday.
            $\sim$ +> John broke a finger yesterday, but it wasn't one of his
         b. John and Mary didn't buy a BMW.
            $\sim$ +> John and Mary bought a BMW, but not together
         c. (Horn 1989: 388–9)
            John wasn't clever enough to solve the problem.
            $\sim$+> John was clever enough to solve the problem, but he didn't do it

> Try doing Exercise 12 on p. 62.

Finally, we come to Levinson's (2000) M-principle.

(2.78)   Levinson's M-principle
         Speaker's maxim:
         Indicate an abnormal, non-stereotypical situation by using marked expressions that contrast with those you would use to describe the corresponding normal, stereotypical situation.
         Recipient's corollary:
         What is said in an abnormal way indicates an abnormal situation, or marked messages indicate marked situations.
         Specifically:
         Where S has said p containing marked expression M, and there is an unmarked alternate expression U with the same denotation D which the speaker might have employed in the same sentence frame instead, then where U would have I-implicated the stereotypical or more specific subset d of D, the marked expression M will implicate the complement of the denotation d, namely d' of D.

The M-principle can be simplified as follows (Levinson 2000, Huang 2004b).

(2.79)   The M-principle
         Speaker: Do not use a marked expression without reason.
         Addressee: What is said in a marked way is not unmarked.

[15] Provided that metalinguistic negation is applicable. There are cases of I-implicatures where metalinguistic negation does not seem to be pertinent, as in, e.g., (2.60) and (2.63) (Huang 2003, 2004b).

Unlike the Q- and I-principles, which operate primarily in terms of semantic informativeness, the metalinguistic M-principle operates primarily in terms of a set of alternates that contrast in form. The fundamental axiom upon which this principle rests is that the use of a marked expression M-implicates the negation of the interpretation associated with the use of an alternative, unmarked expression in the same set. Putting it another way, from the use of a marked linguistic expression, one infers that the stereotypical interpretation associated with the use of an alternative, unmarked linguistic expression does not obtain (see also Huang 1991, 1994, 2000a, 2003, 2004b, 2006b, Horn 2004, Traugott 2004). Schematically (I use { } to represent an M-scale):

(2.80)   M-scale: {x, y}
         y +>M ~ x

M-implicatures are illustrated by the (b) sentences in (2.81)–(2.83) below, which are marked.

(2.81)   a. The timetable is reliable.
         +> The timetable is reliable to degree n
         b. The timetable is not unreliable.
         +> The timetable is reliable to degree less than n
(2.82)   a. John stopped the car.
         +> John stopped the car in the usual manner
         b. John caused the car to stop.
         +> John stopped the car in an unusual way, for example, by bumping into a wall
(2.83)   a. Mary went from the bathroom to the bedroom.
         +> Mary went from the bathroom to the bedroom in the normal way
         b. Mary ceased to be in the bathroom and came to be in the bedroom.
         +> Mary went from the bathroom to the bedroom in an unusual way, for example, in a magic show, Mary had by magic been made to disappear from the bathroom and reappear in the bedroom

Turn to p. 62 and attempt Exercise 13.

Interaction of the Q-, I-, and M-principles

Given the above tripartite classification of neo-Gricean pragmatic principles, the question that arises next is how inconsistencies arising from these potentially conflicting implicatures can be resolved. According to Levinson (1991, 2000), they can be resolved by an ordered set of precedence, which encapsulates in part the Hornian division of pragmatic labour, discussed above.

(2.84)   Levinson's resolution schema for the interaction
         of the Q-, I-, and M-principles
         a. Level of genus: Q > M > I
         b. Level of species: e.g. Q-clausal > Q-scalar

This is tantamount to saying that genuine Q-implicatures (where Q-clausal cancels rival Q-scalar) precede inconsistent I-implicatures, but otherwise I-implicatures take precedence until the use of a marked linguistic expression triggers a complementary M-implicature to the negation of the applicability of the pertinent I-implicature.

By way of illustration, let us consider (2.85)–(2.88).

(2.85)   Q > I
         If Bill Gates gave you a car for Christmas, it may have been a real one.
         (a) Q-clausal $<$(since p, q), (if p, q)$>$
             $+>$ The car may or may not have been a real car
         (b) I [car for Christmas]
             $+>$ The car was a toy car
         (c) Q > I
             $+>$ Possibly the car was a real car

In (2.85), there is a Q-clausal implicature due to the use of (if p, q). But there is also a potential I-implicature to stereotype arising from the use of *the car for Christmas*. The two implicatures are inconsistent with each other. Now given (2.84), the I-implicature is overridden by the Q-implicature.

(2.86)   Q > M
         It is not unlikely that Oxford will win the next boat race, and indeed
         I think it likely.
         (a) Q-clausal $<$know that p, think that p,$>$
             $+>$ It is possible that it is likely that Oxford will win the next boat race
         (b) M{likely, not unlikely}
             $+>$ It is less than fully likely that Oxford will win the next boat race
         (c) Q > M
             $+>$ It is likely that Oxford will win the next boat race

The same resolution mechanism is responsible for the cancellation of the M-implicature in (2.86). In this example, there is a Q-clausal implicature arising from the use of the semantically weaker $<$think that $p>$. On the other hand, there is also a potential M-implicature associated with the use of the marked double negation *not unlikely*. Since the M-implicature is less powerful than the Q-implicature, it is blocked.

(2.87) M > I

The corners of Mary's lips turned slightly upwards.

(a) M

+> Mary didn't exactly smile; she sort of smirked

(b) I (Mary smiled.)

+> Mary smiled in the normal way by producing a nice, happy expression

(c) M > I

+> Mary didn't exactly smile; she sort of smirked

Next, in (2.87), there is a potential I-implicature generated by the use of *Mary smiled*. But since the speaker has avoided it and has instead opted for a marked form, an M-implicature is created. Again by (2.84), the I-implicature is neutralized by the M-implicature.

(2.88) Q-clausal > Q-scalar

If all of his friends don't love chocolate éclairs, then some of them do.

(a) Q-clausal <(since p, q), (if p, q)>

+> All of his friends may or may not love chocolate éclairs—the speaker doesn't know which

(b) Q-scalar <all, some>

+> Not all of his friends love chocolate éclairs

(c) Q-clausal > Q-scalar

+> Possibly all of his friends love chocolate éclairs

Finally, in (2.88), there is a Q-clausal implicature due to the use of the conditional (if p, q). But there is also a potential Q-scalar implicature due to the use of the semantically weaker quantifier *some*. Once again, given (2.84), the Q-clausal implicature defeats the inconsistent Q-scalar implicature. All this shows that a conversational implicature can also be cancelled if it is inconsistent with a priority conversational implicature, as specified in (2.84).

To sum up, conversational implicatures can be cancelled if they are inconsistent with (i) semantic entailments, (ii) background assumptions, (iii) contexts, and/or (iv) priority conversational implicatures. In addition, Q-implicatures can also be cancelled by metalinguistic negation.

The resolution schema in (2.84) can in fact be assimilated into a more general implicature cancellation procedure put forward by Gazdar (1979). On Gazdar's view, the informational content of an utterance can be considered to be an ordered set of background assumptions, contextual factors, semantic entailments, conversational implicatures, and so on and so forth. Each incrementation of the informational content of an utterance must be consistent with the informational content that already exists, otherwise it will be cancelled according to the following hierarchy (adapted from Gazdar 1979, Huang 1991, 1994, 2000a, 2004b, Levinson 2000).

(2.89)   The implicature cancellation procedure
      a. Background assumptions
      b. Contextual factors
      c. Semantic entailments
      d. Conversational implicatures
         (i)   Q-implicatures
             (1) $Q_{\text{-clausal}}$ implicatures
             (2) $Q_{\text{-scalar}}$ implicatures
        (ii) M-implicatures
       (iii) I-implicatures

2.3. Conventional implicature

2.3.1. What is conventional implicature?

In the last two sections, I have surveyed the classical and neo-Gricean pragmatic theories of conversational implicature. In this section, I shall briefly discuss the second category of implicature put forward by Grice, namely, **conventional implicature** (see also Frege 1892, who, according to Bach 1999b, was perhaps the first modern philosopher to notice the phenomenon). A conventional implicature is a non-truth-conditional inference which is not deductive in any general, natural way from the saying of what is said, but arises solely because of the conventional features attached to particular lexical items and/or linguistic constructions.

A few standard examples follow (I use '+>>' to stand for 'convention-
~~tes'.)

> q follows from p
he therefore knows how to use chopsticks.
contrasts with q
r but he is honest.
have gone up but theirs have gone down.

(2.92)   Even p +>> contrary to expectation
         Even his wife didn't think that John would win the by-election.
(2.93) p moreover q +>> q is in addition to p
         Xiaoming can read German. Moreover, he can write poems in the language.
(2.94) p so q +>> p provides an explanation for q
         Mary is taking Chinese cookery lessons. So her husband has bought her a
         wok.

In (2.90), the conventional implicature triggered by the use of *therefore* is
that being Chinese provides some good reason for knowing how to use
chopsticks. In (2.91), there is a conventional implicature of contrast
between the information contained in p and that contained in q[16] (Grice
1989: 25, 88). In (2.92), *even*, being epistemic in nature, conventionally
implicates some sort of unexpectedness, surprise or unlikeness (e.g., Kempson 1975, Karttunen and Peters 1979, Kay 1990, Barker 1991, Lycan 1991,
Farncescotti 1995). In (2.93), the use of *moreover* brings in the conventional
implicature that the statement made in q is additional to the statement
made in p (Grice 1989: 121). Finally in (2.94), the conventional implicature
contributed by *so* is that the fact that Mary is learning how to cook Chinese
food explains why her husband has bought her a wok.

Other representative lexical items that are considered to engender conventional implicatures in English include *actually*, *also*, *anyway*, *barely*,
besides, *however*, *manage to*, *on the other hand*, *only*, *still*, *though*, *too* and *yet*.

See whether you can tackle Exercise 14 on p. 62.

2.3.2. Properties of conventional implicature

Properties of conventional implicatures can best be characterized in contrast to those of conversational implicatures, discussed above (Grice 1975,
Levinson 1983: 127–8, Horn 1988).

---

[16] It should be pointed out here that *but* seems to have three uses: (i) denial of
expectation, as in (2.91a); (ii) contrastive, as in (2.91b), and (iii) correction, as in (i)
below.

(i)   That's not my father but my uncle.

The main similarity between conventional and conversational implicature is that neither makes any contribution to truth conditions (but see Chapter 7). Recall (1.32) in Chapter 1, repeated here as (2.95) for ease of exposition.

(2.95)   a. We want peace and they want war.
         b. We want peace but they want war.

As mentioned in Section 1.3.3. of Chapter 1, (2.95b) shares the same truth conditions with (2.95a), though it contains the conventional implicature of contrast triggered by the use of the connective *but*. This indicates that like a conversational implicature, a conventional implicature does not contribute to the truth condition of its corresponding sentence. A second similarity is that both conventional and conversational implicatures are associated with speaker or utterance rather than proposition or sentence.

On the other hand, there are a number of important differences between conventional and conversational implicatures. First of all, conventional implicatures are not derived from the co-operative principle and its component maxims, but are attached by convention to particular lexical items or linguistic constructions. They are therefore an arbitrary part of meaning, and must be learned ad hoc. By contrast, conversational implicatures are derived from the co-operative principle and its attendant maxims. Hence, they are non-conventional by definition, that is, they are motivated rather than arbitrary.

The same can be said of *mais* in French (e.g., Anscombre and Ducrot 1977). On Horn's (1989) view, the distinction is mainly one of semantic ambiguity. This analysis can be supported by the fact that there are languages in which the different uses of *but* are lexicalized. For example, German uses *aber* for the denial of expectation/contrastive *but* and *sondern* for the correction *but*. The two *but*s in Finnish, Spanish, and Swedish differ in essentially the same way. In Finnish, the denial of expectation/contrastive *but* is translated as *mutta* and the correction *but* as *vaan*. Spanish utilizes *pero* for the former and *sino* for the latter. Swedish has *men* and *utan*, respectively (Horn 1989: 406–9). Finally, there are also two *but*s in Russian: *no* and *a*, the latter serving the function of marking discontinuity in discourse. Furthermore, as pointed by Anscombre and Ducrot (1977) for *mais* in French, the denial of expectation/contrastive *but* and the correction *but* have syntactic complementary distribution (see also Horn 1989: 407). If the analysis is correct, then the correction *but* is not expected to be accounted for in terms of conventional implicature. But see Blakemore (2000) for a dissenting view.

Second, conventional implicatures are not calculable via any natural procedure, but are rather given by convention, thus they must be stipulated. By comparison, conversational implicatures are calculable using pragmatic principles, contextual knowledge, and background assumptions.

Third, conventional implicatures are not cancellable, that is, they cannot be defeated. By contrast, conversational implicatures are cancellable. Fourth, conventional implicatures are detachable, because they depend on the particular linguistic items used. By comparison, conversational implicatures (except those arising from the M-principle) are non-detachable, because they are attached to the semantic content, but not to the linguistic form of what is said. Fifth, conventional implicatures tend not to be universal. By contrast, conversational implicatures tend to be universal (see also Potts 2005, Feng 2006).

It should be pointed out before we leave this section that unlike the notion of conversational implicature, the notion of conventional implicature does not seem to be a very coherent one. Even Grice himself (1989: 46) warned that 'the nature of conventional implicature needs to be examined before any free use of it, for explanatory purposes, can be indulged in' (see also Horn 2004). Since its inception, conventional implicature has been subject to numerous attempts to reduce it to semantic entailment, conversational implicature, and presupposition (Levinson 1983: 128), and more recently, to part of what is said (Bach 1999b, but see Barker 2003 for a different view), part of tacit performatives (Rieber 1997), vehicles for performing second-order speech acts (Bach 1999b), and procedural meaning in relevance theory (Blakemore 2002, 2004). But see Feng (2006) for a defence of the concept.

By way of summary, meaning$_{nn}$/speaker-meaning or the total signification of an utterance in a Gricean system may be represented schematically as follows (Levinson 1983: 131, 2000: 13, Huang 1994, but see Davis 1998 for a recent critique of Gricean pragmatics).

(2.96)

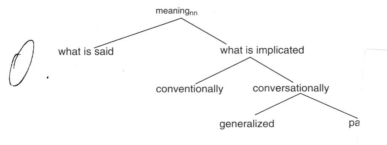

2.4. Summary

In this chapter, I have considered implicature. Section 2.1 discussed the classical Gricean theory of conversational implicature. Section 2.2 presented the latest developments first of the Hornian and then of the Levinsonian neo-Gricean pragmatic theories of conversational implicature. In Section 2.3.1, I examined the notion of conventional implicature. Finally, in Section 2.3.2, I compared and contrasted conventional implicature with conversational implicature.

One final point that is worth mentioning is that in recent years there have been various attempts to integrate the classical and neo-Gricean pragmatic theories of conversational implicature with other current linguistic theories. These linguistic theories include accommodation theory (Thomason 1990), decision theory (Merin 1999), game theory (van Rooy to appear; see also Benz, Jäger, and van Rooy 2006), bidirectional Optimality theory (Blutner 1998, 2004, Blutner and Zeevat 2004),[17] and speech act theory (Vanderveken 2002; see also Martinich 1984).

Key concepts

implicature
$meaning_{nn}$
co-operative principle
maxims of conversation (Quality, Quantity, Relation, Manner)
conversational implicature
$conversational\ implicature_O$
$conversational\ implicature_F$
generalized conversational implicature
particularized conversational implicature
properties of conversational implicature (cancellability/defeasibility, non-detachability, calculability, non-conventionality, reinforceability, universality, indeterminacy)
Q-principle (Horn)
Q- or Horn-scale

[17] For a very brief commentary on Blutner's (1998) bidirectional Optimality-theoretic treatment of the Q- and R-/I-principles, see Huang (2004b).

R-principle
division of pragmatic labour
Q-principle (Levinson)
Q_{scalar} implicature
$Q_{clausal}$ implicature
$Q_{alternate}$ implicature
metalinguistic negation
I-principle
M-principle
interaction of Q-, I-, and M-principles
conventional implicature

Exercises and essay questions

1. Children with pragmatic disorders may often fail to observe the maxims. In the following conversation (adapted from Bishop 1997: 183, cited in Peccei 1999: 29), which maxim did the child violate?

   Speech therapist: So you like ice-cream. What are your favourite flavours?
   Child with a pragmatic disorder: Hamburger . . . fish and chips.

2. Which maxims does the speaker intend to opt out from by using the following hedges?
   (i) I don't think I have sufficient evidence for this, but . . .
   (ii) I'm not at liberty to say any more.
   (iii) I know this is irrelevant, but . . .
   (iv) This is a bit confused, but . . .
   (v) So, to cut a long story short,
   (vi) Not to change the topic, but . . .
   (vii) I'm sure you already know this, but . . .
   (viii) People say . . .

3. Joe and Irving are the two characters in a computer program called Tale-Spin, cited in Mey (2001: 88). In the following passage, what is the conversational implicature Joe failed to work out? Is it a conversational implicature$_O$ or conversational implicature$_F$?

   One day Joe Bear was hungry. He asked his friend Irving Bird where some honey was. Irving told him there was a beehive in the oak tree. Joe threatened to hit Irving if he didn't tell him where some honey was.

4. What is the conversational implicature of Mary's reply in the following conversation? Is it a conversational implicature$_O$ or conversational implicature$_F$? If it is a conversational implicature$_F$, which maxim is flouted?

John: India is the most populous country in the world, isn't it?
Mary: I'm the Queen of Sheba.

Next, how about the clergyman's reply in the following passage from C. P. Snow's *Variety of Men*?

He (Lord Rutherford) said in a speech: 'As I was standing in the drawing-room at Trinity, a clergyman came in. And I said to him: "I'm Lord Rutherford." And he said to me: "I'm the Archbishop of York." '

5. Shortly after the Berlin Wall was erected, President J. F. Kennedy announced in German at a West Berlin rally that he was a Berliner. What he should have said was *Ich bin Berliner* ('I'm a Berliner'), but due to his speech writer's limited knowledge of German, he managed instead to say *Ich bin ein Berliner*, which means that he was a kind of doughnut. However, despite his mistake, his audience did not fail to compute the conversational implicature of what he said (Grundy 2000: 19–20). What is the conversational implicature in question? Which maxim is flouted?

6. Of the following two conversational implicatures, which is the generalized one and which is the particularized one?

   (i)   John: How did yesterday's guest lecture go?
         Mary: Some of the faculty left before it ended.
         +> (a) Not all of the faculty left before it ended
         +> (b) The lecture didn't go well

7. In the following passage taken from a novel set on a Navajo reservation (Tony Hillerman, *Skinwalkers*, cited in Thomas 1995: 76), the speaker is the daughter of a murdered man. She is talking to Officer Jim Chee of the Navajo Tribal Police. Why does she use the vague terms 'the one who got killed' and 'that man' to refer to her father? Is this a real counterexample to the claim of universality for Grice's first submaxim of Quantity?

'Last time you were with the FBI man—asking about the one who got killed,' she said, respecting the Navajo taboo of not speaking the name of the dead. 'You find out who killed that man?'

8. What are the Q-implicatures of the following? Which type of Q-implicatures do they belong to?
   (i)   <Mary's husband, a man>
         Mary is chatting with a man by the lake.

(ii)   <realize, think>
    I think Baird invented television.

(iii)   <Chinese, English, Swahili, ... >
    They teach Swahili here.

(iv)   <adore, love, like>
    John likes Mary.

(v)   <president, prime minister>
    Her uncle is the prime minister.

(vi)   <divorce, separate>
    The Smiths have separated.

(vii)   <and, or>
    John will send it either as an e-mail or as an attachment.

(viii)   <all, most, many, some>
    Many people enjoy a cappuccino with breakfast.

(ix)   <none, not all>
    Not all of her colleagues can speak Italian.

9. What are the Q-implicatures of the following?
   (i)   He can run 100m in 9.9 seconds.
   (ii)   He has cut down his smoking to ten cigarettes a day.

10. Does the following form a Q- or Horn-scale? If not, why not?
    < boiling, hot, warm, lukewarm, cool, cold, freezing>

11. Can you distinguish metalinguistic from descriptive negation in the following?
    (i)   John didn't graduate from Oxford. He graduated from Cambridge.
    (ii)   John didn't have two mon*geese*, he had two mon*gooses*.
    (iii)   He isn't a taxi driver, he is a bus driver.
    (iv)   He's not my dad, he's my father.
    (v)   They don't speak [seltic], they speak [keltic].
    (vi)   Mary doesn't like house sparrows, she likes bullfinches.
    (vii)   We didn't have the party at the cyber café, we had it in the students' common room.
    (viii)   Colin Powell isn't the first black Secretary of State, he is the first Secretary of State who is black.
    (ix)   They don't need six new computer mouses, they need six new computer mice.
    (x)   John hasn't visited some of the nature reserves in the country, he has visited all of them.
    (xi)   Doesn't she [Penelope Cruz] ever yearn for a less hectic life, maybe one where more time is spent in one place? She laughs hard as if the suggestion is quite ridiculous. "Not at all. I love my life. I'm addicted to living like this and traveling all the time. I don't just like hotels, I love them. That's where I get my quiet time and quiet time is golden." (Lesley O'Toole *Lady Penelope. Sunday Express* S, 14 March 2004)

(3.9)   An utterance of a sentence S presupposes a proposition p if and only if
    a. if S is true, then p is true
    b. if S is false, then p is still true

What (3.9) basically says is this: for S to presuppose p, whenever S is true, p is also true, and whenever S is false, p is still true.

There are, however, problems at the very heart of the notion of constancy under negation. On the one hand, constancy under negation may not be necessary. For example, there is a class of sentences which are hard if not impossible to negate, yet they bear presuppositions, as in (3.10) (Green 1996). On the other hand, constancy under negation may not be sufficient. This is illustrated by (3.11) and (3.12). Although (3.11) and (3.12) satisfy the condition of constancy under negation, the inference in the former is standardly analysed as a **felicity condition on the speech act of requesting** (about which more in Chapter 4), and that in the latter as a conventional implicature (e.g., Levinson 1983: 185).

(3.10)   Long live the king of France!
    >> There is a king of France
(3.11)   Do/don't bring the digital camera here.
    ?>> The digital camera is not here
(3.12)   (Chinese)
    nin   yongyuan shi wode laoshi.
    you-HON always   be my   teacher
    'You will always be my teacher.'
    ?>> The addressee is socially superior to or distant from the speaker

---

Now see whether you can tackle Exercise 3 on pp. 91–2.

3.2.2. Defeasibility

Like conversational implicatures, but unlike semantic entailments, presuppositions are cancellable. They are nullified if they are inconsistent with (i) background assumptions, (ii) conversational implicatures, and (iii) certain discourse contexts. Furthermore, they can also drop out in certain intra-sentential contexts, some of which give rise to the projection problem of presupposition. Defeasibility has in general been taken as the second most important property of presupposition.

In the first place, presuppositions can disappear in the face of inconsistency with background assumptions or real-world knowledge. Contrast (3.13) and (3.14). (I use '$\sim$>>' to stand for 'does not presuppose'.)

(3.13)   John got an assistant professorship before he finished his Ph.D.
          \>> John finished his Ph.D.
(3.14)   John died before he finished his Ph.D.
          $\sim$>> John finished his Ph.D.

While (3.13) presupposes that John finished his Ph.D. by virtue of the temporal clause, (3.14) does not carry that presupposition. This is because the putative presupposition conflicts with our real-world knowledge that one cannot do anything after one dies. Consequently, the unwanted presupposition vanishes.[4]

Secondly, presuppositions can be cancelled by inconsistent conversational implicatures. This is illustrated in (3.15).

(3.15)   If John is organizing a stag night, Mary will be angry that he is doing so.
          \+> perhaps John is organising a stag night, perhaps he isn't
          $\sim$>> John is organizing a stag night

---

[4] Compare (3.14) with (i) below.

(i)   John died before he reached the hospital's accident and emergency department.
       \>> John reached the hospital's accident and emergency department
(i) has the presupposition indicated above only on the understanding that *he* means John's body.

More importantly, David Cram has pointed out to me that for some native speakers of English including himself, the presupposition of (3.14) cannot be cancelled. For this group of speakers, only the non-finite alternative to (3.14) allows the presupposition to be defeated. This is given in (ii).

(ii)   John died before finishing his Ph.D.
       $\sim$ \>> John finished his Ph.D.

Furthermore, David Cram has offered a neo-Gricean pragmatic explanation along the following lines: if the speaker had intended the presupposition to be suspended, he or she would have used (ii). If (ii) is not used, but (3.14) is employed instead, then an inference can be drawn, namely, the speaker does not intend the presupposition to be cancelled.

The use of the factive predicate *angry* in (3.15) should give rise to the potential presupposition that John is organizing a stag night. However, there is also a Q-$_{clausal}$ conversational implicature due to the use of the conditional in (3.15), namely, perhaps John is not organizing a stag night (see Chapter 2). In the face of the contradictory conversational implicature, the putative presupposition here is defeated.

Thirdly, presuppositions are contextually cancellable, that is, they can evaporate if they run contrary to what the immediate discourse context tells us. Consider first (3.16), where the putative presupposition is defeated by the inconsistent proposition that is already established in the immediate discourse background.

(3.16)   There is no king of France. Therefore the king of France isn't bald.
　　　　$\sim>>$ There is a king of France

In (3.16) the second sentence should presuppose that there is a king of France. The reason it does not is because such a putative presupposition is inconsistent with the preceding proposition, already established in the immediate discourse background, namely, that there is no king of France. As a result, the unwanted presupposition fails to survive.[5]

Next, presuppositions can be suspended by so-called reduction arguments—arguments that proceed by eliminating each of the possibilities in a discourse. This is exemplified by (3.17), cited from Chierchia and McConnell-Ginet (2000).

(3.17)   A, noticing the open door: Was it you who opened the door to the porch? I closed it at lunch time.

---

[5] Contrast (i) and (ii).

(i)   John doesn't/You don't know that Baird invented television.
　　　$>>$ Baird invented television
(ii)   I don't know that Baird invented television
　　　$\sim >>$ Baird invented television

Here, there is a contrast between the use of a third/second-person subject and that of a first-person subject, in a negative sentence containing the factive verb *know*: while the presupposition in the former gets through, that in the latter (sometimes) drops out. This is because what is presupposed in (ii) is precisely what is denied by what is explicitly said about the speaker's knowledge or beliefs (see Gazdar 1979: 142, 153–4 for an analysis of how the presupposition in (ii) but not (i) is correctly cancelled).

B: Well, it wasn't me who opened it, because I've been gone all afternoon, and it wasn't Joan who opened it, because she was with me, and it wasn't any of the kids who opened it, because they're on a field trip, and I strongly suspect that nobody opened it—there was a lot of wind this afternoon, you know

~>> Someone opened the door to the porch

In this passage, each of the cleft sentences should bear the presupposition that someone opened the door to the porch. However, as pointed out by Levinson (1983: 189) for a similar example, the whole purpose of B's utterance in (3.17) is to convince the addressee that no one opened it. This has the consequence that the presupposition is overridden; 'it was adopted as a counterfactual assumption to argue [for] the untenability of such an assumption' (ibid.).

Finally, presuppositions can disappear in a discourse where evidence for their truth is being weighed and rejected, as in (3.18), due to Levinson (1983: 189).

(3.18)   A: Well we've simply got to find out if Serge is a KGB infiltrator.
         B: Who if anyone would know?
         C: The only person who would know for sure is Alexis; I've talked to him and he isn't aware that Serge is on the KGB payroll. So I think Serge can be trusted.

         ~>> Serge is on the KGB payroll

C's utterance *he isn't aware that Serge is on the KGB payroll* contains the epistemic factive predicate *aware*. Although the use of factive predicates typically presupposes the truth of their complements, the use of it in this example does not. This is because the presupposition clashes with the whole point of C's argument, namely, that since Alexis isn't aware that Serge is on the KGB payroll, he is not a KGB infiltrator. When this happens, the unwanted presupposition is again blocked.

In the fourth place, presuppositions can be blocked in certain intrasentential contexts, that is, they can be defeated by using other clauses in the same complex sentence to increment the local, intrasentential context. Three cases are of particular interest. The first of these is that a presupposition of a sentence can be **overtly denied** in a co-ordinate clause without any apparent contradiction. This is illustrated in (3.19)–(3.21).

(3.19)   The president doesn't regret vetoing the bill because in fact he never did so!
         ~>> The president vetoed the bill

(3.20)   John didn't manage to open an e-savings account, in fact he didn't even try!
　　　　~>>John tried to open an e-savings account
(3.21)   The king of France isn't bald—there is no king of France!
　　　　~>> There is a king of France

Notice that in many cases, outright denial of presupposition is not possible with positive sentences. Contrast (3.19)–(3.21) above with (3.22)–(3.24) below.

(3.22)   *The president regrets vetoing the bill because in fact he never did so!
(3.23)   *John managed to open an e-savings account, in fact he didn't even try!
(3.24)   *The king of France is bald—there is no king of France!

There is thus, at least in these cases, an asymmetry between negative and positive sentences with regard to defeasibility. This asymmetry has led to an entailment analysis for positive sentences, namely, the argument that what is allegedly presupposed in these sentences is actually what is entailed. Since semantic entailments cannot be overtly denied without producing semantic anomaly, the anomaly displayed in (3.22)–(3.24) is entirely expected. A second point to note is that the negation involved in overt denial of presupposition in (3.19)–(3.21) is generally considered as a meta-linguistic negation (see Chapter 2). (See, e.g., Horn 1985, 1989 and Burton-Roberts 1989 for further arguments, but see Carston 2002, Geurts 1998, 1999: 71–2 and Atlas 2004 for scepticism, though for different reasons.)

Next, a presupposition of a sentence can be **explicitly suspended** in an *if* clause that follows. Witness (3.25)–(3.27).[6]

(3.25)   John clearly doesn't regret being an anti-war campaigner, if he actually ever was one.
　　　　~>> John was an anti-war campaigner
(3.26)   John didn't tamper with their computers again, if indeed he ever did.
　　　　~>> John tampered with their computers before
(3.27)   I'm sure John's wife is beautiful, if he has a wife.
　　　　~>> John has a wife

Finally, presuppositions can disappear with certain **verbs of saying** such as *say*, *mention*, *tell*, *ask*, and *announce* and certain **verbs of propositional attitude** such as *believe*, *think*, *imagine*, *dream*, and *want*.

---

[6] The explicit suspension of a presupposition in examples like (3.25)–(3.27) may be regarded as a special case of presuppositional heritability in conditionals of this sort.

(i.e., entailed) by its local context, which is conceived mainly as a set of propositions. The local context is constructed in a dynamic way. This makes it possible for an unwanted presupposition to be filtered out during the derivation of a sentence in a bottom-up manner (see, e.g., Karttunen 1973, 1974, Stalnaker 1973, 1974, 1978, 1999, Karttunen and Peters 1979).

In order to handle the projection problem, Karttunen (1973) classified presupposition operators into three types: (i) **plugs**, which block off all the presuppositions of the lower clauses, (ii) **holes**, which let all such presuppositions ascend to become presuppositions of the matrix sentence, and (iii) **filters**, which prevent some but not all such presuppositions from being projected to the matrix sentence. Examples of plugs include verbs of saying and verbs of propositional attitude, and perhaps presupposition-cancelling metalinguistic negation (Horn 1996: 307) (see Chapter 2). By contrast, factive verbs and modal operators are treated as holes. Descriptive negation is also taken as a hole with respect to presuppositions. Finally, two-place logical connectives are filters. As remarked above, they allow some presuppositions to ascend to become presuppositions of the whole but not others. Further examples of each of the three types of presupposition operators are given below.

(3.37) Plugs
   a. John said/thought that Peter had started buying blue-chip shares.
      ~>> Peter hadn't been buying blue-chip shares
   b. John doesn't regret running the red light, because in fact he never did so.
      ~>> John ran the red light

(3.38) Holes
   a. John knows that George Orwell is the pseudonym of Eric Arthur Blair.
      >> George Orwell is the pseudonym of Eric Arthur Blair
   b. It's unlikely that John will play the piano again.
      >> John played the piano before
   c. The president didn't die of SARS.
      >> There was a president.

(3.39) Filters
   a. John has three children, and all his children are intelligent.
      ~>> John has children
   b. John has three children, and he regrets that he didn't study developmental psychology in university.
      >> John didn't study developmental psychology in university

In (3.37), the plugs, i.e., the verbs *say* and *think*, and the metalinguistic negation block the presuppositions of (embedded) clauses from ascending to the whole sentence. By contrast, in (3.38) the presuppositions under the holes, i.e., the verb *know*, the modal operator *unlikely*, and the descriptive negation, get through unblocked. Finally, filters let presuppositions go through only discriminately. While in (3.39a) the putative presupposition of the second conjunct is cancelled by the filter, in (3.39b) it is projected on to the whole conjunction.

Regarding filters, the question that arises next is under what circumstances a presupposition will be, and under what conditions it will not be, filtered out. The answer provided by Karttunen (1973) is as follows:

(3.40) In a sentence of the form 'if p then q', the presuppositions of the parts will be inherited by the whole unless q presupposes r and p entails r.

(3.41) In a sentence of the form 'p & q', the presuppositions of the parts will be inherited by the whole unless q presupposes r and p entails r.

(3.42) In a sentence of the form 'p or q', the presuppositions of the parts will be inherited by the whole unless q presupposes r and $\sim$ p entails r.

What the filtering condition (3.40) says is this: in the case of a conditional, if the presupposition that would have been engendered by the second clause is entailed by the first clause, then the presupposition will be filtered out, as in (3.30), repeated here for convenience as (3.43). Otherwise, it will survive to be projected to the whole sentence, as in (3.35), repeated here as (3.44).

(3.43) If the bishop promotes the politically incorrect, then he will regret doing so.
    $\sim$>> The bishop will promote the politically incorrect

(3.44) If Susan returned to England, (then) she would be arrested.
    >> Susan was in England before

The same is true of a conjunction, as stated in the filtering condition (3.41). This is illustrated in (3.39a) and (3.39b), repeated here as (3.45) and (3.46), respectively.

(3.45) John has three children, and all his children are intelligent.
    $\sim$>> John has children

(3.46) John has three children, and he regrets that he didn't study developmental psychology in university.
    >> John didn't study developmental psychology in university

In (3.45), the putative presupposition of the second conjunct fails to be inherited by the whole sentence, because the first conjunct entails what the second presupposes. This has the consequence that (3.45) does not presuppose but rather asserts or entails that John has children. By comparison, in (3.46), since the first conjunct does not entail what the second presupposes, the presupposition of the second conjunct is projected to become the presupposition of the whole sentence.

Finally, in the case of a disjunction, the putative presupposition of the second clause will be ruled out if it is entailed by the negation of the first clause. This is the case in (3.31), repeated here as (3.47). Otherwise it will percolate up to the whole sentence, as in (3.36), repeated here as (3.48).[9]

(3.47) Either the bishop will not promote the politically incorrect, or he will regret doing so.
$\sim$>> The bishop will promote the politically incorrect

(3.48) Either Susan returns to England, or she will flee to Spain.
>> Susan was in England before

The filtering-satisfaction analysis represents the first systematic study of presupposition within the context of modern linguistics. As a consequence, it has set the critical background for all subsequent accounts of this important topic in theoretical pragmatics, prefiguring much of the current work such as Heim (1983, 1992), Chierchia and McConnell-Ginet (2000), and Beaver (2001). However, there are problems for this analysis. From a conceptual point of view, the positing of plugs, holes, and filters seems largely to be arbitrarily stipulated rather than independently motivated, thus lacking explanatory power. Somewhat related is the problem that under this analysis, negation is forced to be treated as ambiguous:

---

[9] Faced with examples like (i) and (ii), Karttunen (1974) had to modify (3.40) and (3.41) by replacing 'entail' with 'entail in context', thus allowing access to real-world knowledge.

(i) Geraldine is a Mormon and she has given up wearing her holy underwear!
(ii) If Geraldine is a Mormon, she has given up wearing her holy underwear!
(iii) >> Geraldine used to wear her holy underwear

Here, the second clause in (i) and (ii) presupposes (iii) by virtue of the use of the change-of-state verb *give up*. But whether this presupposition can percolate up unfiltered depends on our beliefs about what Mormons wear. If we have no knowledge whatsoever about what they wear, then this presupposition will get through. On the other hand, if we assume that only Mormons habitually wear holy underwear, then this presupposition inheritance will be blocked. This is because in that context, the presupposition of the second clause is (indirectly) entailed by the first clause.

descriptive negation as a hole but metalinguistic negation as a plug. Clearly this runs against the spirit of Occam's razor (see Chapter 2).

Turning next to empirical considerations, counterexamples are not difficult to find. First of all, a presupposition embedded under a plug, for example, can sometimes survive unscathed, contra the predictions of the filtering-satisfaction analysis. This is the case in (3.49).

(3.49)   (Levinson 1983: 196)
         Churchill said that he would never regret being tough with Stalin.
         >> Churchill was tough with Stalin

In this example, as pointed out by Levinson (1983: 196), in spite of the presence of the verb *say*, which is a plug in Karttunen's analysis, the presupposition of the embedded clause is inherited by the whole sentence.

Next, the filtering conditions also make wrong predictions. Consider (3.50), due to Gazdar (1979).

(3.50)   It's possible that John has children and it's possible that his children are away.
         ~>> John has children

The use of *his children* in the embedded clause of the second conjunct presupposes that John has children, and this presupposition is inherited by the second conjunct as a whole, *possible* being a hole. However, the presupposition is not locally satisfied in (3.50) because it is not entailed by the first conjunct. This has the consequence that given the filtering condition for conjunction (3.41), (3.50) should presuppose that John has children—a prediction that is intuitively incorrect (e.g., Gazdar 1979, Levinson 1983: 209–10, Kadmon 2001: 134; see also Levinson 1983: 210–11 for further counterexamples to the filtering conditions).

Finally, the filtering-satisfaction theory cannot accommodate defeasibility of presupposition—the second most important property of presupposition. This is particularly true of those putative presuppositions that are contextually defeated, as exhibited in examples such as (3.16)–(3.18), repeated here as (3.51)–(3.53).

(3.51)   There is no king of France. Therefore the king of France isn't bald.
         ~>> There is a king of France
(3.52)   A, noticing the open door: Was it you who opened the door to the porch? I closed it at lunch time.
         B: Well, it wasn't me who opened it, because I've been gone all afternoon, and it wasn't Joan who opened it, because she was with me, and it wasn't

any of the kids who opened it, because they're on a field trip, and I strongly suspect that nobody opened it—there was a lot of wind this afternoon, you know.

~>> Someone opened the door to the porch

(3.53)   A: Well we've simply got to find out if Serge is a KGB infiltrator.

B: Who if anyone would know?

C: The only person who would know for sure is Alexis; I've talked to him and he isn't aware that Serge is on the KGB payroll. So I think Serge can be trusted.

~>> Serge is on the KGB payroll

Take, for example, (3.51) as an illustration. As we have already seen, the sentence *Therefore the king of France isn't bald* does not here presuppose that there is a king of France because the putative presupposition is defeated by the contradictory proposition that there is no king of France, which has already been established in the immediate discourse context. But under the filtering-satisfaction theory, on the assumption that descriptive negation is a hole, the unwanted presupposition is wrongly predicted to get through (for some recent, more technical critiques of the filtering-satisfaction analysis, see, e.g., van der Sandt 1988 and Geurts 1999).[10]

3.3.2. The cancellation analysis

In contrast to the filtering-satisfaction analysis, underlying Gazdar's (1979) **cancellation analysis** is the crucial assumption that a presupposition is cancellable (see also Soames 1979, 1982). On this theory, what a presupposition trigger engenders is merely a potential presupposition. A potential presupposition will become an actual one, unless it is defeated. With respect to the projection problem, what the cancellation analysis predicts is that each and every presupposition of the embedded clause will become an actual presupposition of the complex sentence, unless it is nullified by certain linguistic and non-linguistic factors.

[10] On the basis of the presuppositional behaviour of *even*, *too*, and *manage to*, Karttunen and Peters (1979) took the view that all kinds of presupposition are conventional implicatures in the sense articulated by Grice. One problem for such an analysis is that many types of presupposition are cancellable (e.g., Levinson 1983: 210, Soames 1989: 581, 603).

How, then, can a potential presupposition be cancelled? Like a conversational implicature, a potential presupposition is defeated if it is inconsistent with (i) background assumptions, (ii) contextual factors, and (iii) semantic entailment (see Chapter 2). In addition, a potential presupposition is cancelled if it clashes with conversational implicatures.

In the first place, a potential presupposition is cancelled if it is inconsistent with background assumptions or real-world knowledge. Recollect (3.14) above and consider (3.50) below.

(3.54)   John hasn't discovered that Angola is in Asia.
            ~>> Angola is in Asia

The use of the factive verb *discover* should give rise to the potential presupposition that Angola is in Asia. But this proposition runs against our real-world knowledge that Angola is an African country. Consequently the unwanted presupposition is defeated by the contradictory real-world knowledge.

Secondly, a potential presupposition is defeated if it is at variance with contextual factors. In addition to (3.16) above, there is (3.55).

(3.55)   John: I don't have a car.
            Mary: So at least you don't need to worry about where to park your car.
            ~>> John has a car

The potential presupposition that John has a car is in contradiction to the assertion that has already been put in the context. Since the assertion in the context is more powerful, the inconsistent potential presupposition fails to become an actual presupposition.

Next, a potential presupposition disappears if it is not in keeping with semantic entailments. Consider (3.19)–(3.21) above and (3.56) below.

(3.56)   John doesn't know that Mary is a hay fever sufferer: she isn't.
            ~>> Mary is a hay fever sufferer

In (3.56), for instance, there should be a potential presupposition, namely, Mary is a hay fever sufferer. But there is also a conflicting semantic entailment, namely, Mary is not a hay fever sufferer. Now, given that a potential presupposition has to be consistent with any existing semantic entailment, the potential presupposition vanishes.

Finally, a potential presupposition is abandoned if it clashes with a conversational implicature. We have already seen an example in (3.15) above. Another example is given below.

(3.57) (Gazdar 1979 crediting Karttunen)
        If I realize later that I haven't told the truth, I will confess it to everyone.
        +> I will not realize later that I haven't told the truth
        ~>> I haven't told the truth

The whole sentence in (3.57) carries a potential presupposition that the speaker hasn't told the truth. But (3.57) also has a conversational implicature to the effect that the speaker doesn't know that he hasn't told the truth (Gazdar 1979: 150, 153–4, Soames 1989; see also Stalnaker 1974). As a result of this conflict, the presupposition is defeated by the inconsistent conversational implicature. Notice further that presupposition-cancelling conversational implicatures are usually $Q_{-clausal}$ ones.

It should be mentioned at this point that there are two important characteristics of Gazdar's presupposition cancellation mechanism. First, a potential presupposition is overridden if it conflicts with any of the factors we have discussed above, but the cancellation must proceed in a fixed order of priority, which is stated in (3.58) (cf. Chapter 2).

(3.58) Gazdar's presupposition cancellation procedure
        a. Background assumptions
        b. Contextual factors
        c. Semantic entailments
        d. Conversational implicatures
        e. Presuppositions

Put the other way round, the augmentation of the Gazdarian context (i.e., **common ground**), which consists of a set of non-controversial propositions, runs according to the following order of priority: first the relevant background assumptions are placed in the context, then the contextual information is added, then the entailments of what is said, then the conversational implicatures, and only finally the presuppositions. The second, related point is that at each step in the process of augmentation, the additional proposition can be added only if it does not contradict any proposition that is already put in the context (see Gazdar 1979 for further discussion).

From a conceptual point of view, the cancellation analysis is preferable to the filtering-satisfaction analysis. There is no need to postulate arbitrary notions such as plugs, holes, and filters on Gazdar's theory.[11]

---

[11] A possible conceptual problem for this analysis, though of a different kind, is why given that presuppositions are commonly taken to be more conventional than conversational implicatures, they should be defeated by the latter (e.g., Landman 1986, Kadmon 2001: 136).

Empirically, many of the counterexamples to the filtering-satisfaction analysis, as we have already seen, fall out naturally from the cancellation theory. Recollect (3.50), repeated here as (3.59).

(3.59)   It's possible that John has children and it's possible that his children are away.
         ~>> John has children

In this example, the presupposition of the second conjunct that John has children is not projected on to the whole sentence. On Gazdar's analysis, this is correctly accounted for by the fact that (3.59) bears a Q-$_{\text{clausal}}$ conversational implicature, namely, the speaker is not sure whether John has children or not. This implicature, which is inconsistent with the potential presupposition, is added to the context prior to the potential presupposition, thus ensuring the loss of the latter. The same story can be told of (3.51). Since the entailment that there is no king of France is already present in the immediate discourse context, given Gazdar's cancellation mechanism, the inconsistent potential presupposition that there is a king of France cannot be added to the context, which correctly explains why the potential presupposition is cancelled.

However, the cancellation analysis is not without its own counterexamples. As an illustration, consider (3.60), which represents the class of examples on which the cancellation theory fails that was first pointed out by Soames (1982).

(3.60)   If someone in the linguistics department won the research grant, it was John who won it.
         ~>> Someone won the research grant

The problem is this: the consequent of (3.60) bears the potential presupposition that someone won the research grant, but this presupposition is not inherited by the whole conditional, as correctly predicted by the filtering-satisfaction theory. By contrast, under any cancellation theory, the disappearance of the potential presupposition is dependent on the cancelling conversational implicature generated by the *if* clause. But the relevant conversational implicature here is that the speaker is not sure that someone in the linguistics department won the research grant, and as such it is not inconsistent with the potential presupposition under consideration (because someone outside the linguistics department might have won the grant), hence the failure to prevent the potential presupposition from becoming the actual presupposition—an incorrect outcome (see Heim 1983, Landman 1986, and van der Sandt 1988 for other counterexamples).[12]

On the basis of counterexamples like (3.60) above, and of the observation that the filtering-satisfaction and cancellation analyses are complementary in their coverage of data, Soames (1982) suggested a synthesis of the two theories, arguing that a correct account of presupposition projection requires both Karttunen's local filtering and Gazdar's global cancelling mechanisms. Two models of incorporation are considered: (i) filter first and cancel afterwards and (ii) cancel first and filter afterwards. Soames adopted the second alternative (see also Soames 1989, Beaver 2001: 70–2, and Kadmon 2001: 139–42 for further discussion).

Gazdar's cancellation analysis is a very influential theory of presupposition projection. In recent years, this theory has generated other cancellation accounts such as van der Sandt (1988), Bridge (1991), Mercer (1992), Marcu (1994), and Schötter (1995). While these analyses differ considerably in their technical details, they are all based on Gazdar's central insight that presuppositions are cancellable.

3.3.3. The accommodation analysis

In an attempt to combine the strengths of both the filtering-satisfaction and cancellation theories, Heim (1983, 1992) developed a particular version of the filtering-satisfaction model, couched in her dynamic semantic theory of context change (see also van der Sandt 1992).[13] Let us dub this model the **accommodation analysis**.

On Heim's view, the meaning of an expression, including the presupposition of a sentence, is its context change potential. The notion of

---

[12] One solution proposed by Landman (1986) is to strengthen the notion of conversational implicature to cancel the unwanted presupposition. But such a proposal seems to create as many problems as it solves.

[13] Notice that both Karttunen and Stalnaker's filtering-satisfaction and Gazdar's cancellation analyses are dynamic in nature, too. One advantage of Heim's approach, however, is that it can handle presupposition projection below the level of the clause. For a textbook introduction, see, e.g., Kadmon (2001), especially Chapter 10.

accommodation is generally attributed to Lewis (1979), but it was originated by Strawson (1950, 1964). Other scholars who made important con-
tributions to the concept before Lewis include Karttunen (1974), Stalnaker
(1974), and Ballmer (1975, 1978). Simply put, accommodation provides a
theory of how deviant usages are brought back into line with expectations
by a co-operative interlocutor (e.g., Huang 2000a: 239, Levinson 2000:
60–1). Thus, in the case of presupposition, it refers to a dynamic process
of 'repair' in discourse, whereby a 'tacit extension' is made to the discourse
context to allow for update with otherwise unfulfilled presuppositions
(Beaver 1997, 2001). As an illustrating example, consider (3.61), due to
Gazdar (1979: 106), when uttered by John who is late for a meeting.

(3.61)   I'm sorry I'm late, my car broke down.
         >> The speaker has a car and he came by car

Even if no one in the audience previously knew the presupposition of
(3.61), they will let the proposition get through unblocked, that is, they
will accommodate the assumption that the speaker has a car and he came
by car. What seems to happen here is that the presupposition in question is
simply added to the discourse context as if it had been there all along.

Needless to say, accommodation is constrained by certain conditions,
one of which is that what is accommodated must be non-controversial and
consistent with all the propositions already placed in the context (e.g.,
Soames 1979, 1989: 567, Atlas 2004). Suppose that John had uttered
(3.62) (due to Levinson 1983: 205) instead of (3.61) in the above scenario.

(3.62)   I'm sorry I'm late, my fire-engine broke down.
         >> The speaker has a fire-engine and he came by fire-engine

The reason that the required presupposition of (3.62) would probably be
much more difficult to accommodate is that it runs contrary to real-world
knowledge for an average person to own a fire-engine and drive it to a
meeting.[14] All this shows that new information can be, and frequently will
be, conveyed by way of presupposition and that accommodation is essentially a mechanism to increment the discourse context with new, non-
controversial assumptions. Looked at in this way, accommodation can be

---

[14] Another important constraint on accommodation is 'bridging': the requirement that new information added to the discourse context be related to the
information already there. See, e.g., Kadmon (2001: 20–1) for discussion.

regarded as a special case of Gricean exploitation: the speaker exploits the maxims of conversation to engender pragmatic inferences (see Chapter 2) (Stalnaker 1974, Horn 1996; see also Thomason 1990).[15]

On Heim's analysis, two types of context are identified, corresponding to two types of accommodation: (i) **global context**, the context against which a sequence of sentences/clauses are evaluated and (ii) **local context**, the context against which parts of a sentence are evaluated. The former gives rise to **global** (or in Soames' 1989 terms, *de facto*) **accommodation**, and the latter gives rise to **local** (or again to use Soames' 1989 terminology, *de jure*) **accommodation**.[16] By way of illustration, take (3.63).

(3.63)   The king of France isn't bald.
            >> There is a king of France

In performing global accommodation, we amend the initial context to a new context that contains the assumption that France has a king. This leads to the interpretation that there is a king of France and he isn't bald, thus retaining the expectable presupposition. By contrast, in performing local accommodation, we don't amend the initial context in a global way. Instead we amend it only at the point where it has to be amended. This gives rise to the interpretation to the effect that it is not the case that there is a king of France and he is bald.

The question that comes up next is when global accommodation is used and when local accommodation is employed. The answer provided by Heim is that global accommodation is *ceteris paribus* preferred over local

---

[15] As pointed out by Horn (1996), the connection between accommodation and exploitation is forged by Grice himself, as can be seen from the following passage.

[I]t is quite natural to say to somebody, when we are discussing some concert, *My aunt's cousin went to that concert*, when we know perfectly well that the person we are talking to is very likely not even to know that we have an aunt, let alone know that our aunt has a cousin. So the supposition must be not that it is common knowledge but rather that it is noncontroversial, in the sense that it is something that we would expect the hearer to take from us (if he does not already know). (Grice 1989: 274)

[16] According to Soames (1989: 578), in *de facto* accommodation, apparent violations of presuppositional requirements are accommodated by adjusting the existing conversational facts to fit the requirements. By contrast, in *de jure* accommodation, these violations are accommodated by adjusting the requirements to fit the conversational facts.

accommodation. In other words, global accommodation is normally per-formed unless it is forced out by, say, threat of contradiction. Only in the latter case is local accommodation performed (see also van der Sandt 1992).[17] This can be illustrated by a consideration of (3.55) above, and (3.64) below.

(3.64)   John: Auntie Anna doesn't have a cat.
         Mary: So at least you don't have to look after her cat when she is on holiday.
         ∼>> Auntie Anna has a cat

Here, if we employ the strategy of global accommodation, that is, if we make the global assumption that Auntie Anna has a cat, the proposition will clash directly with what is already in the context engendered by John's utterance in the previous turn in the mini-conversation, namely, Auntie Anna does not have a cat. Consequently, global accommodation is forced out, and local accommodation is performed. The latter will produce an interpretation to the effect that Auntie Anna doesn't have a cat and John does not have to look after her cat when she is on holiday, hence the disappearance of the putative presupposition—an empirically correct pre-diction. The same can be said of examples (3.50) and (3.57) above, repeated here as (3.65) and (3.66), respectively.

(3.65)   It's possible that John has children and it's possible that his children are away.
         ∼>> John has children
(3.66)   If I realize later that I haven't told the truth, I will confess it to everyone.
         +> I will not realize later that I haven't told the truth
         ∼>> I haven't told the truth

In (3.65), local accommodation of *his children* in the embedded clause of the second conjunct will result in the interpretation in (3.67) below, allow-ing for the putative presupposition to disappear. In (3.66), if we locally accommodate the assumption that the speaker hasn't told the truth in the antecedent, an interpretation like the one in (3.68) below will ensue, again allowing for the putative presupposition to drop out.

---

[17] In van der Sandt's (1992) accommodation analysis, which is formulated within the framework of Discourse Representation Theory (DRT), in addition to local and global accommodations there is a third type of accommodation, labelled **intermediate accommodation.**

(3.67)   It's possible that John has children and it's possible that John has children and his children are away

(3.68)   If I haven't told the truth and I realize later that I haven't told the truth, I will confess it to everyone

There are, however, problems at the very core of the accommodation analysis. One main problem centres on the relationship between global and local accommodation. In the first place, as pointed out by Soames (1989: 601), the preference for global accommodation will make the wrong prediction that (3.69) presupposes that someone solved the problem.

(3.69)   Either it was Susan who solved the problem, or no one at the conference did.
~>> Someone solved the problem

Secondly, following Roberts (1996), Kadmon (2001: 172) argued that on the assumption that (3.70) does not bear the presupposition that Sue smoked, both global and local accommodations are possible.

(3.70)   If Sue stopped smoking yesterday, for example, that would explain why she is chewing candy all the time today.
~>> Sue smoked

If this is correct, then the argument that local accommodation is legitimate only if global accommodation is not plausible has to be abandoned (see, e.g., Soames 1989, Geurts 1999 for further arguments against the accommodation analysis, and Asher and Lascarides 1998 for an attempt to replace accommodation with discourse update through rhetorical links; see also Bauerle, Reyle, and Zimmerman 2003).[18]

---

[18] Mention should be made here of another important analysis of presupposition, namely, the neo- or post-Gricean analysis. Deriving ultimately from the ideas of Grice (1981), the central tenet of the neo- or post-Gricean analysis is to reduce the presupposition of a positive sentence to an entailment on the one hand, and that of a negative sentence to a conversational implicature on the other. Early attempts along this line include Atlas (1975), Kempson (1975), Wilson (1975), and Atlas and Levinson (1981). A current advance of the analysis can be found in Atlas (2004, 2005), who also argued for a paradigmatic shift in the study of presupposition. This work also contains many insightful comments on presupposition. The neo- or post-Gricean theory of presupposition may be seen as an instantiation of what Levinson (1983: 216–17) dubbed the re-allocation programme.

3.4. Summary

In this chapter I have examined presupposition. I discussed the general phenomena of presupposition in Section 3.1 and proceeded to consider the properties of presupposition in Section 3.2. Finally, in Section 3.3 I surveyed three important analyses of presupposition.

One consensus to be reached is that, as so nicely summed up by Soames (1989: 556, 606), 'presupposition may not be a single phenomenon with a unitary explanation, but rather a domain of related issues involving the interaction of several semantic and pragmatic principles', and therefore 'theories of presupposition are neither exclusively semantic nor exclusively pragmatic, but rather require the integration of both kinds of information'.

One main weakness can also be identified. There has virtually been no cross-linguistic study of presupposition. It is not unreasonable to speculate that while presupposition exhibits universal properties, it could also display language-specific ones. In my view, a better understanding of presupposition can be attained only if the phenomena are approached from a cross-linguistic perspective.

Key concepts

presupposition
presupposition trigger (lexical trigger, constructional/structural trigger)
properties of presupposition (constancy under negation, defeasibility)
presupposition projection problem
plug
hole
filter
filtering condition (for conditionals, conjunctions, disjunctions)
potential presupposition
actual presupposition
presupposition cancellation procedure
accommodation
global accommodation
local accommodation

Exercises and essay questions

1. What presuppositions do the following constructions give rise to?
   (i) The burglar realized that he had been filmed on closed circuit television.
   (ii) John forgot to do the washing up.
   (iii) John hasn't driven a car since he had the accident.
   (iv) Professor Huang was glad that he had solved one of evolution's great mysteries.
   (v) John isn't off cigarettes again.
   (vi) It wasn't John who moved to Spain.
   (vii) Susan discovered that her husband was having an affair.
   (viii) Mary started emptying the shopping bags.
   (ix) It's odd that John doesn't know how to telnet.
   (x) Jane never remarried.
   (xi) If John hadn't missed the interview, he would have got the job.
   (xii) John hasn't found out that his brother used all the printer paper.
2. Can you work out the presuppositions of the following?
   (i) John pretended that he was a professional footballer.
   (ii) John, who read mathematics at Harvard, was a friend of mine.
   (iii) Susan has fed all the rabbits.
   (iv) That John hadn't had a bath for more than three weeks bothered Susan.
   (v) John criticised Susan for wearing a fur coat.
3. In each of the following sentences/utterances, I have identified an inference in (b). Using constancy under negation as a diagnostic, can you tell which inference is a presupposition and which is not?
   (i)   a. John has three girlfriends.
         b. John does not have, for example, four girlfriends
   (ii) a. John understands that raised cholesterol level will increase the risk of heart disease.
         b. Raised cholesterol level will increase the risk of heart disease
   (iii) a. It was in August that John found his brother.
         b. John found his brother sometime
   (iv) a. Even John's mother likes surfing the net.
         b. Others, besides John's mother, likes surfing the net; and of those under consideration, John's mother is among the least likely to do so
   (v)   a. Please open the window.
         b. The window is not open
   (vi) a. All of her children believe in marriage.
         b. Some of her children believe in marriage
   (vii) (French)
         a. Vous êtes en vacances?
            'You are on holiday?'
         b. The addressee is socially superior to or distant from the speaker

(viii)   a. John is rich but humble.

b. There is a contrast between being rich and being humble

4. What are the putative presuppositions of the following? How is each of them cancelled?

   (i) Manchester United didn't regret losing the game, because in fact they won!

   (ii) Dr Smith left the university before being promoted to an associate professor.

   (iii) You say that somebody in this room fancies Henry. Well, it isn't Mary who fancies Henry, it isn't Lucy, and it certainly isn't Jane. In fact, nobody in this room fancies Henry!

   (iv) John doesn't know that Neil Armstrong was the first man to travel in space.

   (v) John was in his office when the news was announced, if it was in fact ever announced.

   (vi) He is proud that he is the tsar of Russia, but of course there isn't any such tsar anymore!

   (vii) If Cambridge wins the boat race, John will be happy that Cambridge is the winner.

5. If (i) below is negated, or put in modal contexts, will its entailment survive? (I use '‖-' to stand for 'entail'.) Contrast it with the behaviour of presuppositions under the same circumstances, as shown in (3.32)–(3.34). What conclusions can you reach?

   (i)   The nursery teacher sold nine Christmas raffle tickets.

   ‖- The nursery teacher sold eight Christmas raffle tickets

6. What are the essential properties of presupposition?

7. To what extent is presupposition a pragmatic phenomenon?

8. What is the projection problem for presupposition?

9. What are the similarities and differences between conversational implicature and presupposition?

10. Critically assess one of the three analyses of presupposition discussed in this chapter.

Further readings

Karttunen (1973).

Gazdar (1979).

Beaver (2001). Part I.

Atlas (2004) or Atlas (2005) Chapter 4.

4

Speech acts

Speech act theory, though foreshadowed by the Austrian philosopher Ludwig Wittgenstein's views about **language-games**, is usually attributed to the Oxford philosopher J. L. Austin.[1] The basic ideas, which were formed by him in the late 1930s, were presented in his lectures given at Oxford in 1952–54, and later in his William James lectures delivered at Harvard in 1955. These lectures were finally published posthumously as *How to do things with words* in 1962. After his death in 1960, Austin's ideas were refined, systematized, and advanced especially by his Oxford pupil, the American philosopher John R. Searle. Simply stated, the central tenet of speech act theory is that the uttering of a sentence is, or is part of, an action within the framework of social institutions and conventions. Put in slogan form, saying is (part of) doing, or words are (part of) deeds.

[1] For a history of speech acts, see, e.g., Smith (1990).

Section 4.1, I discuss Austin's dichotomy between performatives and constatives. The focus of Section 4.2 is on his felicity conditions on performatives. In Section 4.3, I examine Austin's tripartite distinction between locutionary, illocutionary, and perlocutionary speech acts. Section 4.4 looks at Searle's felicity conditions on speech acts. Then, in Section 4.5, I present Searle's classification of speech acts. Next, in Section 4.6, I consider indirect speech acts. Finally, Section 4.7 discusses some cultural aspects of speech acts.

4.1. Performatives versus constatives

4.1.1. The performative/constative dichotomy

In the 1930s, a very influential school of thought in philosophy was **logical positivism**, developed by a group of philosophers and mathematicians principally in Vienna. One of the central doctrines of logical positivism is what is now called the **descriptive fallacy**, namely, the view that the only philosophically interesting function of language is that of making true or false statements. A particular version of the descriptive fallacy is the so-called **verificationist thesis** of meaning, namely, the idea that 'unless a sentence can, at least in principle, be verified (i.e., tested for its truth or falsity), it was strictly speaking meaningless' (Levinson 1983: 227; see also Lyons 1995: 173). On such a view, sentences like those in (4.1) are simply meaningless, because they are not used to make verifiable or falsifiable propositions. Instead they express subjective judgments.

(4.1) a. Shouting and screaming at your children is wrong.
      b. Elizabeth is more beautiful than Mary.
      c. Getting married and having children is better than having children and getting married.

It was against this philosophical background that Austin set about developing his theory of speech acts (Austin 1962). He made two important observations. First, he noted that some ordinary language sentences such as those in (4.2) are not employed to make a statement, and as such they cannot be said to be true or false.

(4.2) a. Good morning!
      b. Is she a vegetarian?
      c. Put the car in the garage, please.

Secondly and more importantly, Austin observed that there are ordinary language declarative sentences that resist a truth-conditional analysis in a similar fashion. The point of uttering such sentences is not just to say things, but also actively to do things. In other words, such utterances have both a descriptive and an effective aspect. Accordingly, Austin called them **performatives**, and he distinguished them from assertions, or statement-making utterances, which he called **constatives**.

Put slightly differently, in Austin's view, an initial distinction was made between performatives and constatives. Performatives are utterances that are used to do things or perform acts, as in (4.3). By contrast, constatives are utterances that are employed to make assertions or statements, as in (4.4).

(4.3) a. I christen/name this ship the *Princess Elizabeth*.
　　　 b. I now pronounce you man/husband and wife.
　　　 c. I sentence you to ten years in prison.
　　　 d. I promise to come to your talk tomorrow afternoon.
　　　 e. I command you to surrender immediately.
　　　 f. I apologize for being late.
(4.4) a. My daughter is called Elizabeth.
　　　 b. The children are chasing squirrels in the park.
　　　 c. Maurice Garin won the first Tour de France in 1903.

Unlike those in (4.4), the declarative sentences in (4.3) have two characteristics: (i) they are not used intentionally to say anything, true or false, about states of affairs in the external world, and (ii) their use constitutes (part of) an action, namely, that of christening/naming a ship in (4.3a), that of pronouncing a couple married in (4.3b), that of sentencing a convicted criminal in (4.3c), that of promising in (4.3d), that of ordering in (4.3e), and finally that of apologizing in (4.3f). In addition, as pointed out in Huang (2006a), there are two further differences between (4.3a–c) and (4.3d–f). The first is that while (4.3a–c) is part of a conventional or ritual behaviour supported by institutional facts (see also Strawson 1964), (4.3d–f) is not. Secondly, while the **performative verb**, that is, the verb naming the action while performing it in (4.3a–c) is in general an essential element and cannot be omitted, it can in (4.3d–f). In other words, whereas, for example, we cannot christen/name a ship without using the verb *christen* or *name*, we can make a promise without using the verb *promise*, as in (4.5).

(4.5)   I'll come to your talk tomorrow afternoon.

This would be a good point at which to attempt Exercise 1 on p. 128.

Explicit versus implicit performatives
Performatives can further be divided into two types: explicit and implicit
(or in Austin's 1962: 69 term for the latter, primary). **Explicit performatives**
are performative utterances which contain a performative verb that makes
explicit what kind of act is being performed. By contrast, **implicit performatives** are performative utterances in which there is no such a verb. This
contrast is illustrated by the explicit performatives in (4.3) above and the
implicit performatives in (4.5) above and (4.6) below.

(4.6)   a. Surrender immediately.
        b. How about going to New York on Saturday?
        c. Leave me alone, or I'll call the police.

Now turn to p. 128 and try Exercise 2.

Syntactic and semantic properties of explicit performatives
Austin also isolated a number of syntactic and semantic properties of
explicit performatives in English. They are: (i) explicit performatives contain a performative verb,[2] (ii) the performative nature of such a verb can be
reinforced by adding the adverb *hereby*, and (iii) explicit performatives
occur in sentences with a first-person singular subject of a verb in the
simple present tense, indicative mood, and active voice.

However, as Austin himself was aware, there are exceptions. Explicit
performatives can sometimes take a first-person plural subject, as in (4.7); a
second-person singular or plural subject, as in (4.8); and a third-person
singular or plural subject, as in (4.9). In addition, there are cases where the
explicit performative verb is 'impersonal', that is, it does not refer to the
speaker, as in (4.10). Furthermore, as (4.8), (4.9), (4.10a), (4.10c), and
(4.11b) show, explicit performatives can also occur in sentences with the

---

[2] Cross-linguistically, the size of the inventory of performative verbs varies from
language to language. English is extremely rich in performative verbs. According to
Lyons (1995), there are hundreds, if not thousands, of such verbs in the language
(see also Verschueren 1985). By contrast, Russian is a languages that contains a
much smaller number of such verbs.

verb in the passive voice. Finally, as the attested examples in (4.11) indicate, they can also occur in sentences of present progressive aspect.

(4.7)   We suggest that you go to the embassy and apply for your visa in person.

(4.8)   You are hereby warned that legal action will be taken.

(4.9)   Passengers are hereby requested to wear a seat belt.

(4.10)   a. *Taken from a company's AGM notice*
             Notice is hereby given that the Annual General Meeting of O2 plc will
             be held at The Hexagon, Queens Walk, Reading, Berkshire RG1 7UA
             on Wednesday, 27 July 2005 at 11.00 am for the following purposes: ...
         b. (Hurford and Heasley 1983: 239)
             The management hereby warns customers that mistakes in change
             cannot be rectified once the customer has left the counter.
         c. (Levinson 1983: 260)
             It is herewith disclosed that the value of the estate left by Marcus
             T. Bloomingdale was 4,785,758 dollars.

(4.11)   (Thomas 1995: 45)
         a. *A radio journalist is interviewing the chairman of Railtrack during a strike
             by signal workers.*
             A: Are you denying that the government has interfered?
             B: I am denying that.
         b. *Taken from a naval disciplinary hearing*
             You are being discharged on the grounds of severe temperamental
             unsuitability for service in the Royal Navy.

[Notice next that performative verbs can also be used descriptively. In this usage, they behave like non-performative verbs.]

(4.12)   a. I baptized John's baby last Sunday.
         b. You are always promising to do housework, but you never do it.
         c. It's the head of department who authorized John to work in our lab.

See whether you can do Exercises 3 and 4 on p. 129.

4.1.2. The performative hypothesis

In order to account for implicit performatives, an analysis known as the **performative hypothesis** was put forward in the 1970s. The basic idea of the hypothesis is that underlying every sentence there is a 'hidden' matrix performative clause of the form given in (4.13).

(4.13)   I (hereby) Vp you (that) S

where Vp is a performative verb, and S is a complement clause. The performative verb, which is in the indicative mood, active voice, and simple present tense (see above), will always make explicit what is implicit, though the matrix performative clause can be deleted without meaning being changed (e.g., Ross 1970, Lakoff 1972, Sadock 1974; see Gazdar 1979 and Levinson 1983 for a more detailed formulation of the hypothesis; see also Sadock 2004 for further discussion). Thus, according to this hypothesis, the performative matrix clause in the deep or underlying structure of (4.14) shows up overtly in (4.15).

(4.14)   Stand up.
(4.15)   I hereby request that you stand up. *Or*,
          I hereby order you to stand up.

There are problems at the very heart of this analysis. One such problem is that there are many cases of implicit performatives which do not have an explicit performative version, even though the relevant verb can be used in a descriptive way. As an illustration, consider (4.16).

(4.16)   a. You're a stupid cow.
          b. ?I hereby insult you that you're a stupid cow.
          c. John insulted Mary by saying that she was a stupid cow.

Intuitively (4.16a) is most naturally interpretable as an insult, but contrary to the prediction of the performative hypothesis, it does not seem to have an explicit performative equivalent, as is shown by the oddness of (4.16b). On the other hand, as (4.16c) indicates, the verb *insult* can be used descriptively without any problem. More or less the same can be said of such speech acts as lying, threatening, and punishing. Faced with this and a variety of other syntactic, semantic, and pragmatic difficulties (see, e.g., Levinson 1983: 243–78, Yule 1996: 52–3, Marmaridou 2000: 187, Cruse 2004, Sadock 2004), the performative hypothesis has long been abandoned.

4.2. Austin's felicity conditions on performatives

As already mentioned, it makes no sense to call a performative true or false. Nevertheless, Austin noticed that for a performative to be successful or 'felicitous', it must meet a set of conditions. For example, one such condition for the speech act of naming is that the speaker must be recognized by his or her community as having the authority to perform that act; for the speech act of ordering, the condition is that the speaker must be in authority over the addressee, and finally, for the speech act of promising, one condition is that what is promised by the speaker must be something the addressee wants to happen. Austin called these conditions **felicity conditions**. In other words, felicity conditions are conditions under which words can be used properly to perform actions.

Austin distinguished three different types of felicity conditions (Austin 1975: 14–15).

(4.17)   Austin's felicity conditions on performatives

A. (i) There must be a conventional procedure having a conventional effect.

(ii) The circumstances and persons must be appropriate, as specified in the procedure.

B. The procedure must be executed (i) correctly and (ii) completely.

C. Often

(i) the persons must have the requisite thoughts, feelings and intentions, as specified in the procedure, and

(ii) if consequent conduct is specified, then the relevant parties must so do.

Violation of any of the conditions in (4.17) will render a performative 'unhappy' or infelicitous. If conditions A or B are not observed, then what Austin described as a **misfire** takes place. For instance, in England, a registrar conducting a marriage ceremony in an unauthorized place will violate condition A (i), thus committing a misfire. The same is true for a clergyman baptizing a wrong baby, because in this case, condition A (ii) is not fulfilled. Next, as an illustration of a violation of condition B (i), consider the case of a bridegroom not saying the exact words that are conventionally laid down at a marriage ceremony.[3] As to condition B (ii), it dictates that the procedure must be complete. Thus, in making a bet, the

---

[3] The standard formula at a Church of England wedding has variants:

(i) The Book of Common Prayer version

Curate: Wilt thou have this woman to thy wedded wife, . . .

Bridegroom: I will.

(ii) The Alternative Service Book version

Curate: (Name), will you take (Name) to be your wife . . .

Bridegroom: I will.

bet is not 'on' unless *You are on* or something with the same effect is uttered by the addressee. In Austin's terminology, this counts as a satisfactory **uptake**,[4] the absence of which will again cause a misfire. Finally, if condition C is not met, resulting in insincerities, then an **abuse** is the outcome. Examples of an abuse include congratulating someone when one knows that he or she passed his or her examination by cheating (condition C (i)), making a promise when one already intends to break it (condition C (ii)), and marrying without intending to consummate the marriage (see also Sadock's 2004 discussion of these conditions in terms of misinvocation, misexecution, and abuse). We will return to the question of felicity conditions when we come to Searle's work.

Now have a go at Exercise 5 on p. 129.

4.3. Locutionary, illocutionary, and perlocutionary speech acts

The initial distinction made by Austin between performatives and constatives was soon to be rejected by him in favour of a general theory of speech acts. In fact, as pointed out by Levinson (1983: 231), there are two internal shifts in Austin's arguments. First, there is a shift from the view that performatives are a special class of sentences/utterances with peculiar syntactic and semantic properties to the view that there is a general class of performatives that encompasses both explicit and implicit performatives, the latter including many other types of sentence/utterance. The second shift is from the performative/constative dichotomy to a general theory of speech acts, of which the various performatives and constatives are just special subcases.

In America, the following is also used:
(iii) Curate: Do you take this woman . . .
      Bridegroom: I do.

[4] Thomas (1995: 40–1) called performatives like betting 'collaborative' performatives, because their success depends on particular uptake by another person. Other collaborative performatives include bequeathing and challenging.

What led Austin to abandon the performative/constative dichotomy? In the first place, he noted that like performatives, constatives are also subject to the felicity conditions stated in (4.17). Recollect so-called Moore's paradox, discussed in Chapter 2, as illustrated by (4.18).

(4.18) ?Princess Diana died in a fatal car crash in Paris with Dodi Al Fayed, but I don't believe it.

This utterance is infelicitous because it violates condition C (i) in (4.17) above. In the same vein, if someone utters (4.19) when he or she knows that John does not in fact have a wife, then its presupposition will not go through (see Chapter 3). The reason the presupposition fails to carry through is that condition A (ii) in (4.17) above is not adhered to.

(4.19) I'm sure John's wife is a feminist.

Secondly, Austin observed that performatives and constatives may be impossible to distinguish even in truth-conditional terms. On the one hand, there are 'loose' constatives that may not be assessed strictly by means of truth conditions, as in (4.20).

(4.20) a. (Austin 1962) France is hexagonal.
        b. John is bald.
        c. London is sixty miles from where I live.

France is not, strictly speaking, hexagonal. John still has quite a few wispy strands of hair on his head. London may not be exactly sixty miles from where the speaker lives. Thus, statements like those in (4.20) can only be said to be more or less, or roughly, true. On the other hand, there are utterances like those in (4.21) that pass the *hereby* test, and therefore are performatives by definition, but that nevertheless are used to state or assert. In these cases, the performatives must be counted simultaneously as constatives.

(4.21) a. I hereby state that John is growing GM crops.
        b. I hereby tell you that the prime minister is not going to stand down.
        c. I hereby hypothesize that there is water on Mars.

On the basis of such evidence, Austin concluded that constatives are nothing but a special class of performatives, and that the two-way distinction between performatives, as action-performers, and constatives, as truth-bearers, can no longer be maintained.

Consequently, Austin claimed that all utterances, in addition to meaning whatever they mean, perform specific acts via the specific communicative force of an utterance. Furthermore, he introduced a threefold distinction among the acts one simultaneously performs when saying something.

(4.22)   Three facets of a speech act
   (i)   Locutionary act: the production of a meaningful linguistic expression.
   (ii)   Illocutionary act: the action intended to be performed by a speaker in uttering a linguistic expression, by virtue of the conventional force associated with it, either explicitly or implicitly.
   (iii) Perlocutionary act: the bringing about of consequences or effects on the audience through the uttering of a linguistic expression, such consequences or effects being special to the circumstances of the utterance.

A **locutionary act** is the basic act of speaking, which itself consists of three related subacts. They are (i) a **phonic** act of producing an utterance-inscription, (ii) a **phatic** act of composing a particular linguistic expression in a particular language, and (iii) a **rhetic** act of contextualizing the utterance-inscription (Austin 1962, Lyons 1995: 177–85). In other words, the first of these three subacts is concerned with the physical act of making a certain sequence of vocal sounds (in the case of spoken language) or a set of written symbols (in the case of written language). The second refers to the act of constructing a well-formed string of sounds/symbols, be it a word, phrase or sentence, in a particular language. The third subact is responsible for tasks such as assigning reference, resolving deixis, and disambiguating the utterance-inscription lexically and/or grammatically. These three subacts correspond broadly to the three distinct levels and modes of explanation in linguistic theory, namely, phonetics/phonology, morphology/syntax, and semantics/pragmatics.

When we say something, we usually say it with some purpose in mind. This is the **illocutionary act**. In other words, an illocutionary act refers to the type of function the speaker intends to fulfil, or the type of action the speaker intends to accomplish in the course of producing an utterance. It is an act defined within a system of social conventions. In short, it is an act accomplished in speaking. Examples of illocutionary acts include accusing, apologizing, blaming, congratulating, giving permission, joking, nagging, naming, promising, ordering, refusing, swearing, and thanking. The functions or actions just mentioned are also commonly referred to as the

illocutionary force or **point** of the utterance. Illocutionary force is frequently conveyed by what Searle (1969) called an **illocutionary force indicating device (IFID)**, the most direct and conventional type of which is an explicit performative in the form of (4.13) above. Indeed, the term 'speech act' in its narrow sense is often taken to refer specifically to illocutionary acts.

It should be mentioned at this point that the same linguistic expression can be used to carry out a wide variety of different speech acts, so that the same locutionary act can count as having different illocutionary forces in different contexts. Depending on the circumstances, one may utter (4.23) below to make a threat, to issue a warning or to give an explanation.

(4.23) The gun is loaded.

In fact, Alston (1994) argued that the meaning of a sentence consists in its having a certain **illocutionary act potential (IAP)** that is closely and conventionally associated with its form. On this view, to know what a sentence means is to know what range of illocutionary acts it can conventionally be used to perform (see also Recanati 2004b).

Conversely, the same speech act can be performed by different linguistic expressions, or the same illocutionary force can be realized by means of different locutionary acts. The utterances in (4.24), for example, illustrate different ways of carrying out the same speech act of requesting.

(4.24) (At ticket office in railway station)
   a. A day return ticket to Oxford, please.
   b. Can I have a day return ticket to Oxford, please?
   c. I'd like a day return ticket to Oxford.

Finally, a **perlocutionary act** concerns the effect an utterance may have on the addressee. Put slightly more technically, a perlocution is the act by which the illocution produces a certain effect in or exerts a certain influence on the addressee. Still another way to put it is that a perlocutionary act represents a consequence or by-product of speaking, whether intentional or not. It is therefore an act performed by speaking. For example, in an armed bank robbery, a robber may utter (4.23) to get the cashier to open the safe. This effect of the act performed by speaking is also generally known as the **perlocutionary effect**.

While there are unclear cases, the main differences between illocutions and perlocutions can be summed up as follows. In the first place, illocutionary acts are intended by the speaker, while perlocutional effects are not always intended by him or her. Secondly, illocutionary acts are under the speaker's full control, while perlocutionary effects are not under his or her full control. Thirdly, if illocutionary acts are evident, they become evident as the utterance is made, while perlocutionary effects are usually not evident until after the utterance has been made (Hurford and Heasley 1983: 247). Fourthly, illocutionary acts are in principle determinate,[5] while perlocutionary effects are often indeterminate. Finally, illocutionary acts are more, while perlocutionary effects are less conventionally tied to linguistic forms (see also Sadock 2004).

At this point, see whether you can tackle Exercise 6 on p. 129.

4.4. Searle's felicity conditions on speech acts

Recall our discussion of the felicity conditions specified by Austin in Section 4.2 above. Just as its truth conditions must be met by the world for a sentence to be said to be true (see Chapter 1), its felicity conditions must be fulfilled by the world for a speech act to be said to be felicitous. Searle (1969) took the view that the felicity conditions put forward by Austin are not only ways in which a speech act can be appropriate or inappropriate, but they also jointly constitute the illocutionary force. Put in a different way, the felicity conditions are the **constitutive rules**—rules that create the activity itself—of speech acts. On Searle's view, to perform a speech act is to obey certain conventional rules that are constitutive of that type of act. Searle developed the original Austinian felicity conditions into a neo-Austinian classification of four basic categories, namely, (i) propositional content, (ii) preparatory condition, (iii) sincerity condition, and (iv) essential condition. As an illustration of these conditions, consider (4.25) and (4.26).

---

[5] But there are situations in which an illocutionary act is not determinate, as the following example shows.

(i) Employer: I'll come back to see how the work is progressing the day after tomorrow.
Employee: Is that a promise or a threat?

(4.25)   Searle's felicity conditions for promising
    (i) Propositional content: future act A of S
    (ii) Preparatory: (a) H would prefer S's doing A to his not doing A, and S so believes (b). It is not obvious to both S and H that S will do A in the normal course of events
    (iii) Sincerity: S intends to do A
    (iv) Essential: the utterance of e counts as an undertaking to do A

where S stands for the speaker, H for the hearer, A for the action, and e for the linguistic expression.

(4.26)   Searle's felicity conditions for requesting
    (i) Propositional content: future act A of H
    (ii) Preparatory: (a) S believes H can do A (b) It is not obvious that H would do A without being asked
    (iii) Sincerity: S wants H to do A
    (iv) Essential: the utterance of e counts as an attempt to get H to do A

Let us now work through these conditions one by one. The **propositional content** condition is in essence concerned with what the speech act is about. That is, it has to do with specifying the restrictions on the content of what remains as the 'core' of the utterance (i.e. Searle's propositional act) after the illocutionary act part is removed. For a promise, the propositional content is to predicate some future act of the speaker, whereas in the case of a request, it is to predicate some future act of the addressee. The **preparatory conditions** state the real-world prerequisites for the speech act. For a promise, these are roughly that the addressee would prefer the promised action to be accomplished, that the speaker knows this, but also that it is clear to both the speaker and the addressee that what is promised will not happen in the normal course of action. In the case of a request, the preparatory conditions are that the speaker has reason to believe that the addressee has the ability to carry out the action requested, and that if the addressee is not asked, he or she will not perform the action. Next, the **sincerity condition** must be satisfied if the act is to be performed sincerely. Thus, when carrying out an act of promising, the speaker must genuinely intend to keep the promise. When making a request, the speaker must want the addressee to do the requested action. Notice that if the sincerity condition is not fulfilled, the act is still performed, but there is an abuse, to use Austin's term. Finally, the **essential condition** defines the act being performed in the sense that the speaker has the intention that his or her utterance will count as the identifiable act, and that this intention is recognized by the addressee. Thus in the case of a promise, the speaker must have the intention to create an obligation to act, and for a request, the speaker must intend that his or her utterance counts as an attempt to get the addressee to do what is requested. Failure to meet the essential condition has the consequence that the act has not been carried out.

Now see what you make of Exercise 7 on p. 129.

4.5. Searle's typology of speech acts

Can speech acts be classified, and if so, how? Austin (1962) grouped them into five types: (i) **verdictives**—giving a verdict, (ii) **exercitives**—exercising power, rights, or influence, (iii) **commissives**—promising or otherwise undertaking, (iv) **behabitives**—showing attitudes and social behaviour, and (v) **expositives**—fitting an utterance into the course of an argument or conversation. Since then, there have been many attempts to systematize, strengthen, and develop the original Austinian taxonomy (e.g., Bach and Harnish 1979, Allan 2001, Bach 2004). Some of these new classifications are formulated in formal/grammatical terms, others in semantic/pragmatic terms, and still others on the basis of the combined formal/grammatical and semantic/pragmatic modes (see, e.g., Sadock 2004 for a review). Of all these (older and newer) schemes, Searle's (1975a) **neo-Austinian typology of speech acts** remains the most influential.

Under Searle's taxonomy, speech acts are universally grouped into five types along four dimensions: (i) **illocutionary point** or speech act type, (ii) **direction of fit** or relationship between words and world, (iii) **expressed psychological state**, and (iv) propositional content (see also Searle 1979, 2002, but see Section 4.7.1 below). The five types of speech act are further explained below.

(i) **Representatives** (or **assertives**; the constatives in the original Austinian performative/constative dichotomy) are those kinds of speech act that commit the speaker to the truth of the expressed proposition, and thus carry a truth-value. They express the speaker's belief. Paradigmatic cases include asserting, claiming, concluding, reporting, and stating. In performing this type of speech act, the speaker represents the world as he or she believes it is, thus making the words fit the world of belief. Representatives are illustrated in (4.27).

(4.27) a. Chinese characters were borrowed to write other languages, notably Japanese, Korean and Vietnamese.
b. Francis Crick and Jim Watson discovered the double helix structure of DNA.
c. The soldiers are struggling on through the snow.

(ii) **Directives** are those kinds of speech act that represent attempts by the speaker to get the addressee to do something. They express the speaker's desire/wish for the addressee to do something. Paradigmatic cases include advice, commands, orders, questions, and requests. In using a directive, the speaker intends to elicit some future course of action on the part of the addressee, thus making the world match the words via the addressee. Directives are exemplified in (4.28).

(4.28) a. Turn the TV down.
b. Don't use my electric shaver.
c. Could you please get that lid off for me?

(iii) **Commissives** are those kinds of speech act that commit the speaker to some future course of action. They express the speaker's intention to do something. Paradigmatic cases include offers, pledges, promises, refusals, and threats. In the case of a commissive, the world is adapted to the words via the speaker him- or herself. Examples of commissives are presented in (4.29).

(4.29) a. I'll be back in five minutes.
b. We'll be launching a new policing unit to fight cyber crime on the internet soon.
c. I'll never buy you another computer game.

(iv) **Expressives** are those kinds of speech act that express a psychological attitude or state in the speaker such as joy, sorrow, and likes/dislikes. Paradigmatic cases include apologizing, blaming, congratulating, praising, and thanking. There is no direction of fit for this type of speech act.[6]

(4.30) a. Well done, Elizabeth!
b. I'm so happy.
c. Wow, great![7]

---

[6] Alternatively, one might claim, as Yule (1996: 55) did, that in performing the act of an expressive, the speaker makes known what he or she feels, thus rendering the words to fit the world of feeling.

[7] In many languages including English, sentences with the import of the following are often used to express one's strong emotions.

(v) **Declarations** (or **declaratives**) are those kinds of speech act that effect immediate changes in some current state of affairs. Because they tend to rely on elaborate extralinguistic institutions for their successful performance, they may be called institutionalized performatives. In performing this type of speech act, the speaker brings about changes in the world; that is, he or she effects a correspondence between the propositional content and the world. Paradigmatic cases include bidding in bridge, declaring war, excommunicating, firing from employment, and nominating a candidate. As to the direction of fit, it is both words-to-world and world-to-words.[8]

(4.31)   a. President: I declare a state of national emergency.
          b. Chairman: The meeting is adjourned.
          c. Jury foreman: We find the defendant not guilty.

Illocutional point, direction of fit, and expressed psychological state can be summarized in (4.32) (see Vanderveken 1994 for a formalization in terms of illocutionary logic).[9]

(4.32) | *Illocutionary point* | *Direction of fit* | *Expressed psychological state* |
|---|---|---|
| Representative | words-to-world | belief (speaker) |
| Directives | world-to-words | desire (addressee) |
| Commissives | world-to-words | intention (speaker) |
| Expressives | none | variable (speaker) |
| Declarations | both | none (speaker) |

Now attempt Exercise 8 on p. 129.

(i) a. I don't know what to say.
     b. I'm absolutely speechless.
     c. No words can express my . . . !

[8] Notice that some performative verbs in English can fit into more than one of Searle's categories. They include *advise*, *confess*, *suggest*, *tell*, and *warn*.

(i)   I warn you not to dance/against dancing on the table. (directive)
(ii) I warn you that there are no train services on Sundays. (assertive)

[9] In Searle (1983), there were also three directions of fit between mind and the world: (i) the mind-to-world direction of fit, (ii) the world-to-mind direction of fit, and (iii) the empty direction of fit. De Sousa Melo (2002) proposed that a fourth direction of fit—the double direction of fit—be added to Searle's typology, paralleling the four directions of fit between words and the world.

4.6. Indirect speech acts

4.6.1. What is an indirect speech act?

Most of the world's languages have three basic sentence types: (i) declarative, (ii) interrogative, and (iii) imperative.[10] In some languages, the three major sentence types are distinguished morphologically and/or syntactically. Somali provides an example of such a language.

(4.33) (Saeed 2003: 237)
      a. Warkii   waad   dhegeysatay.
         news the   DECL-you   listen to-2SG-PAST
         'You listened to the news.'
      b. Warkii   miyaad   dhegeysatay?
         news the   Q-you   listen to-2SG-PAST
         'Did you listen to the news?'
      c. Warkii   dhegeyso.
         news the   listen to-2SG-IMPV
         'Listen to the news.'

In (4.33), the declarative format is marked by *waa*, the interrogative format is indicated by *ma*, and the imperative format is indicated with a zero marking (Saeed 2003: 237). Another example is provided by Greenlandic.

(4.34) (Sadock and Zwicky 1985)
      a. Igavoq.
         cook-INDIC-3SG
         'He cooks.'
      b. Igava.
         cook-Q-3SG
         'Does he cook?'

In (4.34), the declarative and interrogative are differentiated by means of separate personal suffixes (Sadock and Zwicky 1985). Finally, in Lakhota, the difference between a 'declarative' with an indefinite pronoun and an interrogative with an interrogative pronoun is marked by the adding of a sentence-final question particle. (Notice that the indefinite and interrogative pronouns are identical.) This is illustrated in (4.35).

---

[10] There are languages in the world that lack a genuine declarative. One such language is Hidatsa, as described in Sadock and Zwicky (1985).

(4.35)   (Croft 1994)

   a. Mniluzahe Othuwahe ekta tuwa ya.
      Rapid   City   to   who go-3SG
      'Someone went to Rapid City.'

   b. Mniluzahe Othuwahe ekta tuwa ya   he?
      Rapid   City   to   who go-3SG Q
      'Who went to Rapid City?'

The three major sentence types are typically associated with the three basic illocutionary forces, namely, asserting/stating, asking/questioning, and ordering/requesting, respectively. Thus, the three Somali sentences in (4.33), for instance, may be paraphrased using explicit performatives.

(4.36) a. I (hereby) state that you listened to the news.
      b. I (hereby) enquire whether you listened to the news.[11]
      c. I (hereby) order you to listen to the news.

Now, if there is a direct match between a sentence type and an illocutionary force, we have a **direct speech act**. In addition, explicit performatives, which happen to be in the declarative form, are also taken to be direct speech acts, because they have their illocutionary force explicitly named by the performative verb in the main part (or 'matrix clause') of the sentence. On the other hand, if there is no direct relationship between a sentence type and an illocutionary force, we are faced with an **indirect speech act**. Thus, when an explicit performative is used to make a request, as in (4.37), it functions as a direct speech act; the same is the case when an imperative is employed, as in (4.38). By comparison, when an interrogative is used to make a request, as in (4.39), we have an indirect speech act.

[11] Some native speakers of English may find sentences like (4.36b) odd (e.g. Sadock and Zwicky 1985). For this group of speakers, the interrogative is a sentence type for which there is no explicit performative equivalent. A better example may be provided by the exclamation in English.

(i) a. What a beautiful girl she is!
     b. ?I (hereby) exclaim what a beautiful girl she is.
     c. I exclaimed what a beautiful girl she was.

As shown by (ia) and (ib), the exclamation in English does not have a corresponding explicit performative, though the verb *exclaim* can be used descriptively (see, e.g., Cruse 2004 for further discussion).

(4.37)   I request you to pass the salt.
(4.38)   Pass the salt.
(4.39)   Can you pass the salt?

In short, the validity of the distinction between direct and indirect speech act is dependent on whether or not one subscribes to what Levinson (1983: 264, 274) called the **literal force hypothesis**—the view that there is a direct structure–function correlation in speech acts and that sentence forms are by default direct reflexes of their underlying illocutionary forces.

There are, however, problems at the very heart of the literal force hypothesis. One is that there are cases of speech acts where even the direct link between performative verbs and speech acts breaks down. Consider (4.40).

(4.40)   I promise to sack you if you don't finish the job by this weekend.

In (4.40), the performative verb is *promise*, but the illocutionary force that is most naturally ascribed to this speech act is that of either a threat or a warning. This shows that contrary to the main prediction of the literal force hypothesis, we cannot always identify speech acts even with sentences that contain a performative verb.

Secondly and more importantly, as pointed out by Levinson (1983: 264), most usages are indirect.[12] The speech act of requesting, for example, is very rarely performed by means of an imperative in English. Instead, it is standardly carried out indirectly, and there is probably an infinite variety of sentences that can be used to make a request indirectly, as shown in (4.41) (adapted from Levinson 1983: 264–5; see also Bertolet 1994, Holdcroft 1994).

(4.41)   a. I want you to close the window.
         b. Can you close the window?
         c. Will you close the window?
         d. Would you close the window?
         e. Would you mind closing the window?
         f. You ought to close the window.
         g. May I ask you to close the window?
         h. I wonder if you'd mind closing the window.

See whether you can tackle Exercise 9 on pp. 129–30 now.

---

[12] As we will shortly see in Section 4.7 below, the degree of directness/indirectness may vary cross-linguistically.

4.6.2. How is an indirect speech act analysed?

Roughly, there are three main approaches. The first is to assume the existence of a dual illocutionary force (as proposed by Searle 1975b). On this assumption, indirect speech acts have two illocutionary forces, one literal or direct, and the other non-literal or indirect. While the literal force is secondary, the non-literal force is primary. Next, whether an utterance operates as an indirect speech act or not has to do with the relevant felicity conditions. For example, (4.39) above both infringes the felicity condition for the speech act of questioning and queries the preparatory condition for that of requesting. This explains why it can function as an indirect speech act whereas (4.42), for example, cannot. The reason is that in the case of (4.42), felicity conditions are irrelevant.

(4.42)   (Searle 1975b)
         Salt is made of sodium chloride.

Finally, on Searle's view, a speaker's performing and an addressee's understanding an indirect speech act always involves some kind of inference. The question that arises next is how this inference can be computed. Searle's suggestion is that it can be computed along the general lines of the rational, co-operative model of communication articulated by Grice (see Chapter 2).[13]

One interesting characteristic of indirect speech acts is that they are frequently conventionalized (Morgan 1978). This can be illustrated by the fact that of various, apparently synonymous linguistic expressions, only one may conventionally be used to convey an indirect speech act. Consider (4.43).

(4. 43)   a. Are you able to pass the salt?
          b. Do you have the ability to pass the salt?

Under Searle's analysis, both (4.43a) and (4.43b) would be expected to be able to perform the indirect speech act of requesting, because (i) they are largely synonymous with (4.39), and (ii) they, too, inquire about the satisfaction of the addressee-based preparatory condition for making a request. But this expectation is not fulfilled.

---

[13] See, e.g., Vanderveken (2002) for an attempt to reformulate Grice's maxims in terms of speech acts. See Dascal (1994) for a comparison between speech act theory and Gricean theory of conversational implicature.

Searle's response to this puzzle is that there is also a certain degree of conventionality about indirect speech acts, and this may be accounted for in terms of convention of use/meaning. Inspired by this insight of Searle's, Morgan (1978) developed a notion of **short-circuited implicature** to cover inference involved in cases like (4.39). In these cases, while the relevant conversational implicature is in principle calculable, it is not in practice calculated (see also Horn and Bayer 1984, Horn 1988). From a linguistic point of view, then, the conventionality here is correlated with the possible occurrence of *please*. While *please* can be inserted before the verb *pass* in (4.37)–(4.39), it cannot in (4.43), as shown in (4.44).

(4.44)   a. I request you to please pass the salt.
   b. Please pass the salt.
   c. Can you please pass the salt?
   d. ?Are you able to please pass the salt?
   e. ?Do you have the ability to please pass the salt?

Furthermore, the conventionality indicated by *please* in (4.44a) and (4.44b) is one of meaning, hence the speech act of requesting is performed directly. By contrast, the conventionality signalled by *please* in (4.44c) is one of usage, and thus we have an indirect speech act.[14]

A second, rather similar, approach is due to Gordon and Lakoff (1975). In their analysis, there are inference rules called **conversational postulates** that reduce the amount of inference needed to interpret an indirect speech act. Thus in the case of (4.39), if the interpretation as a question cannot be intended by the speaker, then the utterance will be read as being equivalent to his or her having said (4.37), thus resulting in the performance of the indirect speech act of requesting. Stated this way, the conversational postulates proposed by Gordon and Lakoff can be seen as another reflection of the conventionality of indirect speech acts. As to the similarities and differences between Searle's and Gordon and Lakoff's analyses, the major similarity is that both accounts assume that the interpretation of indirect speech acts involves both inference and conventionality; the major difference concerns the question of balance, namely, how much of the work

---

[14] As Searle (1975b) and Green (1975) showed, the use of the *Can/Would you . . .* type question to indirectly express requests and orders varies cross-linguistically (see also Wierzbicka 1991). According to Horn (1988), given that a short-circuited implicature is itself a matter of convention, this is precisely to be expected.

involved in computing an indirect speech act is inferential and how much is conventional. ⎦

Finally, in contrast to the **inferential model** we have just discussed, there is the **idiom model**. In this model, sentences like (4.39) are semantically ambiguous, and the request interpretation constitutes a speech act idiom that involves no inference at all. On this view, (4.39) is simply recognized as a request with no question being perceived. This is the position taken by Sadock (1974). There are, however, problems with this analysis, too. One is that it fails to capture the fact that the meaning of an indirect speech act can frequently (at least in part) be derived from the meaning of its components. The technical term for this is compositionality (see Chapter 3). In addition, these would-be idioms turn out to be quite comparable cross-linguistically. For example, like their English equivalent in (4.45), (4.46)–(4.49) can all be used to indirectly request the addressee to turn on the central heating system, depending on context.[15]

(4.45)   It's cold in here.
(4.46)   (Arabic)
         ?na-hu   barid   huma.
         it's-3-M-S cold   in here
         'It's cold in here.'
(4.47)   (Chinese)
         zher   zhen   leng.
         here   really   cold
         'It's really cold in here.'
(4.48)   (German)
         Es   ist   sehr   kalt   hier   drin.
         it   is   very   cold   here   in
         'It's very cold in here.'
(4.49)   (Modern Greek)
         Kani   krio   edo   mesa.
         it is doing cold   here   in
         'It's cold in here.'

---

[15] Intuitively, the requests in (4.45)–(4.49) are more indirectly conveyed than that in (4.39). As noted by Green (1975) and Horn (1988), in contrast to the request in (4.39), the requests in (4.45)–(4.49) are non-short-circuited, and hence non-detachable implicatures. Consequently, they are not subject to cross-linguistic variation.

A further problem is that in the idiom model, an interpretation that takes into account the literal meaning or the direct illocutionary force of an indirect speech act is not allowed. This, however, leaves examples like (4.50) unexplained.

(4.50)   A: Can you pass the salt?
          B: Yes, I can. (Here it is.)

4.6.3. Why is an indirect speech act used? Some remarks on politeness

Why, then, do people use indirect speech acts? One answer is that the use of indirect speech acts is in general associated with **politeness**. Indirect speech acts are usually considered to be more polite than their direct counterparts. Furthermore, the more indirect a speech act, the more polite.[16]

There is an extensive literature on politeness (see, e.g., DuFon et al. 1994 for a bibliography on politeness covering publications up to the early 1990s), and this is not the place for me to give a full review of it. Instead,

---

[16] This can be illustrated by English. Consider (i)–(v).

 (i) Call Lucy a taxi, please.
 (ii) Will you call Lucy a taxi?
 (iii) Would you call Lucy a taxi?
 (iv) Would you mind calling Lucy a taxi?
 (v) I wonder if you'd mind calling Lucy a taxi?

The speech act of requesting is performed more indirectly, for example, using (iii) than using (i), and therefore the utterance in (iii) is considered more polite than that in (i). But this may not be the case with, say, Polish, as argued by, e.g., Wierzbicka (1991). Jaszczolt (2002: 307) pointed out that (vi) and (vii) in Polish are equivalent in politeness and in commonality to (viii) in English (see also Sifianou 1992 on Greek).

(vi) Siadaj.
     sit down
(vii) Usiądź,   proszę.
      sit down   please
(vii) Will you sit down?

This raises the question of whether or not indirect speech acts are universally more polite than their direct counterparts.

in what follows, I shall provide a brief discussion of politeness with special reference to speech acts.

Currently, there are four main theoretical models of politeness: (i) the 'social norm' model, (ii) the 'conversational maxim' model (e.g., Leech 1983, 2003) (see note 12 in Chapter 2), (iii) the 'face-saving' model (Brown and Levinson 1978, 1987), and (iv) the 'conversational contract' model (e.g., Fraser 1990). (See also Watts 2003 for a 'social practice' model.[17]) Of these four models, the most influential and comprehensive is Brown and Levinson's now classic 'face-saving' model.

At the heart of Brown and Levinson's theory of politeness lies Goffman's (1967) sociological notion of **face**.[18] Simply put, face is 'the public self-image that every member wants to claim for himself' (Brown and Levinson 1987: 61). Stated in another way, face means roughly an individual's self-esteem. Furthermore, there are two aspects to face. First, **positive face**, which represents an individual's desire to be accepted and liked by others. **Positive politeness** orients to preserving the positive face of others. When one uses positive politeness, one tends to choose the speech strategies that emphasize one's solidarity with the addressee. These strategies include claiming 'common ground' with the addressee, conveying that the speaker and the addressee are co-operators, and satisfying the addressee's wants (Brown and Levinson 1987: 101–29). Second, there is **negative face**, which refers to an individual's right to freedom of action and his or her need not to be imposed on by others. **Negative politeness** orients to maintaining the negative face of others. When one employs negative politeness, one tends to opt for the speech strategies that emphasize one's deference to the addressee. Typical linguistic realizations of the strategies of negative politeness involve, for example, the use of conventional indirectness, hedges on illocutionary force, and apologies (Brown and Levinson 1987: 130). Defined thus, face is considered to be a universal notion in any human society. As rational agents, conversational participants will ideally try to preserve both their own face and their interlocutors' face in a verbal interaction.

---

[17] According to DuFon et al. (1994), the earliest book on politeness in the Western tradition is *Libro del cortegiano* (The book of the courtier) by Baldesar Castiglione, published in 1528.

[18] The notion of 'face' and its related English expressions such as *losing/saving/gaining face* seem to originate from the Chinese expression *mianzi*. The concept of 'face' seemed to be introduced to the West by the Chinese anthropologist Hu Hsien Chin in 1944 (Hu 1944).

Many types of speech acts such as complaints, disagreements (e.g., Locher 2004), and requests intrinsically threaten face. Hence they are called **face-threatening acts (FTAs)**. In the first place, FTAs can threaten positive face, negative face, or both. Acts that threaten positive face include expressions of disapproval, accusations, criticism, disagreements, and insults; those that threaten negative face include advice, orders, requests, suggestions, and warnings; those that threaten both positive and negative face include complaints, interruptions, and threats. Furthermore, a second distinction can be made between acts that primarily threaten the speaker's face and those that primarily threaten the addressee's face. The speaker can threaten his or her own face by performing, for example, the acts of accepting compliments, expressing thanks, and making confessions. On the other hand, acts such as advice, reminding, and strong expression of emotions threaten primarily the addressee's face wants (Brown and Levinson 1987: 67–8).

Brown and Levinson (1987: 74) posited three independent and culturally sensitive social variables according to which the strength or weightiness of an FTA can be measured. First, there is the **social distance (D)** between the speaker and the addressee. Second is the **relative power (P)** of the addressee over the speaker. Finally, the third variable is the **absolute ranking (R)** of imposition in a particular culture (see also Scollon and Scollon 1995). The strength of an FTA is measured by adding together the three variables D, P, and R, on the basis of which the amount of face work needed or the degree of politeness required can be worked out.

On Brown and Levinson's model, there is a set of five strategies one can choose from to avoid or weaken an FTA. The strategies are given in (4.51).

(4.51)   Brown and Levinson's (1987: 60) set of FTA-avoiding strategies

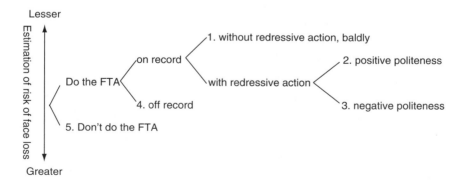

Notice that in the set of strategies given in (4.51), the more threatening an FTA is, the more polite (i.e. the higher-numbered) the strategy the speaker must employ to mitigate its effects.

Let me now explore these strategies in somewhat greater detail. In the first place, one can perform an FTA on record, that is, directly; or off record, that is, indirectly, for example, by dropping a verbal hint. Secondly, an FTA on record can be performed either baldly, i.e. without redress; or with redress. In the latter case, there are two further choices: an FTA can be performed with a face-saving act using either positive politeness redress (such as emphasizing solidarity with the addressee) or negative politeness redress (such as giving deference to the addressee). Finally, there is also the option for one not to perform the FTA at all, for instance, by dropping a non-verbal hint. These five strategies can be illustrated in (4.52).

(4.52)   Situation: John, a student asks Mary, another student to lend him her lecture notes
    1. *On record, without redress, baldly*:
       Lend me your lecture notes.
    2. *On record, with positive politeness redress*:
       How about letting me have a look at your lecture notes?
    3. *On record, with negative politeness redress*:
       Could you please lend me your lecture notes?
    4. *Off record*:
       I didn't take any notes for the last lecture.
    5. *Don't perform the FTA*:
       [John silently looks at Mary's lecture notes.]

It will be apparent that the use of indirect speech acts serves to diminish FTAs and thereby to satisfy face needs.

You may now be ready to tackle Exercise 10 on p. 130.

Since its publication in 1978, Brown and Levinson's 'face-saving' theory has generated an enormous amount of research on politeness (see Brown and Levinson 1987 for a survey of the literature up to the mid-1980s). From an empirical point of view, while Brown and Levinson's model is based on an in-depth study of three unrelated languages/cultures, namely, Tamil, Tzeltal, and English (both British and American), politeness phenomena in a much wider array of languages/cultures ranging from Catalan through Japanese to Turkish have in the meantime been carefully studied. Conceptually, many of the recent studies have focused on the universality of the

Brown and Levinson theory, in particular the notion of face, the social variables, and the set of five politeness strategies. Sifianou (1992), for example, in a cross-cultural comparison between the politeness systems in England and Greece, argued that the politeness system in Greek is more positive-face oriented, whereas in British English it is more negative-face oriented. While arguing for such differences, her study nevertheless showed that Brown and Levinson's theory provides a very good general theoretical and descriptive framework for the study of politeness. On the other hand, a number of scholars have found it difficult to apply Brown and Levinson's model directly to the politeness systems in Eastern, collective cultures (see, e.g., Gu 1990, Mao 1994, and Lee-Wong 2000 on Chinese; Matsumoto 1988, 1989, and Ide 1989 on Japanese; Hwang 1990 on Korean; Bayraktar-oglu 2001 and Zeyrek 2001 on Turkish; Koutlaki 2002 on Persian). The same can be said of some African languages/cultures. Nwoye (1989, 1992), for example, carried out a study of the notion of face in Igbo. According to this study, Igbo society is more concerned with the collective self-image of a group than the individualistic self-image of any one member of the group. The 'group face' is defined as '[t]he avoidance of behavior capable of lowering the public self-image or self-worth[iness] (*iru*) of one's group, dictated by the fear of *imecu iru* (to darken face)' (Nwoye 1992: 314) (see also Agyekum 2004 on the concept of face in Akan). Strecker (1993) also argued that the politeness system of the Hamer in south Ethiopia presents a challenge to Brown and Levinson's theory. All this seems to indicate that while politeness itself is a universal phenomenon, politeness strategies and individual speech acts may to some extent vary from one language/culture to another.

4.7. Speech acts and culture

4.7.1. Cross-cultural variation

Many speech acts are culture-specific. This is particularly so in the case of institutionalized speech acts, which typically use standardized and stereo-typed formulae and are performed in public ceremonies. A good example is provided by the speech act of divorcing. In some Muslim cultures, under the appropriate circumstances, the uttering of a sentence with the import of

(4.53) three times consecutively by a husband to his wife will *ipso facto* constitute a divorce. By contrast, in Western cultures, no one (no matter what his or her religion is) can felicitously use (4.53) to obtain a divorce.[19]

(4.53)   'I hereby divorce you.'

But how about non-institutionalized speech acts? First of all, as said above, any given speech act may be culture-specific. Rosaldo (1982), for example, observed that the speech act of promising has no place among the Ilongots—a tribal group of hunters and horticulturalists in the Philippines. She attributed the absence of this speech act in the conceptual repertoire of the Ilongots to a lack of interest in sincerity and truth in that community. The Ilongots, argued Rosaldo, are more concerned with social relationships than with personal intentions. On the basis of anthropological evidence such as this, Rosaldo claimed that the universality of Searle's typology of speech acts cannot be maintained. Another example of this kind has been reported for the Australian aboriginal language Yolngu. According to Harris (1984: 134–5), there does not seem to be any speech act of thanking in the Yolngu speaker's repertoire.

Conversely, a given speech act may be present only in certain cultures. For example, in the Australian aboriginal language Walmajarri, one finds a speech act of requesting that is based on kinship rights and obligations. The verb in question is *japirlyung* (Hudson 1985), and the speech act may be called 'kinship-based requesting', because it conveys a message meaning

---

[19] In some Muslim cultures, even an unintentional use of (4.53) can effect a divorce, as can be shown by the following incident in Pakistan, cited from Thomas (1995: 43).

A terrible tangle has arisen in Pakistan over a local soap opera. Soap star Usman Pirzada divorced his television wife in traditional Muslim style, pronouncing *Talaq*—I divorce thee—three times. The trouble was that his TV spouse was played by his real wife, Samina. Now the ulemas are saying that the divorce is binding, even though the formula was spoken in the interest of art. Their decree maintains that the Prophet ordained that in three matters (marriage, divorce and the freeing of slaves) words uttered unintentionally or even in jest cannot be withdrawn. Divorced they are and divorced they must remain.

It has been reported in the media that in some Muslim cultures, husbands now can even use e-mails and/or text messages to divorce their wives.

roughly 'I ask/request you to do X for me, and I expect you to do it simply because of how you are related to me'. Thus, for the speakers of Walma-jarri, it is very difficult to refuse a kinship-based speech act of requesting (see also Wierzbicka 1991: 159–60, Goddard 1998: 370). 'Exotic' speech acts such as kinship-based requesting do not seem to be present in either the Chinese-type East Asian or the European-type Western cultures.

Second, given a particular speech situation, pertinent speech acts are carried out differently in different languages/cultures. For instance, in some East Asian and Western cultures, if one steps on another person's toes, one normally performs the speech act of apologizing. But apparently this is not the case among the Akans, a West African culture. As reported by Mey (2001: 287 crediting Felix Ameka), in that culture, such a situation does not call for an apology but calls for an expression of sympathy. 'The focus is on the person to whom the bad thing has happened rather than the person who has caused the bad thing' (Mey 2001: 287). Another example: while in English, thanks and compliments are usually offered to the hosts when leaving a dinner party, in Japanese society, apologies such as *o-jama itashimashita* 'I have intruded on you' are more likely to be offered by the guests. A similar speech act of apologizing is performed in Japanese upon receiving a present, when a Japanese speaker is likely to say something like *sumimasen*—the most common Japanese 'apology' formula or one of its variants (e.g., Coulmas 1981; see also Goddard 1998). Putting the matter the other way round, as is pointed out by many Japanese scholars, apologies can be used in a much broader range of speech situations in Japanese than in English.

Third, in different languages/cultures, the same speech act may meet with different typical responses. For example, a compliment normally generates acceptance/thanking in English, but self-denigration in Chinese, Japanese, or even Polish. A typical compliment response formula in Chinese would be something like (4.54).

(4.54) A: ni cai zuode zhen hao!
        B: nali, nali, wo bu hui zuocai.
        A: bie keqi, ni cai zhende zuode hen hao!
        B: ni tai keqi le.

        A: 'You cook really well!'
        B: 'No, no, I don't really know how to cook properly.'
        A: 'Please don't be too modest. You really cook very well.'
        B: 'You're too kind.'

The same is more true in Japanese. According to Mizutani and Mizutani (1987: 43), '[T]he Japanese will never accept a compliment without saying *iie* ["no"]'. This is vividly illustrated by the following conversation conducted between two women in so-called women's speech (Miller 1967: 289–90).

(4.55)   A: Ma, go-rippa na o-niwa de gozaimasu wa ne. Shibafu ga hiro biro to shite ite, kekko de gozaimasu wa ne.
B: Iie, nan desu ka, chitto mo teire ga yukitodokimasen mono de gozaimasu kara, mo, nakanaka itsumo kirei ni shite oku wake ni wa mairimasen no de gozaimasu yo.
A: A, sai de gozaimasho ne. Kore dake o-hiroin de gazaimasu kara, hito tori o-teire asobasu no ni datte taihen de gozaimasho ne. Demo ma, sore de mo, itsumo yoku o-teire ga yukitodoite irasshaimasu wa. Itsumo honto ni o-kirei de kekko de gozaimasu wa.
B: Iie, chitto mo sonna koto gozaimasen wa.

A: 'My, what a splendid garden you have there—the lawn is so nice and big, it's certainly wonderful, isn't it!'
B: 'Oh, no, not at all, we don't take care of it at all any more, so it simply doesn't always look as nice as we would like it to.'
A: 'Oh, I don't think so at all—but since it's a big garden, of course it must be quite a tremendous task to take care of it all by yourself; but even so, you certainly do manage to make it look nice all the time; it certainly is nice and pretty any time one sees it.'
B: 'No, I'm afraid not, not at all.'

Given the general Japanese reluctance to say 'no' under almost any other circumstances, this compliment response pattern, though considered as rather traditional by the younger generation in present-day Japan, is quite striking.

Leech (2003) regarded (4.54) and (4.55) as cases of what he dubbed '**pragmatic quasi-paradoxes**'. Pragmatic quasi-paradoxes arise from the asymmetry of politeness: what is polite for the speaker (for example, the speaker invites the addressee to dinner) may be 'impolite' for the addressee (that is, the addressee accepts the speaker's invitation to dinner). If both the speaker and the addressee were equally determined to be polite and not to give way, then this asymmetry would never be resolved, hence the paradox of politeness (Leech 2003).

However, in an actual speech event, the pragmatic quasi-paradoxes of this sort are often resolved by means of implicit negotiations between the speaker and the addressee. Thus, after a few rounds of, say, compliment followed by ritual denial, the addressee will 'reluctantly' accept the compliment, as in (4.54), or he or she will continue to deny the compliment, as in (4.55). Another example: after a few exchanges of offer and ritual refusal, the addressee will 'reluctantly' accept the gift offered by the speaker in certain cultures (see, e.g., Zhu, Li, and Qian 2000 on Chinese; see also Barron 2003 on Irish English, about which in the next subsection). This pragmatic quasi-paradoxical mechanism of offer–refusal can be schematized in (4.56).

(4.56) A: offer 1
        B: ritual refusal 1
        A: offer 2
        B: ritual refusal 2
        A: offer 3
        B: acceptance

As our final example, there is the following exchange of insisting on repaying a debt and ritually refusing to accept repayment between two male speakers in Persian (Koutlaki 2002: 1747).

(4.57) A: bezær mæn ... [takes out money] ta færamuš nækærdæm
        B: aqa vel kon tora xoda
        A: næ næ xaheš mikonæm
        B: be vallahe nemixam
        A: xaheš mikonæm
        B: nemixam
        A: pænjai hæm bærat gereftæm æz bank
        B: næ nemixam axe

        A: 'Let me ... er ... [takes out money] before I forget.'
        B: 'Leave it, really.'
        A: 'Please.'
        B: 'I don't need it now, really.'
        A: 'Please.'
        B: 'I don't need it.'
        A: 'I even got it in fifty pound notes for you.'
        B: 'But I don't need it I say!'[20]

---

[20] In terms of **conversation analysis**, (4.54)–(4.57) are instantiations of what is called **adjacency pairs**—a sequence of two structurally adjacent utterances, produced by two different speakers and ordered as a **first pair part** and a **second pair part**. Taking the compliment response pattern as an example, the first pair part is

Fourthly, the same speech act may differ in its **directness/indirectness** in different cultures. Since the late 1970s, a great deal of research has been conducted on how particular kinds of speech acts, especially such FTAs as requests, apologies, and complaints, are realized across different languages. Of these investigations, the most influential is the large-scale Cross-Cultural Speech Act Realization Project (CCSARP) (e.g., Blum-Kulka, House, and Kasper 1989; see also Blum-Kulka and Olshtain 1984). In this project, the realization patterns of requesting and apologizing in German, Hebrew, Danish, Canadian French, Argentinian Spanish, and British, American, and Australian English were compared and contrasted. In the case of requests, the findings were that from among the languages examined, the Argentinian Spanish speakers are the most direct, followed by the speakers of Hebrew. The least direct are the Australian English speakers, while the speakers of Canadian French and German are positioned at the mid-point of the directness/indirectness continuum.

Building on the CCSARP, strategies for the performing of certain types of FTAs in a much wider range of languages have since been examined. These languages include Catalan, Chinese, Danish, Dutch, German, Greek, Hebrew, Japanese, Javanese, Polish, Russian, Thai, Turkish, four varieties of English (British, American, Australian, and New Zealand), two varieties of French (Canadian and French), and eight varieties of Spanish (Argentinian, Ecuadorian, Mexican, Peninsular, Peruvian, Puerto Rican, Uruguayan, and Venezuelan). Recently, there have been a number of new comparative studies. Sifianou (1992) studied requests in British English and Greek. Van Mulken (1996) compared the use of the politeness strategies in Dutch and French requests. Hong (1998) explored requests in Chinese and German. Fukushima (2002) compared requests in British English and Japanese. Márquez-Reiter (2000) investigated requests and apologies in British English and Uruguayan Spanish. Bayraktaroglu and Sifianou (2001) collected a number of comparative studies of speech act realization patterns in Greek and Turkish, including advice-giving, correcting, and complimenting, to mention but a few. Most of these studies adopted a

the complement and the second pair part is the acceptance or rejection. From a cultural perspective, the main difference here is that while the acceptance is the **preferred second pair part** in some languages/cultures (e.g., English or Western), the ritual denial is the preferred second pair part in other languages/cultures (e.g., Chinese or East Asian) (Huang 1987).

methodology which is at least partially compatible and comparable with that used in the CCSARP.

As a result of these studies, it has now been established that there is indeed extensive cross-cultural/linguistic variation in directness/indirectness in the expression of speech acts, especially in FTAs such as requests, complaints, and apologies,[21] and that these differences are generally associated with the different means that different languages utilize to realize speech acts. These findings have undoubtedly contributed to our greater understanding of cross-cultural/linguistic similarities and differences in face-redressive strategies for FTAs.

4.7.2. Interlanguage variation

In the above subsection we looked at cross-cultural variation in speech acts. In this subsection I turn to interlanguage variation.

Simply put, an **interlanguage** is a stage on a continuum within a rule-governed language system that is developed by L2 learners on their path to acquire the target language. This language system is intermediate between the learner's native language and his or her target language. For example, when a native speaker of Chinese is learning German as a second language, then the German used by him or her is an interlanguage.

A number of studies have recently appeared that explored speech acts in interlanguage pragmatics. These include Blum-Kulka, House, and Kasper (1989), Kasper and Blum-Kulka (1993), Ellis (1994), Trosborg (1995), le Pair (1996), Baba (1999), Gass and Houck (2000), Achiba (2003), and Barron (2003). Some of these studies investigated how a particular type

---

[21] The cultural differences in directness versus indirectness in the expression of a speech act frequently lead speakers from one culture to misinterpret speakers from another culture, as the following incident, reported in Takahashi and Beebe (1987), shows.

In 1974, President Nixon asked Prime Minister Sato if Japan would agree to self-imposed restrictions on the export of fabrics to the United States. Prime Minister Sato replied: 'Zensho shimasu', which literally means 'I'll take care of it'. However, when it is used by a politician, the uttering of this expression actually performs the speech act of a polite refusal in Japanese. President Nixon failed to understand it as a polite refusal and became very angry later on, when the Japanese simply took no action at all.

of speech act is performed by non-native speakers in a given interlanguage; others compared and contrasted the similarities and differences in the realization patterns of given speech acts between native and non-native speakers in a particular language. The best-studied interlanguage is that developed by speakers of English as a second language. Other interlanguages that have been investigated include Chinese, German, Hebrew, Japanese, and Spanish.

Kasper and Blum-Kulka (1993) contained five studies of interlanguage expression of FTAs, namely, apologizing, correcting, complaining, requesting, and thanking. Of these studies, Bergman and Kasper's (1993) research showed that in performing apologies, Thai learners of English in general 'do too much of a good thing'—a phenomenon dubbed as 'gushing' by House (1988) and less benevolently as 'waffling' by Edmondson and House (1991). Takahashi and Beebe (1993) observed that American English speakers are most likely, and Japanese speakers of Japanese are least likely, to use a positive remark before making a correction, with Japanese speakers of English falling in between. Olshtain and Weinbach (1993) found that non-native speakers' complaints in Hebrew are less offensive and less face-threatening. Eisenstein and Bodman (1993) pointed out that while expressing gratitude is a universal speech act, it is carried out differently in different languages/cultures. More or less the same is true of interlanguage hints in requests (Weizman 1993). One of the common findings of the studies collected in Kasper and Blum-Kulka (1993) was that the expression of interlanguage speech acts tends to be more verbose. Next, Ellis (1994) focused on the interlanguage FTAs of requesting, apologizing, and refusing. Trosborg (1995) studied requests, complaints, and apologies by Danish learners of English. Le Pair (1996) observed that Dutch learners of Spanish use fewer direct request strategies than native speakers of Spanish. Baba (1999) made a comparative study of compliment responses by Japanese learners of English and American English learners of Japanese. Gass and Houck (2000) studied the speech act of refusal as performed in English by native speakers of Japanese. Finally, Barron (2003) took a detailed look at Irish learners' acquisition of German, especially of the pragmatics of requests, offers, and refusals. Many of her findings are of interest. For example, in Irish English, the ritual refusal of an offer is typically followed by re-offers and acceptances, but this discourse sequence is not characteristic of German. However, Irish learners attempt to implement this pattern in German, although this pragmatic transfer tends to decrease over time. All these studies have made an important contribution to speech act theory, second language acquisition, and second language teaching and learning.

Finally in this chapter, try Exercise 11 on p. 130.

4.8. Summary

In this chapter, I have considered speech acts and speech act theory. Section 4.1 looked at Austin's performative/constative dichotomy. In section 4.2, I examined Austin's felicity conditions on performatives. The focus of section 4.3 was on the three dimensions of speech acts, namely, locutionary, illocutionary, and perlocutionary acts. Section 4.4 discussed Searle's felicity conditions on speech acts. In section 4.5, I presented Searle's fivefold typology of speech acts. Section 4.6 was concerned with indirect speech acts, including a discussion of politeness. Finally, in section 4.7, I discussed cultural and interlanguage variations in speech acts. A few recent formal and computational approaches to speech acts and speech act theory are worthy of note. One important theoretical development is the integration of speech acts with intentional logic, resulting in what is called **illocutionary logic** (Searle and Vanderveken 1985, and Vanderveken 1990, 1991, 1994, 2002). Finally, recent formalizations of various aspects of speech act theory in artificial intelligence and computational linguistics can be found in Perrault (1990), Bunt and Black (2000), and Jurafsky (2004).

Key concepts

speech act theory
speech act
performative
constative
explicit performative
implicit performative
performative verb
properties of explicit performative
performative hypothesis

locutionary act

illocutionary act/force

perlocutionary act/effect

felicity condition (Austin's, Searle's)

representative

directive

commissive

expressive

declaration

direct speech act

indirect speech act

literal force hypothesis

politeness

face

positive face

negative face

face-threatening act (FTA)

interlanguage

Exercises and essay questions

1. Of the following utterances, which are performatives and which are constatives?

C (i) The couple live in a house on the corner of Henry Street.

P (ii) I object, your honour.

C (iii) John's future is full of hope.

P (iv) I declare this bridge open.

P (v) I second the motion.

C (vi) John is growing a beard.

P (vii) *As a call in bridge*
        Three clubs.

2. Of the following performatives, which are explicit and which are implicit?

I (i) All applications must be submitted to the dean by 31st March.

I (ii) Who do you tip for the post?

E (iii) You are hereby forbidden to leave this room.

I (iv) How about going to the British Museum this afternoon?

I (v) Keep all medicines out of reach of children.

E (vi) *One British MP to another in Parliament*
        I apologize for calling my honourable friend a liar.

3. Which of the following are performative verbs?

Y (i) resign
Y (ii) deny
Y (iii) nominate
N (iv) threaten
N (v) punish
Y. (vi) ask

4. In the following, which performative verbs are used performatively, and which are used non-performatively?

N (i) We thanked them for their hospitality.
P (ii) I hereby declare Tony Benn the duly elected member for this constituency.
P (iii) I'm warning you not to spend too much on alcohol.
N (iv) John withdraws his application.
P (v) All passengers on flight number thirty-six to Paris are requested to proceed to gate number nine.
N (vi) The managing director congratulated everyone in the room.

5. At the wedding of Prince Charles and Lady Diana, Diana stumbled over Charles's many names, getting one of his names out of order. Which of Austin's felicity conditions do you think Diana violated? Is it a misfire or an abuse in Austin's term? *B(i) misfire.*

6. What are the locutionary, illocutionary, and perlocutionary acts of the following?
   (i) Mother to son: Give me that *Playboy* magazine.
   (ii) Dean's secretary to professor: Coffee?

7. Can you work out the Searlean felicity conditions for (i) questioning, (ii) thanking, and (iii) warning?

8. Using Searle's typology, classify the following speech acts:
   (i) pleading *directive.*
   (ii) welcoming *expressive*
   (iii) recommending *directive.*
   (iv) undertaking *commissive*
   (v) baptizing a child into the Christian faith *declaration*
   (vi) appointing a minister *declaration.*
   (vii) stating *representative*
   (viii) apologizing *expressive.*

9. Of the following utterances, which are direct and which are indirect speech acts?
   (i) Would all drivers please proceed to the car deck and return to their vehicles, as we will be docking shortly? *indirect.*
   (ii) (At a fitness club in Oxford) *direct.*
        Please shower before entering the pool. Please observe pool rules located at poolside. You are advised against swimming alone.
   (iii) Who cares! *(No one cares.) indirect*
   (iv) Have a nice weekend! *indirect.*

(v) Why don't we go to the new Italian restaurant near the museum? *[handwritten: indirect]*

(vi) (The following example is taken from a letter which I received from
Marquis Who's Who in the World in May 2003.)
[handwritten: direct] Once again, because our publication cycle operates within a firm timetable, we
respectfully request that you return your verified sketch by June 27.

10. John and Mary are watching TV. John has accidentally blocked the TV screen.
In (i)–(v) below, there are five possible ways that Mary could get John to stop
blocking the screen (adapted from Peccei 1999: 90). Can you analyse them in
terms of Brown and Levinson's set of FTA-avoiding strategies? Can you also
rank them in order of politeness, starting with the most polite.
   (i) [Mary keeps shifting on the sofa or craning her neck.]
   (ii) Would you mind moving just a bit?
   (iii) What an interesting programme!
   (iv) Move out of the way.
   (v) How about moving over just a teensy bit?

11. The following is a typical interlanguage compliment response by Chinese L2
learners of English (Huang 1987). *[handwritten: Interlanguage compliment response.]*
   (i) Foreign visitor to China: Your English is excellent.
      Chinese student: No, no. My English is very poor. There's much room for
      improvement. I still have a long way to go in my study . . .

What is the main pragmatic error here? To what extent do you think that
the Chinese L2 learner's native language has influenced his or her inappropriate realization of the speech act of responding to compliments in
English?

12. What is a performative, and what is a constative? Can a performative be
distinguished from a constative? If yes, how; if no, why not?. *[handwritten Chinese characters]*

13. What are locutionary, illocutionary, and perlocutionary acts? Illustrate with
examples. *[handwritten: the difference between them.]*

14. What are the main types of speech act?

15. Critically assess the notion of indirect speech acts.

16. To what extent is Brown and Levinson's theory of politeness universal?

17. Compare and contrast the realization pattern of any one FTA in any two
languages you are familiar with. An example might be to compare and contrast
the realization pattern of refusals in English and Spanish.

18. What are the similarities and differences between speech act theory and
Gricean/neo-Gricean theory of conversational implicature?

Further readings

Austin (1975).
Searle (1969).
Sadock (2004).
Brown and Levinson (1987). Especially Introduction t
recent work, and Chapters 1, 2, and 3.

5

Deixis

The term '**deixis**' is derived from the Greek word meaning 'to show' or 'to point out'. Deixis is directly concerned with the relationship between the structure of a language and the context in which the language is used. It can be defined as the phenomenon whereby features of context of utterance or speech event are encoded by lexical and/or grammatical means in a language. Linguistic expressions that are employed typically as **deictic expressions** or **deictics**[1] include (i) demonstratives, (ii) first- and second-person pronouns, (iii) tense markers, (iv) adverbs of time and space, and (v) motion verbs.

Deixis is a universal linguistic phenomenon, that is, all human languages contain deictic terms. Why is this the case? The reason is straightforward: a language without deictics cannot serve the communicative needs of its users as effectively and efficiently as a language which does have them. Example

---

[1] Deictic expressions or deictics are commonly called **indexical expressions** or **indexicals** in the philosophy of language literature. For further discussion, see, e.g., Lyons (1982: 106), Kaplan (1989), Nunberg (1993), Manning (2001), and Levinson (2004).

(5.1), adapted from Fillmore (1997: 60), illustrates what would happen in the absence of deictic information.

(5.1)   (Found in a bottle in the sea)
        Meet me here a month from now with a magic wand about this long.

Without the relevant deictic information, one would not know who to meet, where or when to meet the writer of the message, or how long a magic wand to bring.

In this chapter I provide a descriptive analysis of deixis. Section 5.1 presents preliminaries of deixis, including deictic versus non-deictic expressions (5.1.1), gestural versus symbolic use of deictic expressions (5.1.2), and deictic centre and deictic projection (5.1.3). In Section 5.2 I discuss the three basic categories of deixis, namely, person (5.2.1), space (5.2.2), and time (5.2.3). Finally, in Section 5.3 the other two categories of deixis, namely, social deixis and discourse deixis, will be examined. Data will be drawn from a wide variety of genetically unrelated and structurally distinct languages to show the diversity and richness of the deictic systems in the world's languages.

5.1. Preliminaries

5.1.1. Deictic versus non-deictic expression

Deictic expressions or **deictics** are expressions that have a deictic usage as basic or central; non-deictic expressions are expressions that do not have such a usage as basic or central. For example, while second-person pronouns are deictic expressions, as in (5.2), third-person pronouns are not, as in (5.3).[2]

(5.2)   *You* and *you*, but not *you*, go back to *your* dorms!
(5.3)   Mary wishes that *she* could visit the land of Lilliput.

It should be pointed out, however, that a deictic expression can be used non-deictically, as in (5.4), and conversely a non-deictic expression can be used deictically, as in (5.5).

---

[2] But this is not the case for Diyari, Kwakwa'la, and many South Asian languages. See Section 5.2.3 below.

(5.4)   If *you* travel on a train without a valid ticket, *you* will be liable to pay a penalty fare.

(5.5)   *She*'s not the principal; *she* is. *She*'s the secretary.

In (5.4), *you* is used as impersonal, similar in function to lexical items such as *on* in French or *man* in German;[3] in other words it is used non-deictically. On the other hand, in (5.5), the interpretation of each of the three instances of *she* depends crucially on a direct, moment by moment monitoring of the physical context in which the sentence is uttered. Hence the third-person pronoun here serves as a deictic expression.

5.1.2. Gestural versus symbolic use of a deictic expression

Within deictic use, a further distinction can be drawn between **gestural** and **symbolic** use (Fillmore 1971, 1997: 62–3). Gestural use can be properly interpreted only by a direct, moment by moment monitoring of some physical aspects of the speech event. For example, in (5.2) and (5.5) above, the deictic expressions can be interpreted only if they are accompanied by a physical demonstration (such as a selecting gesture or eye contact) of some sort. By contrast, interpretation of the symbolic use of deictic expressions only involves knowing the basic spatio-temporal parameter of the speech event. If you hear someone uttering (5.6), you do not expect the utterance to be accompanied by any physical indication of the referent. Provided that you know the general location of the speaker, you can understand it without any problem.

(5.6)   *This* town is famous for its small antiques shops.

Clearly, gestural use is the basic use, and symbolic use is the extended use. It seems that in general if a deictic expression can be used in a symbolic way, it can also be used in a gestural way; but not vice versa. Thus, there are deictic expressions in the world's languages that can only be used gesturally. The presentatives *voici/voilà* in French, *ecce* in Latin and *vot/von* in Russian, for example, belong to this category.

---

[3] There are languages in which the impersonal function is distinctively marked via verbal inflection. One such language is Breton (Anderson and Keenan 1985: 260).

We can summarize the uses of deictic expressions as in (5.7).

(5.7)   Uses of a deictic expression

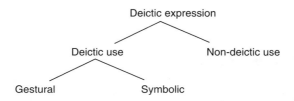

Start work in this chapter by doing Exercise 1 on p. 175.

5.1.3. Deictic centre and deictic projection

Generally speaking, deixis is organized in an egocentric way (Lyons 1977: 646). The default **deictic centre**, or the deictic *origo* (ground zero) in the terminology of Bühler (1934), of the three major categories is the following: (i) the central anchorage point for person is the person who is speaking, (ii) that for time is the time at which the speaker produces the utterance, and (iii) that for place is the place where the speaker produces the utterance (see also Levinson 1983: 63–4). Put informally, we may say that deixis is a 'self-centred' phenomenon, its centre being typically 'I-here-now'.

However, this 'egocentric' organization of deixis is not always adhered to, which gives rise to what Lyons (1977: 579) called a **deictic projection**. As an illustration, consider (5.8).

(5.8)   a. Can I go to your office tomorrow at 12:00?
        b. Can I come to your office tomorrow at 12:00?

Go and *come* are both motion verbs. In (5.8a), the use of *go* encodes movement away from the deictic centre, therefore we do not have a deictic projection. By contrast, in (5.8b), the use of *come* marks movement toward the deictic centre, therefore we have a deictic projection, namely, the deictic centre has been projected from the speaker on to the addressee.[4] We shall have more to say about motion verbs in Section 5.2.3.

> Now see whether you can tackle Exercises 2 and 3 on pp. 175–6.

5.2. Basic categories of deixis

Traditionally, three basic categories of deixis are discussed in the linguistics and the philosophy of language literature, namely, person, place, and time. The *raison d'être* behind this tripartition is that all 'pointing' is done by human beings, and therefore all 'pointing' expressions have to be related to the uttering person, the place of utterance, and the time of utterance (e.g., Mey 2001: 54).

5.2.1. Person deixis

Person deixis is concerned with the identification of the interlocutors or participant-roles[5] in a speech event. It is commonly expressed by (i) the traditional grammatical category of person, as reflected in personal pronouns and if relevant, their associated predicate agreements, and (ii) vocatives, which can be encoded in, for example, kinship terms, titles, and proper names, and in combinations of these.

Personal pronouns
Let me begin with **personal pronouns**. Personal pronouns usually express person, number and gender, so-called φ-features in the generative syntax literature. They sometimes also encode distance and social relations. In this subsection, I shall concentrate on person, number, and gender. I shall

---

[4] Deictic projection is formally marked in some languages, including Inukitut. In this language, when the deictic centre is shifted from the speaker to another person in the speech event, the 'field shifting prefix' *ta-* is used (Denny 1982, Diessel 1999: 47).

[5] Following Goffman (1979) and Fillmore (1971, 1997: 62), Levinson (1983: 68, 72, 1988) argued that interlocutors or participant-roles can be further discriminated on a more accurate basis. Thus, the speaker can be differentiated as between source and transmitter of the message/utterance, and the addressee between recipient and overhearer (see Levinson 1988 for a more elaborated system).

discuss distance in relation to place deixis in Section 5.2.3, and social relations in relation to social deixis in Section 5.3.1.

Person

Personal pronouns generally exhibit a three-way distinction of first, second, and third person. The category first-person is the grammaticalization of the speaker's reference to him- or herself, that is, the participant-role with speaker inclusion [+S]. Second person is the encoding of the speaker's reference to one or more addressees, that is, the participant-role with addressee inclusion [+A]. Third person is the grammaticalization of reference to persons or entities which are neither speakers nor addressees in the situation of utterance, that is, the 'participant-role' with speaker and addressee exclusion [−S, −A] (Ingram 1978, Levinson 1983: 69). Notice that third person is unlike first or second person in that it does not necessarily refer to any specific participant-role in the speech event (Lyons 1977: 638, Levinson 1983: 69). Therefore, it can be regarded as the grammatical form of a residual non-deictic category, given that it is closer to non-person than either first or second person (e.g., Huang 2000a: 178). This is why all of the world's languages seem to have first- and second-person pronouns, but some appear to have no third-person pronouns. Dyirbal (Dixon 1972: 51), Hopi (Malotki 1982), Yélî Dnye (Levinson 2004), Yidiɲ (Dixon 2003), and the Ngaanyatjara dialect of the Western Desert of Australia (Dixon 1980: 357) are examples of such languages. Lack of third-person pronouns is also common in the Caucasian languages (Corbett 1991: 132).[6]

Number

Languages vary greatly here, ranging from those like Pirahã, Kawi, and perhaps Classical Chinese that have no number category, through those like Yimas, Murik, and Meryam Mir that have a singular–dual–paucal–plural distinction (where 'paucal' signals 'a few'), to those like Lihir that have a singular–dual–trial–paucal–plural system (see Corbett 2000: 9–53 for

---

[6] At this point, mention should be made of what is referred to in the literature as **obviation**. As pointed out in Huang (2000a: 10–11), within obviation, proximate and obviative (also often misleadingly termed third- and fourth-person, respectively) are assigned to different third-person NPs on the basis of their relative salience in a discourse. In general, NPs which are contextually and/or rhetorically more prominent are encoded by means of proximate morphology; contextually

detailed discussion of the full range of number categories). Examples of the two most common number systems are given below.

(5.9) Singular–plural
  a. (Chinese)

Person	Singular	Plural
1	wo	women
2	ni	nimen
3	ta	tamen

  b. (West Dani, Voorhoeve 1975: 403)

Person	Singular	Plural
1	an	nit
2	kat	kit
3	at	it

  c. (Mizo, Lalitha Murphy and Subbarao 2000)

Person	Singular	Plural
1	kei	keni
2	nang	nangni
3	ani	anni

(5.10) Singular–dual–plural
  a. (Arabic)

Person	Singular	Dual	Plural
1	'anaa		nah.nu
2	'anta	'antumaa	'antum
3	huwa	huma	hum

  b. (Tok Pisin, Mühlhäusler and Harré 1990: 51)

Person	Singular	Dual	Plural
1	mi	mitupela	mipela
2	yu	yutupela	yupela

and/or rhetorically less central NPs are put in obviative form. This proximate/obviative opposition is indicated not only on NPs, but if relevant, on verbs as well. Consequently, only proximates can be interpreted as coreferential with proximates, and obviatives as coreferential with obviatives. Obviation can thus be seen as representing a natural extension of the gender/class system to the category of person, with proximates indicating the unmarked third-person category and obviates marking a subsidiary 'fourth person', or in the case of Potawatomi even a further-obviative 'fifth-person' category (Anderson and Keenan 1985). Obviation is found in many American Indian languages, including Algonquian (such as Blackfoot, Cree, and Fox), Apachean (such as Navajo), Eskimo, Keresan, and Kutenai (e.g., Comrie 1989).

c. (Yankunytjatjara, Goddard 1998: 298)

Person	Singular	Dual	Plural
1	ngayulu	ngali	nganana
2	nyuntu	nyupali	nyura

Two points are worth mentioning regarding non-singular of first person. In the first place, plural of first person does not mean the same as plural of third person. For example, in English, *we* does not mean plural speakers in the same way that *they* means more than one third-person entity (Levinson 1983: 69). Secondly, many of the world's languages have two non-singular first-person pronouns, one meaning 'we-inclusive-of-addressee' and the other meaning 'we-exclusive-of-addressee'.[7] The languages in (5.11) exemplify the **inclusive/exclusive** distinction with regard to plural first-person pronouns, those in (5.12) illustrate the opposition with relation to dual and plural first-person pronouns, and finally those in (5.13) exemplify the distinction with regard to pronouns with more 'exotic' number systems. (See Harley and Ritter 2002, Cysouw 2003, Bhat 2004, and Siewierska 2004 for further discussion of person and number in pronouns.)

(5.11) Plural 'we'

	Inclusive	Exclusive
Gujarati	aapNe	ame
Malay	kita	kami
Zayse	nuy	nii

(5.12) Dual–plural 'we'

a. (Diyari, Austin 1982: 274)

Singular	Dual	Plural	
	ngalda	ngayani	Inclusive
nganhi			
	ngali	ngayana	Exclusive

b. (Palaung, cited in Goddard 1998: 299)

Singular	Dual	Plural	
ɔ	ar	ε	Inclusive
	yar	y ε	Exclusive

---

[7] In some languages, the inclusive–exclusive distinction is marked on the verb. This is the case of Oriya (Ray 2000: 576).

(i) aame   jibaa
    we   will go-INC

(ii) aame   jibũ
     we   will go-EXC

c. (Tongan, adapted from Mühlhäusler and Harré 1990: 66)

Singular	Dual	Plural	
kita (e)	kitaua (ta)	kiautolu (tau)	Inclusive
au	kimaua (ma)	kimautolu (mau)	Exclusive
	(ou~ku~u~kau)		

(5.13) 'Exotic' number systems

a. (Singular–dual–trial–paucal–plural, Lihir, cited in Corbett 2000: 25)

Person	Singular	Dual	Trial	Paucal	Plural
1 exclusive	yo	gel	getol	gehet	ge
1 inclusive	–	kito	kitol	kitahet	giet
2	wa	gol	gotol	gohet	go
3	e	dul	dietol	diehet	die

b. (Singular–dual–plural–greater plural, Mokilese, Harrison 1976: 88)

Person	Singular	Dual	Plural	Greater plural
1 exclusive	ngoah(i)	kama	kamai	kimi
1 inclusive	–	kisa	kisai	kihs
2	koah	kamwa	kamwai	kimwi
	koawoa			
3	ih	ara/ira	arai/irai	ihr

Try to complete Exercises 4 and 5 on p. 176.

Gender

Personal pronouns may also mark semantic or natural, and grammatical or conventional gender. Cross-linguistically, the general pattern for pronominal gender marking may be captured in the following implicational universal. In all languages with pronominal gender marking, gender can be distinguished on third person, where commonly two (that is, masculine and feminine) or three (that is, masculine, feminine, and neuter) genders may be identified; in some, gender assignment can also be for second person; in a few, gender can be marked on first person as well (e.g., Greenberg 1963: 96, Anderson and Keenan 1985: 269). For example, a gender distinction in Catalan, English, Marathi, and Russian can be indicated on third-person only. By contrast, in Arabic, Modern Hebrew (Anderson and Keenan 1985: 269), Tunica, and Shilha (Corbett 1991: 129), gender marking is for third and second but not for first person (and not for first person singular in the case of Shilha). Finally, Nagla is a language in which gender can be distinguished on first person as well (Trudgill 2000: 63). But there are exceptions to this implicational universal. As reported in Burquest (1986), Angas, an Afro-Asiatic language, has a gender distinction in the second person only, except in reported speech.

Also worth mentioning is that gender can be marked in verbal morphology, especially when the pronoun itself fails to make a gender distinction. This is illustrated in (5.14)–(5.16).

(5.14)   Modern Hebrew (Anderson and Keenan 1985: 270)
    a. Ani   medaber.
       I   speak-M-SG
      'I speak.' (male speaker)
    b. Ani   medaberet.
       I   speak-F-SG
      'I speak.' (female speaker)

(5.15)   Punjabi
    a. mai   aura.
       I   come-M
      'I'm coming.' (male speaker)
    b. mai   auri.
       I   come-F
      'I'm coming.' (female speaker)

(5.16)   Russian (Corbett 1991: 128)
    a. ja   čital-Ø.
       I   read-PAST-M
      'I was reading.' (male speaker)
    b. ja   čital-a.
       I   read-PAST-F
      'I was reading.' (female speaker)

Finally, gender can also be indicated on adjectives and nouns. The following examples are from French.

(5.17)   a. Je   suis   heureux.
       I   am   happy-M
      'I'm happy.' (male speaker)
    b. Je   suis   heureuse.
       I   am   happy-F
      'I'm happy.' (female speaker)

(5.18)   a. Je   suis   le   président.
         I   am   the-M   president-M
         'I'm the president.' (male speaker)
      b. Je   suis   la   présidente.
         I   am   the-F   president
         'I'm the president.' (female speaker)

Next, while in most languages, the unmarked gender is masculine, there are languages in which the unmarked gender is feminine. These include a group of Australian languages (such as Kala Lagaw Ya) (Alpher 1987), a few North American Indian languages (such as Iroquois) (Brown 1975), and perhaps Arakul, a Caucasian dialect (see also Mühlhäusler and Harré 1990: 242–5).

A further point of interest is that with regard to person-gender marking, languages tend to encode more gender distinctions in the singular than the plural. This is because less marked categories are likely to be more differentiated internally than more marked ones (e.g., Greenberg 1966, Anderson and Keenan 1985). A familiar language that confirms this principle is English (third-person singular: M: *he*, F: *she*, N: *it*; third-person plural: *they*). Another, less familiar one is Moni (third-person singular: M: *ogo*, F: *oa*; third-person dual: *uiya*; third-person plural: *ui*) (Voorhoeve 1975: 409). Counterexamples, however, are afforded by, say, Spanish, in which gender is distinguished in all persons in the plural but only in third person in the singular.

Finally, in some of the world's languages, personal pronouns may not need to be realized phonetically at all. In other words, they can be encoded in terms of an empty category or a zero anaphor. Languages which allow the dropping of a personal pronoun in the subject position of a finite clause have come to be known as '**null subject**' or '**pro-drop**' languages in the generative syntax literature. Generally speaking, pronouns can be omitted in a language if their content can be recovered either morphologically (e.g., via rich verbal agreement), as in (5.19); or from the discourse in one way or anther, as in (5.20) (see Huang 2000a for a detailed discussion).

(5.19)   (Pashto, cited in Huang 2000a: 55)
         Ø   mana   xwr-əm.
             apple   eat-1-M-SG
         '(I) ate the apple.'

(5.20) (Chinese)

Ø	qu	guo	Beijing	ma?
	go	EXP	Beijing	Q

'Have (e.g., you) been to Beijing?'

Vocatives

Person deixis can also be accomplished by **vocatives**. Vocatives are NPs that refer to the addressee, but form no part of the arguments of a predicate. Prosodically, they are separated from the body of an utterance that may accompany them. Vocatives in general are grouped into two types, **calls** or **summonses**, as in (5.21); and **addresses**, as in (5.22).

(5.21) a. Hey *Daddy*, look, a spider in the corner!

b. *John*, if we don't leave now, we'll be late for our next appointment.

c. *Doctor Williams*, do you think I need a blood test?

(5.22) a. I'm afraid, *Sir*, we are closing.

b. Do you fancy going to a concert of African music, *Lucy*?

c. My view, *Dean*, is that we should set up a new department of linguistics.

Three points may be briefly mentioned here. First of all, calls/summonses, being gestural in nature, are utterance-initial; addresses, on the other hand, being symbolic in character, are parenthetical, and can occur wherever other parentheticals can occur. The second point to note is that while all addresses can be used as calls/summonses, only some calls/summonses can be used as addresses (Zwicky 1974, Levinson 1983: 70–1, Brown and Levinson 1987: 292, Marmaridou 2000: 78–80). Finally, as (5.21) and (5.22) show, vocatives are in general socially marked. I shall return to this issue in Section 5.3.1, where I shall discuss social deixis.[8]

---

[8] According to Fillmore (1997: 119), in English *Miss* can be used in polite attention-calling, *Mr* can be used in impolite attention-calling, but *Mrs* cannot be used in attention-calling at all. We can offer a partial neo-Gricean pragmatic analysis here. The use of *Madam* as a vocative pre-empts *Mrs* used in that way. The use of *Sir* as a polite vocative has the priority over that of *Mr* as a polite vocative, thus relegating it to an impolite vocative. Finally, since there is nothing to pre-empt it, *Miss* is free to be used as a polite vocative.

5.2.2. Time deixis

We move next to **time deixis**. Time deixis is concerned with the encoding of temporal points and spans relative to the time at which an utterance is produced in a speech event.

Time
Before considering how time deixis is grammaticalized in language, let us first take a look at the concept of time. As pointed out by Fillmore (1997: 45–6), time is one-dimensional and unidirectional. Generally speaking, the passage of time is represented in two distinct ways: (i) to regard time as constant and the 'world' as moving through time from the past into the future, and (ii) to think of the 'world' as stable and of time as flowing through the 'world' from the future to the past. Thus, in terms of the 'moving world' metaphor (i), we can talk about 'the years ahead'; on the other hand, in terms of the 'moving time' metaphor (ii), we can talk about 'the coming years'.

A distinction can be made between time points such as 'eight o'clock' and time periods such as 'tomorrow evening'. Time periods can be uniquely defined in terms of their beginning and ending points. They are most commonly encoded in the world's languages on the basis of the natural and prominent recurring cycles of days and nights, weeks, months, seasons, and years. Such time units can be **calendrical** or **non-calendrical**. In the calendrical usage, time measure periods designate a fixed-length sequence of naturally given time units. 'July', for example, is such a calendrical unit. On the other hand, in the non-calendrical usage, time measure periods are used only as units of measure relative to some fixed points of interest. 'Fortnight', for instance, is an example of a non-calendrical unit (Fillmore 1997: 48–50; see also Levinson 1983 and Anderson and Keenan 1985: 296). Calendrical units can further be divided into **positional** ones like 'Monday', 'January', and 'morning', and **non-positional** ones like 'week', 'month', and 'year' (Fillmore 1997: 50, 52, 69).

Another distinction we need to make is between the moment of utterance, to be called **coding time (CT)**, and the moment of reception, to be called **receiving time (RT)**. Under normal circumstances, assuming the default deictic centre, RT can be taken to be identical to CT; in this case, we have what Lyons (1977: 685) called **deictic simultaneity**. But there are situations of utterance, such as the writing of letters and the pre-recording of media programmes, where messages are not sent and received at the same time.

In these cases, the speaker has to decide whether the deictic centre will remain on the speaker and CT, as in (5.23), or will be shifted to the addressee and RT, as in (5.24) (Levinson 1983: 73–4, Fillmore 1997: 67–8).

(5.23)   This interview is being recorded today, Wednesday 3 July, to be relayed on Sunday 7 July.

(5.24)   This interview was recorded last Wednesday, 3 July, to be relayed today, Sunday 7 July.

The encoding of time deixis

Time deixis is commonly grammaticalized in (i) deictic adverbs of time and (ii) tense.

Deictic adverbs of time

Let us start with **deictic adverbs of time**. Consider first *now* and *then* in English, the two pure time deictics which Anderson and Keenan (1985: 297) called temporal demonstratives. *Now* designates '**proximal**' time, and following Levinson (1983: 74) it can be defined as the 'pragmatically given (time) span including CT'. By contrast, *then* refers to '**distal**' time, and can be reduced to meaning 'not now' (see also Section 5.2.3 below). It can indicate time either in the past or in the future.

Look next at deictic calendrical unit terms such as *today*, *tomorrow*, and *yesterday*. These deictic names of days divide time into diurnal spans. Thus *today* can be glossed as 'the diurnal span including CT', *tomorrow* as 'the diurnal span following today', and *yesterday* as 'the diurnal span preceding today' (see also Levinson 1983: 74). Note further that both *now/then* and *today/tomorrow/yesterday* can relate to either a time point, as in (5.25), or an interminable time period within the relevant span, as in (5.26), or the whole span itself, as in (5.27).

(5.25)   Start the engine *now*!
(5.26)   John is *now* working as a government's spin-doctor.
(5.27)   *Yesterday* was a public holiday.

Another interesting point is that the use of *today/tomorrow/yesterday* pre-empts, that is, it has priority over, the use of the calendrical terms for the relevant days. Thus, speakers of English would normally avoid saying (5.28) if either today or tomorrow is Saturday. This is because on a Saturday they would use *today*, and on a Friday they would use *tomorrow* (Levinson 1983: 75, Fillmore 1997: 72).

(5.28)   I'll test-drive a BMW on Saturday.

Finally, languages differ in precisely how many deictically anchored terms of days they lexicalize. For example, while English names only one day in either direction from today, Arabic, Chinese, and German go two days in each direction. There are languages which display a richer system. Greek, Hausa (Anderson and Keenan 1985: 300), and Japanese (Fillmore 1997: 71), for instance, have three lexicalized deictic names of days on either side of the present day. Chinantec is reported by Fillmore (1997: 71) to go even four days both ahead and back.

Also of interest is that some languages use the same word for tomorrow and yesterday, thus reducing the number of lexicalized names of days. The major dialects of Igbo, for example, belong to this type of language. The relevant word employed in the language is *eci* (Anderson and Keenan 1985: 300). More interestingly, Punjabi has a single word *kall* for tomorrow and yesterday, and another single word *parso* for the day after tomorrow and the day before yesterday. The same, according to Fillmore (1997: 73), is true of Hindi. Put slightly differently, in these languages the same words are utilized to indicate times both one day and two days from today in either direction. The potential interpretative difficulties caused by these lexically ambiguous day names can normally be avoided either grammatically (e.g., via tense) or pragmatically (e.g., by shared knowledge).

Furthermore, the distribution of lexicalized deictic names of days in a language can be asymmetric. Spanish seems to be such a case. It names one day ahead from the present day but two days back. Persian is said to go two days ahead but four days back, and Vietnamese, three days ahead but four days back (Fillmore 1997: 71). The following are some of the examples I have collected.

(5.29)   *Lexicalized deictic names of days*

Finally, there are complex deictic adverbs of time such as *this month*, *next Monday*, and *last year*. These deictic adverbs of time contain two components, a deictic component like *this*, *next*, and *last*, and a non-deictic component like *month*, *Monday*, and *year*. As pointed out by Fillmore (1997: 69–71) and Levinson (1983: 75–6), the interpretation of such adverbs is systematically determined by two distinctions: (i) the distinction between calendrical and non-calendrical modes of reckoning of time, and (ii) the distinction between positional and non-positional calendrical units.

LANGUAGE	0–3	0–2	0–1	0	0+1	0+2	0+3
English			yesterday	today	tomorrow		
Diyari			waldawirti	karrari	thang-kuparna		
Arabic		albarahati	albaraha	alioum	ghuden	bada-ghuden	
Chinese		qiantian	zuotian	jintian	mingtian	houtian	
German		vorgestern	gestern	heute	morgen	über-morgen	
Greek	antipro-chthes	prochthes	chthes	sinera	avrio	methavrio	anti-mentha
Punjabi		parso	kall	ajj	kall	parso	
Spanish		anteayer	ayer	hoy	mañana		

This X, where *X* is a non-positional calendrical unit such as week, month, and year, normally refers to the unit including CT. Furthermore, the adverb of time is ambiguous between a calendrical and a non-calendrical interpretation. Thus, *this year* refers to the same year as the moment of utterance, and is ambiguous between the calendrical unit that runs from 1 January to 31 December,[9] and the non-calendrical measure of 365 days that starts on the day including CT. More or less the same can be said of *this week* and *this month*, and perhaps *this decade* and *this century*. By contrast, *this Y*, where *Y* is a positional calendrical unit such as Thursday, July, and evening, which is included in a larger calendrical unit *Z*, usually means the unit which is included in the larger unit, which includes CT. Thus, *this July* does not necessarily make reference to the month the speaker is now in. Instead, it refers to the July of the same calendar year as the moment of utterance. Moreover, the July in question is by preference taken to be the future rather than the past July. In the similar vein, we can say *this morning* either during the morning or during the rest of the day (Levinson 1983: 75–6, Fillmore 1997: 69–73).[10]

---

[9] There are, of course, other culturally specific calendrical units such as the academic year, the tax year, and the Chinese (lunar) year.

[10] There are languages that use different lexical items to refer to 'this morning' in the morning and in the afternoon or evening. One such language is Chinantec (Fillmore 1997: 71). There are also languages that utilize different words to refer to 'evening'. Punjabi, for example, has two expressions for 'evening': *numasha* and *shami*. The former can only be used in the evening and the latter can be used outside the evening.

Tense

We move next to a brief discussion of **tense**. Following Lyons (1977: 682) and Levinson (1983: 77), one can distinguish between **metalinguistic tense (M-tense)** and **linguistic tense (L-tense)**. By M-tense is meant the theoretical category of tense, whereas by L-tense is meant the linguistic realization of M-tense, typically through verbal inflection but also in the form of other periphrastic constructions in a particular language. Generally speaking, all languages have M-tense, but some lack L-tense. In the latter case, M-tense may be lexically realized by means of adverbs of time or the like—expressions equivalent to *yesterday*, *this week*, and *next year*. This contrast can be illustrated by a consideration of (5.30).

(5.30)   a. The giant panda lives on bamboo shoots.
   b. (Chinese)
     Xiaoming qunian jielehun.
     Xiaoming last year get married
     'Xiaoming got married last year.'

Note that the English example (5.30a) is M-tenseless but L-tensed, in that its verb form is morphologically marked for simple present tense. By contrast, the Chinese example (5.30b) is M-tensed but L-tenseless, in that no L-tense is morphologically marked on its verb form.

M-tense can be given a purely deictic interpretation. In such a system, one can easily distinguish past tense (i.e. time earlier than CT), from present tense (time coinciding with or including CT), from future tense (time later than CT). Furthermore, one can also distinguish time points from time spans (Lyons 1977: 683).

It is unclear, however, to what extent L-tense can be marked in a purely deictic way. In the first place, L-tense may include aspectual and modal elements. For example, future tense nearly always has modal overtones. Secondly, L-tense may not distinguish past from future. A typical example is the Shiriana languages of South America (Fillmore 1997: 73–4). Thirdly, L-tense may make use of calendrical units. In the Peruvian language Amahaucan, for instance, there is an L-tense form which means 'yesterday' if it is used in the morning but which means 'this morning' if it is used later on in the day (Fillmore 1997: 73). Another interesting case can be found in the Australian language Tiwi, in which verbs are inflected to indicate whether the action denoted took/is taking/will take place in the morning or in the evening (Anderson and Keenan 1985: 300). All this adds complexity to the deictic marking of L-tense in individual languages. (See Comrie 1985 and Dahl 1985 for discussion of tense. See also Fritz 2003 for a Q-scalar implicature analysis of future tense.)

5.2.3. Space deixis

The third and final basic category of deixis I am going to discuss is that of **space deixis**.[11] Space deixis is concerned with the specification of location in space relative to that of the participants at CT in a speech event.

Frames of spatial reference
Frames of reference, as they are called by Gestalt theorists, are coordinate systems used to compute and specify the location of objects with respect to other objects. Cross-linguistically, there are three linguistic frames of reference to express spatial relationships between the entity to be located (referent or figure) and the landmark (or ground): (i) **intrinsic**, (ii) **relative**, and (iii) **absolute**. The first is based on object-centred coordinates, which are determined by the 'inherent features' such as the sideness or facets of the object to be used as ground. This can be illustrated by (5.31), where 'the dog' is the figure and 'the car' is the ground. The second, relative frame of reference is roughly an egocentric system. It expresses a ternary spacial relation between a viewpoint, and a figure and a ground that are distinct from the viewpoint. It uses the coordinates fixed on the viewpoint to assign directions to the figure and the ground. This can be exemplified by (5.32), where the point of view is given by the location of a perceiver, in this case, the speaker. The deictic use of this frame is prototypical. Finally, the absolute frame of reference also involves a coordinate system, but one that is based on absolute coordinates like north/south/east/west. This can be shown by (5.33), where the fixed bearing 'east' is used to specify the relationship between the figure and the ground (Levinson 1996, 2003, 2004, Majid et al. 2004).

(5.31)   The dog is behind the car.
(5.32)   The dog is to the left of the car.
(5.33)   The dog is (to the) east of the car.

Languages vary greatly in the use of the three universal spatial coordinate systems. Some utilize all of them. This is the case of Balinese, Belhare,

---

[11] Other terms include place, spatial, local, and locational deixis.

English, Ewe, French, Kgalagadi, and Yukatek, among many others. Other languages—good examples are Arrernte, Mopan, Tzeltal, and Warwa—employ only two of the three systems. Still others rely predominantly on one frame only. Guugu Yimidhirr, for example, is a language that utilizes the absolute frame almost exclusively (Levinson 2003, 2004, Majid et al. 2004). This is partially due to the fact that spatially orientational terms such as *up/down*, *front/back*, and *left/right* are absent from many, perhaps a third of the world's languages. There are also languages, like many of those spoken in Australia, which adopt an absolute frame in place of topological terms such as *in*, *on*, or *above/below/over/under* (Levinson 1996: 134).

Of further interest is the fact that cross-linguistic variations have been observed in how the spatial coordinate systems are instantiated in a language. Hausa, for example, is a language that is well known for using a relative spatial reference frame. But in constructing such a system, the language enters into a 'tandem' rather than a 'mirror' spatial configuration, as does English when used in the same system. Another way of putting it is that in Hausa, the front of, say, a calabash is sometimes not facing the speaker, but is away from him or her. Thus, the Hausa sentence in (5.34) below is semantically equivalent to the English sentence *There's a spoon in front of the calabash* (Hill 1982: 21; see also Levinson 2004).

(5.34)   Ga   cokali   can   baya   da   k'warya.
         look   spoon   there   back   with   calabash
         Literally: 'There's a spoon behind the calabash.'

Note next that (5.31) can also be put in the relative frame, and (5.32) in the intrinsic frame. In other words, both sentences are ambiguous between the intrinsic and the relative frame readings. Put slightly differently, in terms of the deictic versus non-deictic distinction, *behind* in (5.31) and *left* in (5.32) can have both a deictic and a non-deictic function. *Behind* in (5.31) is deictic if the car intervenes between the dog and the speaker's location, and it is non-deictic if the dog is at the intrinsic rear-end of the car. As for *left* in (5.32), under the deictic interpretation, the dog is to the left of the car from the speaker's point of view, and under the non-deictic reading, the dog is to the car's own left (Levinson 1983: 82–3, Fillmore 1997).

The grammaticalization of space deixis
Spatial deictic notions are commonly expressed by the use of (i) demonstratives including both demonstrative pronouns and demonstrative

adjectives, (ii) deictic adverbs of space, (iii) deictically marked third-person pronouns, and (iv) verbal affixes of motion and verbs of motion.[12, 13]

[12] Two other typologies of demonstratives are worth mentioning here. Diessel (1999: 57–92) classified demonstratives into four types: (i) demonstrative pronouns, (ii) demonstrative determiners (i.e. our 'demonstrative adjectives'), (iii) demonstrative adverbs (i.e. our 'deictic adverbs of space'), and (iv) demonstrative identifiers. Demonstrative identifiers are demonstratives used in copular and non-verbal clauses, as in the Ambulas example below (cited in Diessel 1999: 80).

(i) kén   bakna   walkaum   taalé.
     this   just   little   place
     'This is just a little place.'

Some languages (e.g., Acehnese) do not distinguish any of the four types of demonstratives. Others (e.g., Korean) have only two categories. Others (e.g., Nunggubuyu) have three. Still others (e.g., Pangasinan) distinguish all the four types (Diessel 1999: 89–92).

Another typology is presented by Dixon (2003), who posited three types of demonstratives: (i) nominal demonstratives including both demonstrative pronouns and adjectives, (ii) local adverbial demonstratives, and (iii) verbal demonstratives. Dixon claimed that the first two types of demonstrative occur in every language, except in Jul'hoan. But this claim may not stand (see Diessel 1999: 89). Only two languages (i.e., Boumaa Fijian and Dyirbal) have been reported as containing verbal demonstratives. However, in each case there is just one such verbal demonstrative meaning 'do it like this' (Dixon 2003).

Dixon (2003) also noted an interesting inverse correlation between the size of demonstratives and deictic adverbs of space and that of the language community: the smaller the number of speakers of a language, the more complex the system of demonstratives and deictic adverbs of space in that language. Consequently, languages that are spoken by a large number of speakers tend to have just a two-term system. Supporting evidence can be drawn from Dravidian languages. Within this language family, systems with three or four terms are found in small tribal languages. By contrast, in each of the four major languages with tens of millions of speakers (i.e., Kannada, Malayalam, Tamil, and Telugu), there are only two-term spatially deictic systems (Dixon 2003).

See also Diessel (1999: 115–55) for discussion of the diachrony of demonstrative pronouns and deictic adverbs of space in a range of languages. The discussion covers both sides of the diachrony coin: on the one hand, how demonstratives and deictic adverbs of space develop into a wide variety of grammatical markers such as definite articles, third-person pronouns, and complementizers; on the other, what is the historical source of demonstratives and deictic adverbs of space.

[13] There are, of course, other means to express space deixis. One such way, as already noted above in Section 1.2, is to use deictic presentatives such as *voici/voilà* in French, *ecce* in Latin, and *vot/von* in Russian. See also note 19 below.

Demonstratives and deictic adverbs of space

I shall begin with **demonstratives** and **deictic adverbs of space**. I shall examine them in terms of four deictic parameters: (i) distance, (ii) visibility, (iii) elevation, and (iv) side, which Hanks (1992), Agha (1996), and Manning (2001) considered to belong to the relational type of the indexical category of deixis.

Distance

Following Anderson and Keenan (1985), languages can be classified according to the number of terms demonstratives and deictic adverbs of space display.

One-term systems. A number of languages have only one demonstrative pronoun or adjective, unmarked for distance. Possible candidates for such a system are *dies/das* in German (Himmelmann 1997, Levinson 2004), *ten* in Czech, and *ce-cet/cette* in French (Anderson and Keenan 1985: 280). But as pointed out by Diessel (1999: 36) and Levinson (2004), most and perhaps all such one-term systems of demonstratives are supplemented by a two-term system of deictic adverbs of space.[14]

Two-term systems. Many languages possess a bipartite system of demonstratives and deictic adverbs of space. In such a language, a fundamental distinction between **proximal** (or relatively close to the speaker) and **distal** (or non-proximal, sometimes relatively close to the addressee) is grammaticalized. This two-term system (of deictic adverbs of space) seems to be the most typical and universal system of space deixis (e.g., Diessel 1999: 38, Levinson 2004). Catalan, Chinese, Diyari, English, French, Guugu Yimidhirr, Modern Hebrew, Hopi, Hungarian, Nama Hottentot, Italian, Spoken Portuguese,

---

[14] This indicates that there are languages which have different numbers of terms with regard to demonstratives and deictic adverbs of space. Indonesian, for example, has two demonstratives but three deictic adverbs of space. Yagua has two demonstratives but its deictic adverbs specify four degrees of distance (Dixon 2003). Ewondo has three demonstratives but expresses a four-way contrast in adverbs of space (Diessel 1999: 19). Other such languages include German, the Tuscan dialect of Italian and Malagasy. Dixon (2003) and Levinson (2004) hypothesized that in general deictic adverbs of space make more distinctions than do demonstratives. But two counterexamples have been noted in the literature. In Tariana, there are four spatially distinguished terms in demonstratives but only two for deictic adverbs of space (Dixon 2003). Lillooet has three demonstratives but only two deictic adverbs of space (van Eijk 1997: 168–77).

Punjabi, the Paasaal variety of Sisaala, Russian, and Vietnamese, for example, belong to this type of language. Some examples follow.

(5.35)

	Proximal	*Distal*
Chinese	zheli	nali
Diyari	nhingki	nhaka
English	here	there
Hungarian	itt	ott
Sisaala (P)	nyɛ	ɛɛ

Turn to p. 176 and try Exercise 6.

Three-term systems. There are also many languages which have a basic tripartite system. These include Classic Arabic, Breton, certain dialects of Chinese (e.g., Danyang), Czech, certain dialects of English (e.g., Scottish), Georgian, Greek, certain dialects of Italian (e.g., Tuscan), Japanese, Latin, Old Church Slavonic, Palauan, Portuguese, Southern Sotho, Spanish, Tagalog, Turkish, and Welsh. Of these languages, two types can further be classified. In languages like Ambulas, Classic Arabic, Scottish English, Georgian, Hopi, Southern Sotho, Tiriyo, Lango, Ponapean, Hixkaryana, Yimas, and perhaps Boumaa Fijian, we have a three-way contrast: proximal, **medial**, and distal (extremely far from the speaker and/or the addressee).[15] Note that in such a system, the middle term points to a location relative to the deictic centre, typically the speaker. Following Anderson and Keenan (1985: 282) and Diessel (1999: 39), we call this three-term system **distance-oriented**. Roughly speaking, if a language has a distance-oriented series of demonstratives, it will also have a distance-oriented series of deictic adverbs of space (Levinson 2004).

(5.36)

	Proximal	*Medial*	*Distal*
Classic Arabic	hona	honak	honalik
Scottish English	this	that	yon
Hopi	i	pam	mi
Southern Sotho	see	seo	sane
Yimas	p-k	m-n	p-n

On the other hand, in languages like Basque, Ewondo, Japanese, Korean, Quechua, Swahili, Thai, the Tuscan dialect of Italian, Old Church Slavonic, Palauan, Pangasinan, and Tagalog, the three terms can be

---

[15] Alternatively, the three-way contrast is termed proximal, distal (or mid-distance), and extreme-distal (e.g., Malotki 1982: 234).

identified as proximal to the speaker, proximal to the addressee, and distal from both the speaker and addressee. In this system, the middle term refers to a location that is close to the addressee. Let us follow Anderson and Keenan (1985) and Diessel (1999: 39) and call this three-term system **person-oriented** (but see Fillmore 1997: 49–50).

(5.37)	Proximal (S)	Proximal (A)	Distal (S + A)
Ewondo	ɲɔ	ɲɔlo	ɲɔli[16]
Japanese	kore	sore	are
Palauan	tia	tilechaa	se
Pangasinan	(i)yá	(i)tán	(i)mán

It is claimed that a distance-oriented system tends to have fewer members than a person-oriented one. The former is normally confined to three deictic terms, but there is no such restriction on the latter (Fillmore 1982: 48–9, Diessel 1999: 40, but see Anderson and Keenan 1985: 286–95 for a dissenting view, and the counterexamples below).[17]

In addition, there are languages whose three-term system is not easily assigned as distance- or person-oriented. Latin, Spanish, and Turkish seem to belong to this category (see, e.g., Anderson and Keenan 1985; see also Jungbluth's 2003 rejection of the distance- versus person-oriented distinction based on the analysis of Spanish and Meira's 2003 arguments against it based on the study of Brazilian Portuguese and Tiriyo).[18]

Four-term systems. Some languages present a quadripartite system of space deixis. Hausa, Kusaiean, Marshallese, Samal, Sre, Tlingit, and

---

[16] Note that, as mentioned in note 14 above, the Ewondo adverbs of space express a four-way deictic contrast: (i) close to the speaker, (ii) close to the addressee, (iii) away from both the speaker and the addressee, and (iv) far away from both the speaker and the addressee. Furthermore, they have two sets. Set 1 (the 'precise' set) is used to mark an 'exact location', but Set 2 (the 'vague' set) is used to signal that the location is somewhere 'around' or 'in the vicinity of' the speaker, the addressee or some other reference point (Diessel 1999: 19–20).

[17] Diessel (1999: 167) was of the view that two-term systems are in general derived from three-term systems by dropping the middle term. This is, for example, the case for the Zagreb dialects of Croatian.

[18] It has been claimed that distance- and person-oriented systems cannot co-exist in the same language. Daga seems to be a counterexample to this claim. According to Anderson and Keenan (1985: 291), in this language the demonstratives *uta/utu/use* and *ita/ita/isi/ise* present a distance-oriented three-term system, while the demonstratives *ma* and *ame* contrast on a person-oriented system. Another counterexample is Yéli Dnye (Levinson 2004).

Waray are languages of this type. Of these, Kusaiean and Tlingit represent distance-oriented systems. This can be shown in the four-way contrast in the Kusaiean demonstratives *nge* 'this', *ngacn* 'that', *ngoh* 'that over there', and *ngi* 'that way over there' (Goddard 1998: 312). Clearly, the fourth term points to some entity that is more remote from the speech situation. The same can be said of Tlingt (Anderson and Keenan 1985: 286). By contrast, Hausa, Marshallese, Quileute, Samal, Sre, and Waray are examples of a person-oriented system. In Hausa, the terms are *nân* 'close to the speaker', *nan* 'close to the addressee', *cân* 'away from both, but still visible', and *can* 'further away from both, less visible' (Jaggar and Buba 1994, Saeed 2003: 183). The four demonstratives in Sre are *dɔ* 'close to the speaker', *dɛn* 'close to the addressee', *nɛ* 'not close to the speaker, not close to the addressee' and *hɔʔ* 'remote, out of sight' (Anderson and Keenan 1985: 287). In Quileute, we find *yü'x:o'* 'close to the speaker', *yi'tca'* 'close to the addressee', *sa''a* 'close to the speaker and the addressee', and *ha* 'away from the speaker and the addressee' (Diessel 1999: 41). The same is true of Waray: *adi* 'close to the speaker', *itu* 'close to the addressee', *ini* 'close to the speaker and the addressee', and *itu* 'distal or far away' (Imai 2003). In Marshallese, there are *y&y/yih&h* 'close to the speaker', *yin* 'close to the speaker, close to the addressee', *ney/neyney* 'not close to the speaker, close to the addressee', and *yen/yiyen* 'not close to the speaker, not close to the addressee' (Goddard 1998: 312). Finally, Samal is a language whose four-way distinction can be glossed as 'close to the speaker', 'close to the addressee', 'close to the audience, i.e. the other participants in the conversation', and 'away from all of the above' (Fillmore: 1997: 65–6, but see Levinson 1983: 81 for a different gloss).

See whether you are ready to do Exercise 7 on p. 176.

More than four-term systems. There are also languages with more than four terms. These include Kwakiutl (with six terms), Malagasy (with six terms), Koasati (with seven terms), and Yup'ik. There are even languages which have several hundred terms. One such language is Inuktitut, whose demonstrative and adverb of space system comprises 686 different forms. Another is Santali, in which there are well over 200 distinct forms of demonstratives and adverbs of space (Diessel 1999: 13). While some of the languages with more than four terms (e.g., CiBemba) are defined along the basic, single deictic dimension of distance, most are involved with more than one dimension of contrast, to which I shall now turn.

Visibility

One additional dimension that is deployed by many of the world's languages is that of **visibility**, which is in general concerned with whether the entity in question is within sight of the speaker or not. Demonstratives in Kwakwa'la, for example, show a basic person-oriented three-way contrast along the dimension of distance. But in addition, each of the three persons is marked for visibility. Daga uses the suffix *-t/-m* for visibility marking and the suffix *-pa/-pe* for invisibility marking. The Kashmiri distal demonstrative pronoun has two variants: *hu* for an entity within sight and *su* for an entity out of sight (Anderson and Keenan 1985: 290, 291, 476). Coastal Yidiɲ utilizes a demonstrative stem *yu-* to refer to entities that are both distant and visible (Dixon 1977: 180–1). By contrast, the category of invisibility in Kabardian is marked by *a* (Colarusso 1989: 269). According to Becker and Mary (1997: 156), Moroccan Arabic has three markers for simple/compound locatives: *hna(ya/hafayn)* for proximate, *temma(-yalk/rah)* for distal, and *lheh/dikjih* for invisible entities. Invisibility in Ute is indicated by *'ú/'úru/'úmu*. Other American Indian languages which have particular demonstratives for invisible entities include Epena Pedee, West Greenlandic, Halkomelem, Passamaquoddy-Maliseet, Tümpisa Shoshone, and Quileute. Quileute is particularly interesting in that (while most languages have a single deictic term to refer to invisible objects) it has a set of three adverbs of space to indicate invisibility: *xa'x:e* for entities nearby (which may be partially visible), *tci''tc'* for entities whose location is known, and *xu' xwa'* for entities whose location is unknown (Diessel 1999: 42). Locationals in Khasi (Diessel 1999: 43) and Malagasy (Anderson and Keenan 1985: 288, 293) can also be marked for invisibility.

Imai (2003) distinguished three types of invisibility: (i) invisible-remote, (ii) invisible-occlusion, and (iii) invisible-periphery. The first type of invisibility parameter is used to mark entities that are out of sight and far from the speaker. Most languages which encode invisibility belong to this category. Secondly, invisible-occlusion is employed to refer to entities that are behind an obstacle or inside a container. Finally, there is invisible-periphery, which is utilized to encode entities that are out of sight but audible and/or olfactory, that is to say, things that the speaker can identify by their noise and/or smell but cannot see. The deictic term *anagha* in Muna is said to be used to make reference to some entity that is invisible but audible (Imai 2003). Other languages which mark visibility/invisibility include Bengali, Crow, Jarawara, Kwakiutl, Lillooet, Palikur, Shoshore, and West Greenlandic (Fortescue 1984, Hanks 1992, Dixon 2003). (See also the subsection on deictically marked third-person pronouns on pp. 159 *et passim* below.)

Elevation

Another additional kind of spacial specification is that of what Hyslop (1993) and Diessel (1999) called **elevation**, that is, the physical dimension of height relative to the deictic centre, typically the speaker. In languages that use this **geometric parameter**, to borrow the term from Imai (2003), the deictic centre, typically the speaker, will set a horizontal line as the zero point. When the entity is above the line, 'up' or 'upwards' is used; when it is below the line, 'down' or 'downwards' is employed. Nine languages in Diessel's (1999) sample mark this deictic parameter. They are Byanisi, Khasi, Lahu, Hua, Usan, Tauya, Dyirbal, Ngiyambaa, and Lezgian. Of those languages which signify elevation, most make a basic distinction between 'up' or 'upwards' and 'down' or 'downwards'. Abkhaz, Lahu, and Paamese are such languages. Khasi uses *u-tey* for 'up' and *u-thie* for 'down'. In Lahu, *nô* signifies 'up (there)' and *mô* 'down (there)' (Diessel 1999: 43, Dixon 2003). Tauya utilizes the prefix *pise-* to mark a location above the deictic centre and *tofe-* to indicate a location below the deictic centre (MacDonald 1990). Other languages distinguish three dimensions of space: 'above the speaker', 'below the speaker', and 'level with the speaker'. These include Angguruk, Epo, Daga, Yale, and the Arakul dialect of Lak. Of these languages, the Arakul dialect of Lak uses *ho* to encode 'higher or lower than the speaker' and *hara* to encode 'farther away from but on the same level with the speaker' (Dixon 2003). Daga also marks more than one degree of elevation above and below the speaker.

One variant of elevation is where height is marked in terms of 'uphill' versus 'downhill' and/or 'upriver' versus 'downriver', depending partially on the geographic environments in which a particular language is spoken. The former is usually found in languages that are spoken in mountainous regions, and the latter in languages that are used in areas where there are rivers. This Imai (2003) called the **geographic parameter**. Dyirbal is a language which marks both 'uphill/downhill' and 'upriver/downriver'. In this language, there are two sets of deictic markers which are employed to suffix a noun marker. One set indicates a contrast of height relative to the speaker, but the other set marks both uphill/downhill (*-day/-baydi*) and upriver/downriver/across river (*-dawala/-balbala/-guya*) (Dixon 1972: 48, 2003). Another language is Yup'ik whose large series of demonstratives contains 'upstream/downstream/across river' oppositions (Levinson 2004). Other languages that mark the geographic features of elevation include Eskimo, Hua, Muna, Tepehuan, West Greelandic, and Zayse (Diessel 1999: 44–5, Dixon 2003, Imai 2003).

Side

A further deictic dimension of contrast is involved with the concept of **side**. In Aleut, *ukan* is used to indicate a referent that is 'inside the house', and *sadan* is employed to mark a referent that is 'outside the house'. West Greenlandic uses *qam-* for 'in/out' and *kig-* for 'outside'. It is also a language in which there is a set of deictic terms which encodes on which side a settlement is located along the coastline: *av-* for 'in the north' and *qav-* for 'in the south' (Fortescue 1984: 259–63). There are also languages that distinguish side-proximal from side-distal.

Stance

Finally, there is the deictic dimension of **stance**. According to Ceria and Sandalo (1995), in languages of the Waikurúan family, the demonstratives must indicate the stance or motion of the referent—whether it is 'standing', 'sitting', 'lying', 'coming', or 'going' (see also Dixon 2003 on languages in the Siouan family).[19]

---

[19] Of particular interest is the use of gestures for expressing spatially deictic information such as distance and visibility. The term 'gesture' is interpreted in its broad sense here, since there are cultures (such as the Gunha), in which people point primarily with the lips and eyes rather than the hands (Levinson 2004). As an illustrating example, Dixon (2003) cited the Tucano and Arawak languages of the Vaupes river basin. In these languages, different deictic gestures are used for varying distances and visibility. For example, pointing with the lips is for 'visible and near'; pointing with the lips plus a backwards tilt of the head signifies 'visible and not near'; and pointing with the index finger is for 'not visible' (if the direction in which the object lies is known).

Deictically marked third-person pronouns
We move next to **deictically marked third-person pronouns**. These pronouns specify the location of the intended referent with respect to the speaker. In some languages, the encoding of distance is optional; in others, it is obligatory. Diyari, for example, is a language in which third-person pronouns may be optionally suffixed by -*rda* (indicating that the referent is in the immediate vicinity, usually up to a few meters away), -*ya* (indicating that the referent is close by and visible), or -*wa* (indicating that the referent is distant including distant and visible) (Austin 1982). By contrast, in Kwakwa'la, there are no third-person pronouns which are unmarked for deixis (Anderson and Keenan 1985: 290).

Specially marked deictic third-person pronouns can be found in many South Asian languages. These include Dravidian languages like Kannada, Malayalam, Tamil, and Telugu, Indo-Aryan languages like Bangala, Hindi/Urdu, Kashmiri, Oriya, Punjabi, and Sinhala, and Austro-Asiatic languages like Juang (Lust et al. 2000). A few examples from the South Asian languages are given in (5.38).

(5.38)	Proximal	Distal
Bangala	e	o
Punjabi	eh	oh
Tamil	ivan	avan

The same is also true of some Australian aboriginal languages. For example, the Thargari third-person singular pronoun distinguishes 'near', 'far', and 'remote'. In Pittapitta there are also three third-person forms, marking (i) proximity to the speaker's front or side, (ii) proximity to the speaker's back, and (iii) remoteness anywhere from the speaker. Finally, for the Western Desert language, the third-person pronoun displays a quadripartite system, namely 'near', 'mid-distant', 'distant', and 'not-visible' (Dixon 1972: 8).

There are also languages in which the third-person pronoun encodes visibility. One such language is the Western Desert language, just mentioned. Another is Mantauran (Rukai), spoken in Taiwan. In this language, visibility is marked by *ana* for third-person singular and *ana-lo* for third-person plural, and invisibility by *ona* for third-person singular and *ona-lo* for third-person plural (Zeitoun 1997).

Deictic directionals
We come finally to **deictic directionals**. They can be grouped into two categories: (i) kinetic or deictic motion affixes, morphemes, and particles,

which mean 'hither/thither', and (ii) deictic motion verbs—verbs such as 'come' and 'go' that encode motion to or away from the deictic centre. Many languages in the world do not have motion verbs, and make do instead with motion affixes, morphemes, and particles. In Yélî Dnye, the 'hither' particle can be used with the unmarked 'go' verb *le* to express 'come here'. The interesting point is that this language does not have a 'thither' particle (Levinson 2004). By contrast, in Abaza there are two deictic/directional verbal prefixes: ʕ*a* indicates that the movement denoted by the verb is directed towards the speaker's location at CT, and *na* indicates that it is directed away from the speaker's location at CT (Anderson and Keenan 1985: 277, Manning 2001: 79). Diyari is a language which uses *yarra* (towards the speaker's location) and *yada* (away from the speaker's location) to express the direction of (induced) motion (Austin 1982). In Somali, one combines *soo* and *sii* with a verb to indicate that the motion proceeds towards or away from the speaker, respectively, as can be shown by (5.39) (Saeed 2003).

(5.39) a. Soo   soco.
            hither   walk
            Come this way.
        b. Sii   soco.
            thither   walk
            Go away.

Kiowa has a set of three directional markers: -*dé* indicates movement towards the deictic centre, -*p* movement away from the deictic centre, and -*pé* movement across the visual field of the speaker (Watkins 1984). A similar set of three kinetic suffixes can be found in Nunggubuyu (Heath 1980; see also Diessel 1999: 45–6). Among the set of post-verbal particles reconstructed for Proto-Polynesian, and widely found in its daughter languages, are five which are considered to be directional: *mai* (toward the speaker/venitive), *atu* (away from the speaker/andative), *hake* (upwards), *hifo* (downwards), and *aŋe* (along, obliquely) (Hopper 2002). Finally, many North American Indian languages have rich sets of verbal motion affixes, morphemes, and particles, which express both deictic and absolute coordinate information (Mithun 1999: 139, Levinson 2004).

We turn next to motion verbs such as 'come' and 'go'. Of these two verbs, 'go' is the unmarked one, whose condition of use can be roughly stated as movement away from the speaker's location at the time of speaking, i.e. CT.[20] However, when we consider 'come', we find that its use is more complicated. Following the seminal work of Fillmore (1971, 1997), the conditions for the use of 'come' in English can be summed up as follows: (i) movement towards the speaker's location at CT, (ii) movement towards the speaker's location at **arrival time**, (iii) movement towards the addressee's location at CT, (iv) movement towards the addressee's location at arrival time, and (v) movement towards the **home-base** maintained at CT by either the speaker or the addressee.

These conditions can be illustrated by a consideration of (5.40).

(5.40)   John will come to the library next week.

(5.40) is five-way ambiguous/vague. In the first place, the sentence can be used when the speaker is in the library at the time of speaking. A second possible situation is when the speaker is in the library at arrival time, namely, the time when John will arrive in the library. Thirdly, the sentence can be used when the addressee is in the library at speech time. Fourthly, the sentence can be uttered when the addressee is in the library at arrival time. Suppose that you work in the library but I don't. I can use (5.40) to tell you that John will come to your library next week, either if you are there at the time of speaking or if you will be there when John arrives (see also Marmaridou 2000: 91–3).

The sentence can also be used in a situation where the destination is not the participants' *actual* location, but their *nominative* location such as their home, workplace, or school, at the time of speaking. This nominative location Fillmore called home-base. Suppose that you and I both work in the library. One of us can say (5.40), or even better (5.41) when neither you nor I am in the library (see also Levinson 1983: 83–5 and Goddard 1998: 206–11).

(5.41)   John will come to the library next week, but both of us will be on holiday then.

There are languages which use different deictic items to express movement towards/away from the home-base and non-home-base. One such language is Diuxi Mixtec. In this language, distinct verbal categories are

---

[20] There are languages that do not have a semantic equivalent to the English motion verb *go*. These include German, Polish (Goddard 1998: 205), and Longgu, a language spoken on the Soloman Islands (Wilkins and Hill 1995).

employed to encode the distinction between home-base and non-home-base: *ndisi* for motion towards and *nu?u* for motion away from the home-base, and *vási* for motion towards, and *hi?i* for motion away from the non-home-base (Manning 2001: 75).

At this point, see whether you can do Exercise 8 on p. 176.

The use of 'come' in Catalan, Chinese, French, German, and Punjabi seems to behave like their equivalent in English, though the relevant details need to be worked out. On the other hand, in languages like Hungarian (Batori 1982), Japanese (Coulmas 1982: 212–13), and Spanish (Hottenroth 1982: 144–5), 'go' has to be used if movement is towards the addressee (see also Sinha 1972 on Hindi, Gandour 1978 on Thai, Gathercole 1977 on Turkish, Fillmore 1997 and Levinson 1983: 84 on Chinantec, Wilkins and Hill 1995 and Goddard 1998: 213–18 on Arrernte and Botne 2005 on Chindali).

Recently, Levinson (2004) has suggested that another parameter—specifying whether 'come' is marked for **telicity**—be added to the parameter of whether it requires the destination to be the place of speaking, as discussed above. The suggestion is based on the following observation. Suppose that John comes towards me but stops short before he arrives at the tree over there, I can say 'John came to the tree' in English but not in Longgu or Italian, where I must say 'John went to the tree'. Using the two parameters, one arrives at the classification of the 'come'-type motion verbs in the world's languages (Levinson 2004).

(5.42)   Levinson's (2004) classification of 'come'-type motion verbs

	+*Telic*	−Telic (unmarked)
Destination is place of speaking	Longgu	Italian
Destination need not be place of speaking	Ewe	Tamil

Furthermore, Levinson (2000) put forward a neo-Gricean pragmatic analysis of 'come' and 'go' by arguing that they tend to form a Q_{scalar} opposition. As such, the use of the semantically weaker, unmarked 'go' where the semantically stronger, more informative 'come' might have been used, will Q-implicate that the speaker is not in a position to use 'come'. The reason is that at least one of the conditions specified for 'come' in (5.42) is not met.

5.3. Other categories of deixis

In the last section, I discussed the three main types of deixis, namely, person, time, and space. In this section, I shall take a look at two other types of deixis, namely, social and discourse.

5.3.1. Social deixis

Social deixis is concerned with the codification of the social status of the speaker, the addressee, or a third person or entity referred to, as well as the social relationships holding between them (see, e.g., Levinson 1983: 63, Anderson and Keenan 1985, Fillmore 1997: 111–12, Manning 2001). The information encoded in social deixis may include social class, kin relationship, age, sex, profession, and ethnic group. Defined thus, social deixis is particularly closely associated with person deixis. In fact, there are scholars (e.g., Marmaridou 2000: 79, 81) who argue that person deixis cannot be studied independently of social deixis.[21]

Absolute versus relational social deixis
Following Comrie (1976), Levinson (1983: 90–1), and Brown and Levinson (1987), two main types of socially deictic information can be identified: (i) **absolute** and (ii) **relational**. Absolute information in social deixis can be illustrated by forms that are reserved for authorized speakers or authorized recipients. For example, in imperial China there was a form 朕 *zhen* that was specially reserved for the emperor to refer to himself. The same situation

---

[21] As pointed out by Mühlhäusler and Harré (1990: 264–5), the presence of social deixis implies that of person deixis, but not vice versa. This can be supported by the fact that in the historical reduction of pronoun systems, those pronouns that mark social deixis tend to be lost. Furthermore, the V form is typically replaced by the T form. For example, pidgin German spoken in various parts of the world employs *du* rather than *Sie* as its second-person singular pronoun. The French-derived pidgins of New Caledonia and West Africa use *tu* rather than *vous*. On the other hand, given that pidgins usually develop in contexts where power plays an important role, pronouns encoding differential social status can be introduced relatively early in their developments, as is the case of Tay Boi, the Pidgin French of French Indochina, the Portuguese-derived Kriol of Guiné-Bissau, and Zambuangueño, the Spanish Creole spoken in the Philippines.

is reported by Fillmore (1997) to be true of Japanese. Going next to forms that are reserved for authorized recipients, restrictions are placed on most titles of addressees such as *Your Majesty*, *Mr President*, and *Professor* in English (Levinson 1983: 91).

Four axes of relational social deixis

Relational information in social deixis can be represented between (i) speaker and referent (e.g., referent honorifics), (ii) speaker and addressee (e.g., addressee honorifics), (iii) speaker and bystander (e.g., bystander honorifics), and (iv) speaker and setting (e.g., levels of formality). **Referent honorifics** are forms that are employed by the speaker to show respect towards the referent; **addressee honorifics** are forms that are used by the speaker to show deference towards the addressee. Defined thus, the main difference between the speaker–referent axis and the speaker–addressee axis, according to Comrie (1976), is that while in the former, respect or honour can only be conveyed by referring to the target of the respect, in the latter it can be conveyed without such a direct reference being necessary. Respectful pronouns such as the French *vous* used to address a singular addressee (to be elaborated below) are not addressee honorifics (as has commonly but mistakenly been believed) but referent honorifics which happen to refer to the addressee. By contrast, the Tamil particle *-nka* is an addressee honorific, which can be adjoined freely to any constituent of a sentence, and which conveys respect to addressees only, but not to any referents in the sentence honorifics (e.g., Levinson 1983, 2004, Brown and Levinson 1987: 180). Referent honorifics are more common than addressee honorifics.

Next, **bystander honorifics** are forms that are used by the speaker to signify respect to a bystander, including participants in the role of audience and non-participant overhearers. A classic example is the use of so-called 'mother-in-law' and 'brother-in-law' languages in Australian aboriginal languages such as Dyirbal, Guugu Yimidhirr, and Umpila. This special 'avoidance' language or style/register is used in the presence of someone, especially a relative, prototypically a mother-in-law, with whom close social contact is taboo. One of the interesting characteristics of such a language is that a part or nearly all of its vocabulary has to be replaced by special 'avoidance' lexical items. Dyirbal, for example, has a *guwal* or everyday language, and a *dyalŋuy* or 'mother-in-law' language. While these varieties are identical in phonology and largely identical in grammar, they are entirely different in vocabulary (Dixon 1972: 32–3). More or less the same can be said of Guugu Yimidhirr. In this language, a brother-in-law would typically be the tabooed kin whose presence would trigger the use of alternative lexical items. Contrast (5.43a) in Guugu Yimidhirr everyday language and (5.43b) in its 'brother-in-law' variety.

(5.43) a. Ngayu   mayi   buda-nhu.
            1SG-NOM   food-ABS   eat-PURP
            'I want to eat food.'
        b. Ngayu   gudhubay   bambanga-nhu.
            1SG-NOM   food-ABS   eat-PURP
            'I want to eat food.'

In (5.43b), while the grammatical word *ngayu* is retained, the lexical words *mayi* and *buda*—are replaced by the respectful words *gudhubay* and *bambanga*- respectively (Haviland 1979: 368–9). This kind of grammaticalization of bystander honorifics and/or other bystander social deictic information has been cited also by Levinson (1988: 191, 204) for other, non-Australian languages such as Abipon, Ponapean, and Tojolabal (see also Keating 1998 on Pohnpei and Levinson 2004 on Yélî Dnye).

Finally, the **speaker–setting axis** has to do with the relation between the speaker (and perhaps other participants) and the speech setting or event. Although the formal/informal style can be said to be characteristic of perhaps all languages to a certain extent (for example, many European languages have distinct registers for formal and informal occasions), the distinction is more firmly grammaticalized and/or lexicalized in a number of East, Southeast and South Asian languages including Balinese, Japanese, Korean, Javanese, Thai, and Tibetan. Social deictic information is encoded in Japanese across all levels of grammar including morphology, syntax, and lexicon (e.g., Shibatani 1990). The same is true of Tamil, which has diglossic variants, with distinct morphology for formal and literary styles (Levinson 1983: 91, 93, 2004). Thai has what Diller (1993) called diglossic grammaticality, which differs markedly in its 'high' and 'low' syntax. Javanese is reported to have ten different speech levels. An example is given below.

(5.44) (Javanese, Anderson and Keenan 1985: 275)
        a. *Krama/Keromo* 'Formal'
        Kulo   saweg   maos   buku   Djawi.
        I   be-PROG   read   book   Javanese
        'I'm reading a Javanese book.'

b. *Ngoko* 'Informal'

Aku	lagi	motjo	buku	Djowo.
I	be-PROG	read	book	Javanese

'I'm reading a Javanese book.'

More or less the same is also true of two Austronesian languages, Madurese (Levinson 1983, Brown and Levinson 1987: 180) and Samoan (Milner 1961, Haviland 1979). In addition, many languages in the world have replacement vocabularies. For example, in English, on formal occasions, one may use *dine* to replace *eat*, *residence* to replace *home*, and *bestow* to replace *give* (Brown and Levinson 1987: 181). Many Australian aboriginal languages have replacement vocabularies that are employed only during special initiation rites (Dixon 1980: 65–8; see also Haviland 1979 on Gudadja). Finally, Yélî Dnye is a language where there is a replacement vocabulary that is used only when on the sacred islet of Lów:a (Levinson 2004).

The expression of social deixis

Social deixis can be accomplished by a wide range of linguistic devices including personal pronouns, forms of address, affixes, clitics and particles, and the choice of vocabulary.

Personal pronouns

Personal pronouns can be used to achieve a number of socially deictic effects.

Marking of respect

It is well known that a number of European languages have the familiar *tu/vous* type of distinction in second-person singular pronouns. The distinction has been known as the **T/V distinction** since Brown and Gilman (1960).

In a T/V system, there are two second-person singular pronouns: one familiar or T, and the other polite or V. The following is a list of T/V pronouns in the European languages I have collected.

(5.45)   T/V pronouns in European languages

	T	V
French	tu	vous
German	du	Sie
Italian	tu	lei

Spanish	tu'	usted
Russian	ty	vy
Danish	du/I	De
Dutch	jij	u
Norwegian	du	De
Greek	esi	esis

In fact, the T/V distinction is not restricted to European languages. Based on a study of one hundred of the world's languages, Helmbrecht (2003) divided languages into four types with respect to second-person singular pronouns. First of all, there are languages which do not show the T/V distinction in their personal pronoun systems. Out of his one hundred language sample, seventy-six languages belong to this type. They include English, Manipuri, Mongolian, Burushaski, Hmong Njua, Rama, Imonda, Goonyiandi, Luvukaleve, Acoma, Mapuche, and Zulu. Second is the type of language which displays the European-type binary T/V distinction. In addition to the European languages listed in (5.45), Helmbrecht singled out Basque, Finnish, Persian, Georgian, Turkish, Chinese, Mixtec, Fijian, Quechua, Luvale, Nama, Sango, and Yoruba. To Helmbrecht's list, we can add Ainu, Punjabi, Bangala, Kashmiri, Marathi, Oriya, Telugu, Mparntwe Arrernte, Djaru, Khasi, Usan, Dullay, Tigak, Guarijio, Guugu Yimidhirr, Tamil, and Ponapean (see, e.g., Brown and Levinson 1987: 198–203, Corbett 2000: 220–1, Lust et al. 2000). Note that in Bangala and Oriya, in addition to the T and V forms, there is also a third, **neutral form (N)**. Thirdly, there are languages which show two or more *degrees* in the T/V distinction. Three South Asian languages Hindi/Urdu, Kannada and Tagalog—are considered to be such languages. Finally, there are languages in which second-person pronouns are in general avoided in polite address. Instead, professional titles or kinship terms are used as a mark of respect. Helmbrecht mentioned six East and Southeast Asian languages, namely, Burmese, Indonesian, Japanese, Korean, Thai, and Vietnamese. To this list we can add Dzongkha, and to a less extent Chinese (see also Shibatani 1999).

The V form is most commonly derived from the second-person plural pronoun. This is the case in, for example, French, Persian, Yoruba, Nama, and Fijian. The next most common way is for the V pronoun to be developed out of the third-person plural pronoun, as is exemplified by German, Luvale, and Tagalog. There are other sources. In some languages the V form is borrowed from the third-person singular pronoun.

Italian and Indonesian belong to this category. In others it comes from the first-person plural pronoun, as in Ainu and Nahuatl; or it is derived from the second-person demonstrative pronoun, as in Sinhalese; or it is developed out of the reflexive pronoun, as in Hungarian and Imbabura Quechua. The V form can come from status terms. *Usted* in Spanish, for example, is derived from *vuestra merced* meaning 'your grace'. Other languages which belong to this category include Burmese, Dutch, Rumanian, Vietnamese, and Thai. Finally, there are also languages whose V forms are derived from more than one source. The V form in Hindi comes from both the reflexive and the third-person plural pronoun, and that in Kannada from both the second- and third-person plural pronouns (Helmbrecht 2003). (See also the papers collected in Taavitsainen and Jucker 2003 for discussion of the diachronic development of the T/V system covering English, Anglo-Norman, German (both Middle High and Modern Standard), Swedish, Czech, French, Spanish, and Finnish.)

In addition to languages with second-person polite pronouns, there are languages which have third-person honorific pronouns. This is the case of many Southeast Asian languages like Kashmiri, Malayalam, and Oriya. In Bangala, for example, the T form is *se* for singular and *ta-ra* for plural, and the V form is *tini* for singular and *tã-ra* for plural. Another Southeast Asian language which imposes social restrictions on the use of third-person pronouns is Punjabi. In this language, the spatially deictic contrast in the third-person singular pronoun carries over into the socially deictic domain. While the proximal form *eh* 'he/she' is used to refer to intimates and inferiors, its distal counterpart *oh* is employed to refer to non-intimates and superiors. In other words, whereas the former acts as T, the latter serves the function of V, to signify the social relationship between the speaker and the referent. In Tamil, another Southeast Asian language, the plurality of the T/V distinction is extended to third-person pronouns. *Avaanka* 'they' is used to refer respectfully to a male or (especially) a female. Furthermore, this plurality carries over into the first person, with the use of the royal 'we' (Brown and Levinson 1987: 180). Which brings us to first-person pronouns. Javanese is a language that is well known in this respect. It has three distinct first-person pronouns: *aku* is the form used to talk to equals, *kulo* is employed when talking to intimate superiors, and *kawulo* is used to talk to non-intimate superiors.

Marking of kinship relations

Personal pronouns are used to mark kinship relations. The Australian aboriginal language Parnkalla, for example, has three forms in the first-person dual pronoun: *nadli* is used for general first-person dual; *nadlaga* for mother and child, and uncle and nephew; and *narrine* for father and one of his children. But more systematic is the use of different sets of pronouns in Australian aboriginal languages to distinguish between **harmonic** and **disharmonic** kinship relations. Put rather crudely, two people are considered to be generationally harmonic if they are both members of the same generation (e.g., ego and brother), or of generations that differ by an even number (e.g., grandparent and grandchild). By contrast, two people are disharmonic if they belong to alternate generations (e.g., ego and parent or child), or they are three generation levels apart (e.g., great grandparent and great grandchild). This is the case of Lardil, where there are two sets of pronouns in dual and plural (e.g., Dixon 1980). Finally, even more complicated systems can be found in Australian aboriginal languages. Adnyamadhanha is one such language; Aranda is another. In addition to its harmonic/disharmonic sets, this language has a third set of personal pronouns, which are marked for reference to a group of people non-agnatic to the speaker (e.g., Mühlhäusler and Harré 1990: 165).

Other socially deictic information such as age and sex can also be indicated through the use of personal pronouns. For example, in the Oceanic language Dehu there are four first-person dual pronouns: *n~iho* is used for two young people exclusive, *eaho* for one young and one old person exclusive, *niso* for two young people inclusive, and *easo* for one young and one old person inclusive (Mühlhäusler and Harré 1990: 170). Turning next to sex, there are languages whose personal pronouns differ with the sex of the addressee. An example is provided by Malagasy. In this language, the second-person singular pronoun has two variants that are used according to the sex of the addressee: *ialahy* for males and *indriaku* for females (Anderson and Keenan 1985).

Forms of address

Forms of address are another common way of realizing social deixis. They include different types of name such as first name (e.g., *James*), last name (e.g., *Bond*), and a combination of first and last names (e.g., *James Bond*), kinship terms (e.g., *uncle*), titles borrowed from names of occupations (e.g., *doctor*), ranks in certain social/professional groups (e.g., *colonel*), and other sources (e.g., *madam*), and a combination of titles and names (e.g., *Professor Sir John Lyons*). Terms of address can be used to perform a variety of socially deictic functions. First, in English and many other languages, the use of address forms which include a title and the last name but not the first name, such as *Mr Lakoff*, *Dr Cram*, and *Lady Huxley*, marks the higher social status of the addressee and signals the social distance between the speaker and the addressee. For example, when I was a visiting professor at the Zentrum für Allgemeine Sprachwissenschaft Typologie und Universalienforschung (ZAS) in Berlin, I was always addressed as 'Sehr geehrter Herr Prof. Dr. Yan Huang' in writing. Second, many languages in the world utilize generalized forms of address such as *ayi* 'aunt' in Chinese, *sir* in English, and *bankilal* 'elder brother' in Tzeltal to show respect to strangers. Third, certain modes of address are used in many languages to claim in-group solidarity. Typical examples are *huoji* 'mate' in Chinese, *pal* in English, and *tampi* 'younger brother' in Tamil (see, e.g., Brown and Levinson 1987: 107–11, 182–5 for further discussion). In conclusion, it is not unreasonable to say that in human languages there is no such thing as a socially neutral form of address.

Affixes, clitics, and particles

Socially deictic information can also be encoded by **affixes, clitics**, and **particles**. Verb forms in Korean, for example, may select one of the following suffixes attached to them: *-na* marking intimate, *-e* familiar, *-ta* plain, *-eyo* polite, *-supnita* deferential, and finally *-so* authoritative (Trudgill 2000: 93). Another language which signals social relations by means of verbal affixes is Nahuatl. In this language, different affixes may be attached to verbs to indicate such social relations as (i) intimacy, (ii) neutral or somewhat formal, (iii) respect, and (iv) 'compadrazgo'[22] between the speaker and the addressee. An unusual variant of this socially deictic mechanism has also

---

[22] Compadrazgo is a social relation which exists between persons standing in a ritual relation of kinship by virtue of being parent/godparent or godparent/godparent of the same child (Anderson and Keenan 1985).

been reported for the Basque 'familiar voice' forms of non-second-person verbs (Anderson and Keenan 1985).

Choice of vocabulary

Finally, socially deictic information can also be reflected in the choice of the vocabulary used. We have already seen the use of the so-called 'avoidance' language and 'replacement' vocabulary in certain Australian aboriginal languages. Another case in point involves the use of 'triangular kin terms'. These terms encode the kinship relations not only between the speaker and the referent, and between the propositus (typically the addressee) and the referent, but also between the speaker and the propositus. Mayali, for example, has a set of terms for referring to the 'father' of one participant in the speech event, depending on the kinship relations between the speaker and the addressee. *Kornkumo* is employed by a mother to her child, referring to the child's father (i.e., her husband); *na-ngarrkkang* is used by a woman to her son's child to refer to the child's father (i.e., her son); the child in this situation will use *na-rroyngu* back to his/her grandmother to refer to his/her father (i.e., her son). Spouses will employ *na-bolo* to refer to the father of either one of them (and father-in-law to the other). And there are even more elaborate terms (Evans 1993).

More commonly, however, languages have a whole series of '**deferential**' and '**humiliative**' pairs of lexical items in their vocabularies. Thus, in Chinese we have *lingzun* '(your) honorable (father)' / *jiafu* '(my) humble father', *guifu* '(your) honorable residence' / *hanshe* '(my) humble hut', and *guixing* 'What's (your) honorable surname?' / *bixing* '(my) humble surname'. The same holds for Japanese, which contains a large number of honorific/humbling sets of lexical items adopted from Chinese such as *rei-situ* '(your) honorable wife' / *gu-sai* '(my) stupid wife', and *gyoku-koo* '(your) splendid article' / *sek-koo* '(my) humble article'. Similar humble forms are also used in the Urdu of Delhi Muslims and in Ponape. As pointed out by Brown and Levinson (1987: 185, 178–9), the use of the honorific/dishonorific terms has a two-sided nature: the lowering of the self on the one hand, and the raising of the addressee on the other (see Duranti 2002 on the Samoan respect vocabulary; see also Traugott and Dasher 2001 for discussion of diachronic development of social deixis).

5.3.2. Discourse deixis

We come finally to **discourse deixis**.[23] Discourse deixis is concerned with the use of a linguistic expression within some utterance to point to the current, preceding or following utterances in the same spoken or written discourse. Alternatively, discourse deixis can be said to refer to propositions (Lyons 1977, Webber 1991, Grenoble 1994, Herring 1994, Fillmore 1997: 103–6, Diessel 1999: 101). A few illustrative examples from English are given in (5.46).

(5.46)   a. This is how birds evolved from predatory dinosaurs.
      b. That is tonight's evening news.
      c. Here goes the main argument.
      d. In the last section, we discussed conversational implicature, in this section, we consider conventional implicature, and in the next section, we shall compare and contrast them.
      e. As already mentioned, the three main branches of the legal profession in England are solicitors, barristers, and legal executives.

The use of the proximal demonstrative *this* in (5.46a) anticipates information to be conveyed in an upcoming stretch of the discourse. The same is true of the use of the proximal adverb of space *here* in (5.46c). By contrast, the use of the distal demonstrative *that* in (5.46b) refers back to a preceding segment of the discourse. This is also the case with the use of *already* in (5.46e). The terms *last*, *this*, and *next* used in (5.46d) make reference to a preceding, current, and following portion of the discourse, respectively. The use of discourse deictics such as those in (5.46) can be found in most, if not all languages in the world. For example, Ambulas uses the proximal manner demonstrative *kéga* and the medial manner demonstrative *aga* to point to a forthcoming segment of the discourse, and the distal manner demonstrative *waga* to refer back to a preceding stretch of the discourse (Diessel 1999: 17). In Usan, one finds *ende* and *ete*, which are used only as discourse deictics. The former is the backward- and the latter the forward-referring discourse deictic (Reesink 1987: 81). Ainu is another language in which manner demonstratives function as discourse deictics (Diessel 1999: 105). I shall provide more data when we come to the marking of the feature 'previously mentioned in the discourse'.

---

[23] Other terms are text and textual deixis.

Next, some of the lexical expressions in English that are claimed to trigger a conventional implicature, discussed in Chapter 2, can also take a discourse deictic function when they occur at the initial position of an utterance. These may include *actually, anyway, after all, besides, but, even, however, in conclusion, moreover, so, therefore,* and *well*. As pointed out by Levinson (1983: 87–8), a major function of the utterance-initial usage of these words is to indicate that there is a relation between the utterance that contains them and some portion of the prior discourse.

Finally, a number of East and Southeast Asian languages have a special mechanism to mark the **topic** in a **topic construction**. A topic construction usually contains two parts: a topic, which typically occurs first, and a **comment**—a clause which follows the topic and says something about it (e.g., Huang 2000a: 266). This can be illustrated by (5.47).

(5.47)   (Korean, cited in Huang 2000a: 267)
    Kkoch-un   kwukhwa-ka   olaykan-ta.
    flower-TOP   chrysanthemum-NOM   last long
    'Flowers, chrysanthemums last long.'

In (5.47) *kkoch* is the topic, *kwukhwa-ka olaykan-ta* is the comment, and *un* is the topic marker. In similar vein, topics are marked in Japanese by *wa*, in Lahu by ɔ, and in Lisu by *nya* (Li and Thompson 1976, Huang 2000a: 266–76). In terms of information structure, topics are often associated with **given**, and comments with **new**, information. Clearly one of the main functions of topic marking in these East and Southeast Asian languages is 'precisely to relate the marked utterance to some specific topic raised in the prior discourse, i.e. to perform a discourse-deictic function' (Levinson 1983: 88).

In fact, marking of previous mention of an entity or given information in the discourse is not restricted to such East and Southeast Asian languages as Chinese, Japanese, and Lisu, which are considered to be **topic-prominent**. Such marking is found in a range of languages around the world. In Daga, for example, *me(pe)* can be suffixed to any of the fourteen demonstratives to yield a further set of discourse deictics to indicate the feature 'previously mentioned in the discourse' (Anderson and Keenan 1985: 291). Epio is a language which employs *-tebuk* to mark something that has been previously mentioned in the discourse. Yale behaves in a similar fashion (Heeschen 1982: 85, 88, 95). In Hausa, one finds *wànnàn* 'the one previously mentioned' as opposed to *wànnàn* 'this (new)', and *wàncán* 'that other (mentioned) one' as opposed to *wáncàn* 'that (new)' (Anderson and Keenan 1985: 289). In Aina, *tan* is used to mark the new topic of a conversation (Dixon 2003).[24]

Now look at Exercise 9 on pp. 176–7.

5.4. Summary

In this chapter I have provided a cross-linguistic, descriptive analysis of deixis. Section 5.1 discussed deictic versus non-deictic expressions, gestural versus symbolic use of deictic expressions, and deictic centre and deictic projection. In Section 5.2 I examined first-person, then time, and finally space deixis. Lastly, in Section 5.3 I considered social and discourse deixis.

Key concepts

deixis
deictic versus non-deictic expression
indexical expression
gestural versus symbolic use
deictic centre
deictic projection
person deixis
inclusive versus exclusive 'we'
vocative
time deixis
calendrical versus non-calendrical usage
coding versus receiving time
space deixis
frames of spatial reference (intrinsic, relative, absolute)

[24] Recall our discussion of obviation in note 6 above. As pointed out by Bloomfield (1962: 38), '[t]he proximate third person represents the topic of discourse, the person nearest the speaker's point of view, or the person earlier spoken of and already known'. Therefore obviation may be seen as performing the function of discourse deixis of some sort.

distance (proximal, medial, distant)
distance- versus person-oriented system
visibility
elevation
side
social deixis
absolute versus relational social deixis
referent, addressee, bystander honorifics
T/V pronoun
deferential versus humiliative form
discourse deixis

Exercises and essay questions

1. Of the following italicized expressions, which are used deictically and which are used non-deictically? For those used deictically, which are used in a gestural way and which in a symbolic way?
    (i) Hi, is Mary *there*?
    (ii) Press the button *now*.
    (iii) *You* will never fail until *you* give up.
    (iv) Does *that* shirt become *you*?
    (v) John said that *he* was thoroughly exhausted.
    (vi) In 1888, Ivanov moved to Moscow and lived *there* for the rest of *his* life.

2. The following is a Yiddish joke cited in Levinson (1983: 68; see also Mey 2001: 55). What is the 'mistake' made by the Hebrew teacher?

A melamed (Hebrew teacher), discovering that he had left his comfortable slippers back in the house, sent a student after them with a note for his wife. The note read: 'Send me your slippers with this boy.' When the student asked why he had written 'your' slippers, the melamed answered: 'Yold (Fool)! If I wrote "my" slippers, she would read "my" slippers and would send her slippers. What could I do with her slippers? So I wrote "your slippers", she'll read "your" slippers and send me mine.'

3. Of the following utterances, which involve a deictic projection?
    (i) *We* may lose customers if *our* prices are very high.
    (ii) The *next* station is Piccadilly Circus. Please change *here* for the Piccadilly line.
    (iii) Can you prepare a list of hints and tips for safe camping *now*?
    (iv) (To a colleague in New Zealand from England)
        I shall be delighted to lecture in your department *next* (*New Zealand*) summer.

   (v) *Take this there; bring that here!*

   (vi) I'll *bring* the DVD to you tomorrow.

4. Compare (i) and (ii) below, and explain why (ii) is anomalous.

   (i) Let's go to the airport to collect him next Monday.

   (ii) ?Let's go to the airport to collect you next Monday

5. In many languages, 'we' can be used to indicate 'I' or 'you'. Can you explain why 'we' is used in the following sentences?

   (i) (Doctor to patient)

      How are we feeling today? (we = you)

   (ii) (Director of personnel services to job applicant)

      We regret to inform you that your application was not successful. (we = I)

   (iii) (Polish, ticket collector to passenger, Grundy 2000: 27)

      Nie   mamy   bilitu?

      Not   have-(1PL)   ticket

      'We haven't got a ticket?' (we = you)

6. Consider the use of *here* in (i)–(iv) (adapted from Hanks 1992). What are the differences?

   (i) I'm over here! (shouted to companion through the woods)

   (ii) Oh, it's just beautiful here! (with sweeping arm gesture to countryside)

   (iii) Doctor, it hurts here. (with hand on abdomen)

   (iv) They live over here, but we live here. (pointing to a small map)

7. In the following pairs of sentences, which expressions are used deictically and which are not?

   (i) a. Let's go to a *nearby* café.

      b. John took Mary to a *nearby* café.

   (ii) a. There was a fatal car accident in Oxford yesterday. A *local* driver was arrested.

      b. Why not employ a *local* tour guide?

8. As already noted, *we* is ambiguous between an inclusive and an exclusive interpretation. This ambiguity is retained for the *we* in (i) but not for the *we* in (ii), which can only have an exclusive reading. Can you explain this contrast in terms of the conditions for the use of *go* and *come*?

   (i) We'll go there this afternoon.

   (ii) We'll come there this afternoon.

9. Ignoring the tense markers, point out all the deictic expressions in the following sentences and indicate in each case which type of deixis is involved.

   (i) I live here in New York and Lucy lives there in California.

   (ii) Good morning, ladies and gentlemen. This is the 10:15 Thames Express service to London Paddington, calling at Reading, Slough, and London Paddington.

   (iii) We may get a pay cut if sales go down this year. That's what I've been told.

   (iv) I came over several times to visit you last week, but you were never there.

(v) Good afternoon, Sir, how can I help you?

10. Deixis shows that meaning cannot be studied without reference to context. Do you agree?

11. What are the main semantic parameters of space deixis? Of these parameters, which is the most important one?

12. What are the main categories of deixis? Discuss with examples.

13. One view is that spatial expressions are more fundamental than non-spatial ones, and as such they tend to extend into other linguistic domains. This view is known as **localism** (Lyons 1977: 718ff). Regarding deixis, localism amounts to saying that spatial deictics tend to be extended to other categories of deixis such as time, social, and discourse deixis. Is there any evidence in this chapter to support this view?

14. Give a brief description of the deictic system of a language other than English.

Further readings

Fillmore (1997).
Lyons (1977). Chapter 15.
Anderson and Keenan (1985).
Levinson (2004).

Part II

Pragmatics and its interfaces

This part deals with those topics which represent new ground in pragmatics, but which are under-represented in any of the existing pragmatics coursebooks. In particular, it focuses on various interfaces between pragmatics and other (core) areas of inquiry. Chapter 6 discusses the pragmatics–cognition interface, concentrating on Sperber and Wilson's relevance theory. The interface between pragmatics and semantics is the topic of Chapter 7. Finally, Chapter 8 examines the interaction and division of labour between pragmatics and syntax, focusing on anaphora and binding.

6

Pragmatics and cognition:
relevance theory

Relevance theory was originated by the French scholar Dan Sperber and the British scholar Deirdre Wilson.[1] It can best be regarded as both a reaction against, and a development of, the classical Gricean pragmatic theory (see Chapter 2). The main ideas of relevance theory are presented in Sperber and Wilson (1986, 1995), and more recently updated in Wilson and Sperber (2004). Grounded in a general view of human cognition, the central thesis of the theory is that the human cognitive system works in such a way as to tend to maximize relevance with respect to communication. Thus, the communicative principle of relevance is responsible for the

[1] Though a similar concept of relevance can be traced back to the work of the logician Noel Belnap (1969), and the social phenomenologist Alfred Schutz (1970). Belnap (1969) developed a logic of relevance to account for inferences that are relevant but not quite valid. Schutz (1970) was of the view that relevance is a principle according to which an individual organizes his or her cognitive structures into 'provinces of meaning'. See Allwood (2000) for further discussion.

recovery of both the explicit and implicit content of an utterance. Furthermore, it is hypothesized that pragmatics, which incorporates the relevance-theoretic comprehension procedure, is a submodule of the 'theory of mind', that is, a variety of mind-reading (Sperber and Wilson 2002, Wilson and Sperber 2004).[2]

This chapter begins, in Section 6.1, with a discussion of the two principles of relevance. Section 6.2 then examines the concepts of explicature, implicature, and conceptual versus procedural meaning in relevance theory. Next, in Section 6.3, I discuss the recent relevant-theoretic shift from treating pragmatics as a Fodorian central, inferential process to the view that it is a submodule of the 'theory of mind'. Finally, in Section 6.4, I briefly compare and contrast relevance theory and classical/neo-Gricean theory of conversational implicature.

6.1. Relevance

6.1.1. The cognitive principle of relevance

At the heart of Sperber and Wilson's (1986, 1995) relevance theory lies the notion of **relevance**. This is embodied in the two principles of relevance put forward by Sperber and Wilson (1995): a **first**, or **cognitive principle of relevance**, and a **second**, or **communicative principle of relevance**.[3] Let us consider the cognitive principle of relevance first.

---

[2] There are, of course, a number of other cognitive pragmatic theories. One such theory is known as cognitive semantics or experientialist realism, based on the connectionist model of the mind (see note 11 below). This approach is represented by e.g., Lakoff (1987), Sweetser (1990), Johnson (1992), Lakoff and Johnson (1999), Marmaridou (2000), and Fauconnier (2004). A second perspective on cognitive pragmatics can be found in the literature on Construction Grammar (e.g., Goldberg 1995, Kay 2004). Finally, there is also the cognitive pragmatic theory of abductive reasoning, which, though foreshadowed by the ideas of Sir Isaac Newton, the German philosopher Christian Wolff and Charles Pierce, has recently been developed out of research in artificial intelligence and computational pragmatics (e.g., Hobbs 2004).

[3] Notice that in Sperber and Wilson (1986) there was only one principle of relevance, which goes thus: every ostensive stimulus conveys a presumption of its own optimal relevance.

(6.1) Sperber and Wilson's (1995) cognitive principle of relevance
       Human cognition tends to be geared to the maximization of relevance.

What, then, is relevance? According to Sperber and Wilson, relevance is a function (or measure) of two factors: (i) **cognitive** (or **contextual**) **effects** and (ii) **processing effort**. The first factor is the outcome of an interaction between a newly impinging stimulus and a subset of the assumptions that are already established in a cognitive system. The second factor is the effort a cognitive system must expend in order to yield a satisfactory interpretation of any incoming information processed. Defined thus, relevance is a matter of degree. The degree of relevance of an input to an individual is a balance struck between cognitive effects (i.e. reward) and processing effort (i.e. cost). This is given in (6.2) (Sperber and Wilson 1995).

(6.2) Relevance of an input to an individual
       a. Other things being equal, the greater the positive cognitive effects achieved by processing an input, the greater the relevance of the input to the individual at that time.
       b. Other things being equal, the greater the processing effort expended, the lower the relevance of the input to the individual at that time.

Furthermore, Sperber and Wilson isolated three main types of cognitive effects to which the processing of new information in a context may give rise: (i) generating a conclusion derivable from new and old information together, but from neither new nor old information separately, which is called a **contextual implication**, (ii) strengthening an existing assumption, and (iii) contradicting and cancelling an existing assumption. As an illustration, consider the following scenario, taken from Blakemore (2002: 60–1). Suppose that a bus driver is to leave from a bus stop. He sees in his rear mirror the reflection of an anxious-looking woman carrying a bus pass, trying to cross the road behind him. In this situation, the bus driver's overall representation of the world can be improved in the following three ways corresponding to the three types of cognitive effects mentioned above. In the first place, given the assumption that if a person is holding a bus pass, then he or she intends to travel on a bus, the bus driver will derive the new assumption or the contextual implication that the woman in question has the intention of travelling on his bus. Secondly, the bus driver's existing assumption that the woman is trying to cross the road to catch his bus may be supported and strengthened by the assumption that she is carrying a bus pass. Thirdly and finally, the bus driver's existing assumption that the woman intends to take his bus is contradicted and eliminated when he sees the woman walk off in the opposite direction after handing the bus pass to someone who is standing by the bus stop.

Next, processing effort. Consider another scenario. Suppose that Xiaoming, a Chinese student, who has just arrived in England, wants to rent a room from the Smiths, his potential landlords. He wants to know whether the Smiths keep any cats. He could receive either of the replies in (6.3).

(6.3)   a. The Smiths have three cats.
        b. Either the Smiths have three cats or the capital of China is not Beijing.

Here, (6.3a) requires less processing effort than (6.3b). This is because (6.3a) and (6.3b), being logically equivalent, yield exactly the same amount of cognitive effect. However, the effect is much more easily obtained from (6.3a) than (6.3b), since the latter has a second, false disjunct to be computed.

Now, by (6.1) and (6.2), what the cognitive principle of relevance basically says is this: in human cognition, there is a tendency for communicators to achieve as many cognitive effects as possible for as little processing effort as possible. In order to give a complete illustration of (6.1) and (6.2), let me add (6.4) to the two replies Xiaoming could receive in (6.3).

(6.4)   The Smiths have three pets.

Given the cognitive principle of relevance in (6.1), all the three replies in (6.3) and (6.4) are relevant to Xiaoming's question whether the Smiths keep any cats or not. However, according to (6.2), (6.3a) is more relevant than either (6.4) or (6.3b). (6.3a) is more relevant than (6.4) because the processing of it engenders greater positive cognitive effects than does that of (6.4). The reason is that (6.3a) entails (6.4), and hence generates all the conclusions, among other things, deducible from (6.4), together with the context. On the other hand, (6.3a) is more relevant than (6.3b) because, as we have already seen, the processing effort required to compute (6.3a) is smaller than that required to compute (6.3b).

Notice that relevance stated in this way is a trade-off of effect and effort, hence comparative rather than quantitative. One feature of such a comparative notion is that, as Sperber and Wilson were aware, it provides clear comparisons only in some cases. This gives rise to one of the most common criticisms levelled against relevance theory, namely that it fails to provide an explanation of how to measure contextual effects and processing effort in an objective way, how to make them commensurate with each other, or why there is always a unique way to meet the cognitive principle of relevance (e.g., Levinson 1989, Bach 1999a, but see Wilson and Sperber 2004 for a spirited defence).

6.1.2. The communicative principle of relevance

We move next to the **communicative principle of relevance**. Before proceeding, let us first take a look at two general theoretical approaches to communication.

Code versus inferential models of communication
On Sperber and Wilson's (1986, 1995) view, theories of communication can be roughly divided into two models: (i) the **code model** and (ii) the **inferential model**. According to the classical, code model, communication is accomplished by encoding and decoding messages, that is, a communicator encodes his or her intended message into a signal, which is then decoded by the audience utilizing an identical copy of the code. With respect to human verbal communication, there are two main assumptions underlying this model: (i) human languages are codes, and (ii) these codes associate thoughts to sounds.[4]

But the code model is descriptively inadequate. This is because comprehension involves much more than the decoding of a linguistic signal. As already established in Chapter 1, there is a huge gap between the semantic representation of a sentence and the messages that are actually conveyed by the uttering of that sentence. In other words, linguistically encoded meaning radically underdetermines the proposition expressed by an utterance (e.g., Austin 1962, Atlas 1977, 1989, 2005, Searle 1979, 1992, 1996, Travis 1981, 1997, Sperber and Wilson 1986, 1995, Recanati 1989, 1994, 2004a, 2004b, Levinson 2000, Carston 2002, Horn 2004). This is known as the linguistic underdeterminacy thesis. Furthermore, the gap is filled not by more coding, but by inference. I have already given a few examples, (1.2)–(1.5), in Chapter 1. A further example is given in (6.5) below.

(6.5)   *Advice given by the government during an outbreak of salmonella in the UK*
         Fried eggs should be cooked properly and if there are frail or elderly people in the house, *they* should be hard-boiled.

---

[4] On Sperber and Wilson's (2002) view, much animal communication uses the code model. This, for example, is the case for the bee dance employed to indicate the direction and distance of nectar (Hauser 1996).

Intuitively, the preferred antecedent of the pronoun *they* in this example is *eggs* rather than *frail or elderly people*. But the derivation of this reading is dependent not on coding but on what the speaker is most likely to intend to mean, and our real-world knowledge about who or what is or is not likely to be hard-boiled.

Directly opposed to the code model is the inferential model, whose foundation was largely laid by Grice's original theory of meaning$_{nn}$. As pointed out in Chapter 2, the essence of meaning$_{nn}$ is that it is communication which is intended to be recognized as having been intended. In other words, on Grice's view, meaning$_{nn}$ or speaker-meaning is a matter of intention. According to the inferential model, communication is achieved by expressing and recognizing intentions. That is to say, a communicator provides evidence of his or her intention to convey a certain meaning, which is then inferred by the audience on the basis of the evidence presented (see also Recanati 2004b). Both the classical/neo-Gricean pragmatic theory of conversational implicature discussed in Chapter 2 and the relevance theory I am discussing here fall under this model. A further point to note is that while inferential communication can be used on its own, coded communication can be employed only as a means to strengthen inferential communication (Sperber and Wilson 1986, 1995).

Ostensive-inferential communication

In relevance theory, inferential communication is called **ostensive-inferential communication**. Why? This is because inferential communication involves, in addition to a **first-order informative intention**, a higher-order intention, which Sperber and Wilson (1986, 1995) call **communicative intention**. Furthermore, they call the behaviour which yields the attribution of such an intention 'ostensive communication', 'ostensive behaviour', or simply 'ostension'.

(6.6)   Ostensive-inferential communication
   a. The informative intention
      An intention to inform an audience of something.
   b. The communicative intention
      An intention to inform the audience of one's informative intention.

In ostensive-inferential communication, there is generally an ostensive stimulus, the use of which gives rise to an expectation of a particular level of relevance which Sperber and Wilson call **optimal relevance**.

(6.7) Presumption of optimal relevance
  a. The ostensive stimulus is relevant enough to be worth the audience's processing effort.
  b. It is the most relevant one compatible with communicator's abilities and preferences.

Stated in this way, ostension and inference are two sides of the same communication coin: the former is from the perspective of the communicator, and the latter is from the point of view of the audience.

With (6.6) and (6.7) in place, we can now present Sperber and Wilson's (1995) communicative principle of relevance as follows.

(6.8) Sperber and Wilson's (1995) communicative principle of relevance
  Every ostensive stimulus (e.g. an utterance) conveys a presumption of its own optimal relevance.

The specific procedure employed by the comprehension system on the basis of the presumption of optimal relevance is given in (6.9).

(6.9) Sperber and Wilson's (1995) relevance-theoretic comprehension procedure
  a. Follow a path of least effort in computing cognitive effects: test interpretative hypotheses (disambiguation, reference resolution, implicatures, etc.) in order of accessibility.
  b. Stop when your expectations of relevance are satisfied (or abandoned).

6.2. Explicature, implicature, and conceptual versus procedural meaning

In the previous section I discussed Sperber and Wilson's cognitive and communicative principles of relevance. In this section, let us take a look at the notions of explicature, implicature, and conceptual versus procedural meaning in relevance theory.

6.2.1. Grice: what is said versus what is implicated

Recall that in Chapter 2, I pointed out that on a classical Gricean account, meaning$_{nn}$/speaker-meaning or the total signification of an utterance is divided into **what is said** and **what is implicated**. Simply put, what is said is generally taken to be (i) the conventional meaning of the sentence uttered with the exclusion of any conventional implicature, and (ii) the truth-conditional propositional content of the sentence uttered (e.g., Grice 1989: 25, Levinson 1983: 97, 2000: 170, Neale 1992: 520–1, Clark 1996: 141, Carston 2002: 114–15). What is conversationally implicated is then defined in contrast to, and calculated on the basis of, what is said (and in the case of M-implicatures, together with *how* what is said is said). Stated thus, what is said is supposed to provide the input to deriving what is conversationally implicated. But to work out what is said, according to Grice (1989: 25), one has to (i) resolve reference, as in (6.5) above and (6.10) below; (ii) fix deixis, as in (6.11); and (iii) disambiguate expressions, as in (6.12), (6.13), and (6.14).[5]

(6.10)   a. John told Bill that he wanted to date his sister.
                 Preferred interpretation: he = John, his = Bill's
         b. John told Bill that he couldn't date his sister.
                 Preferred interpretation: he = Bill, his = John's
(6.11)   *Accompanied by selecting gestures*
         I don't want to go with *her*, I want to go with *her*.
(6.12)   (Structural ambiguity)
         Flying planes can be dangerous.
         a. The act of flying planes can be dangerous.
         b. Planes that are flying can be dangerous.
(6.13)   (Lexical ambiguity)[6]
         The coach left the stadium after the match.
         a. coach = bus
         b. coach = instructor of athletic team
(6.14)   (Structural-lexical ambiguity)
         John saw her duck.
         a. John saw her lower her head.
         b. John saw the duck belonging to her.

I shall return to Grice's dichotomy between what is said and what is implicated in Chapter 7.

6.2.2. Explicature

On Sperber and Wilson's (1986, 1995) view, Grice failed to recognize that pragmatics contributes to what is said, or using the relevance-theoretic

---

[5] To these, Levinson (2000: 172–86) added (i) unpacking ellipsis and (ii) narrowing generalities. I shall return to these in the next chapter.

[6] Note that all of the examples of ambiguity discussed in the relevance theory literature belong to lexical ambiguity.

terminology, to **explicit content** or **explicature**. Consequently, according to Sperber and Wilson, in the classical Gricean framework, too much attention has been given to the pragmatic contribution to **implicit content** or **implicature**. It is now widely acknowledged, following the earlier work by Cohen (1971), Atlas (1977), and Gazdar (1979), that there is indeed **pragmatic intrusion** of some sort, namely, the intrusion of pragmatically inferred content, into the conventional, truth-conditional content involved in the working out of what Grice called what is said (see, e.g., Travis 1985, 2001, Sperber and Wilson 1986, 1995, Recanati 1989, 1993, 2004a, 2004b, Neale 1992, Levinson 2000, Fodor 2001, Carston 2002, Huang 2004b).

In an attempt to account for the crucial role played by pragmatic inference in explicit content, Sperber and Wilson put forward a notion of explicature, parallel to the classical Gricean notion of implicature. An explicature is an inferential development of one of the incomplete **conceptual representations** or **logical forms** encoded by an utterance. In other words, an explicature functions to flesh out the linguistically given incomplete logical form of the sentence uttered, yielding fully propositional content (but see Bach's 2004 comments on the term 'explicature').

In the current version of relevance theory, explicatures typically serve to complete and enrich conceptual representations or logical forms into propositional forms in the following five areas: (i) disambiguation, (ii) reference resolution, (iii) saturation, (iv) free enrichment, and (v) *ad hoc* concept construction (e.g., Carston 2004). Let me take them one by one.

Disambiguation

Disambiguation usually involves the selection of one sense out of two or more potential senses provided by the linguistic system. Explicatures will complete the incomplete logical form by selecting a particular interpretation, depending on context.

(6.15)   John and Bill passed the port in the evening.
     a. port = harbour
     b. port = wine
     Explicature: e.g., John and Bill passed the harbour in the evening

Reference resolution

In contrast to disambiguation, for **reference resolution**, the candidate referents are not determined by the linguistic system. Reference resolution is achieved by assigning an appropriate contextual value to the relevant referential or anaphoric expression on the explicit side. In addition to (6.5) and (6.10) above, consider (6.16).

(6.16)   John walked into a music room. The piano was made in the nineteenth century.
Explicature: There was a piano in the music room John walked into

(6.16) is an example of what is known as 'bridging cross-reference' in the linguistics literature. As defined in Huang (2000a: 249), a bridging cross-reference anaphoric expression is one that is used to establish a link of association with some preceding expression in the same sentence or discourse via the addition of background assumptions. Defined thus, bridging cross-reference anaphora has three characteristic properties: (i) the anaphoric expression, which is usually a definite NP, must occur in the appropriate context of its 'antecedent', which is usually an indefinite NP, (ii) there is some semantic and/or pragmatic relation between the anaphoric expression and its 'antecedent', and (iii) the anaphoric expression and its 'antecedent' do not stand in a strictly coreferential relation. Rather they are linked to each other via the addition of pragmatic inference of some kind. In Matsui (2000) a relevance-theoretic analysis of bridging cross-reference anaphor was developed. The central idea of her analysis is that the interpretation of bridging cross-reference anaphora is constrained by the communicative principle of relevance. Thus, on this account, in interpreting bridging cross-reference anaphora, one is always making a bridging assumption that yields adequate cognitive effects but without subjecting the language user to unjustifiable processing effort to obtain these effects. Further discussion of the theoretical issues involved in the analysis of bridging cross-reference anaphora, and a comparison between Matsui's relevance-theoretical model and the other two influential models, namely, the topic/focus model and the scenario model, can be found in Huang (2000a: 249–53).

Saturation

Saturation is a pragmatic process whereby a given slot, position, or variable in the linguistically decoded logical form is filled or saturated (Recanati 1989, 1993: 243, 2001, 2002, 2004a, 2004b). A few relatively uncontroversial examples are given in (6.17).

(6.17)   a. Yan works too hard. [for what?]
         b. Chomsky's minimalist program is less promising. [than what?]
         c. Sperber and Wilson's notion of explicature is different. [from what?]

Here, the bracketed questions are taken to be the slots in the incomplete logical forms of the sentences in (6.17). These slots need to be explicitly completed so that their full propositional forms can be obtained. Saturation may yield such explicatures as those in (6.18) for (6.17), depending on context.

(6.18) a. Yan works too hard [for a not terribly well-paid British university professor]

b. Chomsky's minimalist program is less promising [than its principles-and-parameters predecessor]

c. Sperber and Wilson's notion of explicature is different [from Grice's notion of implicature]

Free enrichment

Turning now to **free enrichment**, this term is again borrowed from Recanati (2004a, 2004b). In free enrichment, although there does not seem to be either an overt indexical or a covert slot in the linguistically decoded logical form of the sentence uttered, the logical form nevertheless needs to be conceptually enriched in the explicature. The process of free enrichment is 'free' because it is pragmatically rather than linguistically based (Recanati 2004a, 2004b). In the relevance theory literature, two types of free enrichment are identified. In the first place, we have the type in which the enrichment focuses on a particular lexical item in the utterance and narrows the concept it encodes. Compare (6.19) and (6.20).

(6.19) a. John has a brain.
        b. The university campus is some distance from the rail station.
        c. I haven't washed my face yet.
        d. It's snowing.
        e. The police moved in and the hostages were released.

(6.20) a. John has a [scientific] brain
        b. The university campus is a [considerable] distance from the rail station
        c. I haven't washed my face yet [this morning][7]
        d. It's snowing [in Boston]
        e. The police moved in and [then, as a result, etc.] the hostages were released[8]

---

[7] The enrichment of (6.19c) is dependent on our shared beliefs about the world, in particular about our shared face-washing practices. This would explain, for example, why *I haven't had sex* would be enriched in a different way, as pointed out by Taylor (2001). See Taylor (2001) for a 'roughly but still deeply Gricean' explanation.

[8] Note that (6.20e) is explicitly treated as carrying a generalized (I-)implicature in the Gricean and neo-Gricean framework.

Here, (6.19a) and (6.19b) are truisms or express a trivial truth. It goes without saying that every human being has a brain and that there is distance between any two places. Next, (6.19c) and (6.19d) are so vague that the minimal propositions recovered from both utterances by decoding and reference assignment fall short of what the speakers must have meant. Consequently, the vagueness in both utterances needs to be resolved. Finally, the use of *and* in (6.19e) requires the strengthening of the conjunct relation. On this basis, we will obtain explicatures such as those shown in the brackets in (6.20).

Secondly, there is the type in which a contextually provided conceptual constituent needs to be added in the explicature. Consider (6.21).

(6.21)   a. Everyone wore a new wool cardigan.
         b. There's nothing to watch on TV tonight.
         c. They eat everything.

The process involved here is again that of narrowing or specifying. In the case of (6.21a), the domain of the quantifier *everyone* needs to be narrowed down, hence specified, resulting in an explicature such as (6.22a), depending on context. In the case of (6.21b), the incomplete logical form has to be enriched by something like '(nothing) the speaker considers worth (watching)'. In the case of (6.21c), 'everything' needs to be enriched to 'everything that is edible'.

(6.22)   a. Everyone [at Mary's party] wore a new cardigan
         b. There's nothing [the speaker considers worth] watching on TV tonight
         c. They eat everything [that is edible][9]

Ad hoc concept construction
Finally, we come to ***ad hoc* concept construction**. This notion, introduced by Barsalou (1983), means the pragmatic adjustment of a lexical concept in the linguistically decoded logical form, the adjustment being a narrowing or strengthening, a broadening or weakening, or a combination of both. As an illustration, take (6.23) first.

[9] It should be pointed out that in Recanati's (1989, 1993, 2004b) original analysis, (6.20a)–(6.20c) are taken to be cases of strengthening or logical enrichment, whereas (6.21b) is considered as a case of expansion, *à la* Bach (1987). The main difference between strengthening and expansion is whether the output proposition needs to entail the original input proposition. I shall have more to say about Recanati's work in the next chapter.

(6.23)   John is happy/angry/depressed...

The general concepts expressed by the lexical items *happy*, *angry*, and *depressed* can access a large, if not indefinite number of more specific subconcepts indicating different kinds, degrees, and qualities of the emotions. For example, *John is depressed* can be used to mean that John feels a bit low, John feels very low, or John feels suicidal, depending on context. Explicatures here serve to recover the narrower, more specific concepts in the logical form.

Next, consider (6.24), some of which are taken or adapted from Carston (2002, 2004).

(6.24)   a. There is a rectangle of lawn at the back.
         b. The fridge is empty.
         c. Holland is flat.
         d. Classic FM plays continuous classics.
         e. John is a bulldozer.

All the sentences in (6.24) are used in a broad, 'loose' way. Recall that in Chapter 4, we mentioned Austin's notion of 'loose' use and his example *France is hexagonal*. This is exactly what is happening in (6.24). In (6.24a), the rectangle is likely to be approximately rectangular, hence what is expressed is not the encoded concept RECTANGLE, but a broadened or loosened concept RECTANGLE$'$. More or less the same can be said of the 'loose' use of many other geometrical terms such as *round, triangular*, and *oval*. In (6.24b), there could still be some odd groceries left in the fridge. In (6.24c), Holland is not, strictly speaking, flat. In (6.24d), Classic FM also broadcasts news, commercials, and the listeners' call-ins. Finally, loosening is applicable to cases of metaphor as well, as in (6.24e). In all these cases, the lexical concepts will undergo an *ad hoc* pragmatic adjustment or weakening (see also Carston 2004).

See what you make of Exercise 1 on p. 207.

At this point, mention should be made of a subtype of explicature—what is called **higher-level** or **higher-order explicature** in the relevance theory literature. These are explicatures which involve embedding the propositional form of an utterance under a higher-level description. The higher-level descriptions include propositional attitude descriptions, speech act descriptions, and certain other comments such as evidentiality markers on the embedded propositions. By contrast, non-higher-level explicatures are called **basic explicatures** by Wilson and Sperber (2004). As an illustration of higher-level explicature, consider the explicatures of (6.25) in (6.26).

(6.25) Susan: My husband is a womanizing alcoholic.
(6.26) a. Susan believes that her husband is a womanizing alcoholic
       b. Susan is angry that her husband is a womanizing alcoholic

Here, (6.26a) and (6.26b) may be the higher-level explicatures for (6.25). The propositional form of (6.25) is embedded under a propositional attitude description.

    Next, witness the explicatures of (6.27) in (6.28).

(6.27) John to Bill: Bring me a glass of water, please.
(6.28) a. John is telling Bill to bring him a glass of water
       b. It is moderately desirable to John (and achievable) that Bill bring him a glass of water
       c. John is requesting Bill to bring him a glass of water

The uttering of (6.27) by John performs the speech act of requesting (see Chapter 4). It gives rise to the higher-level explicatures in (6.28) (but see Bird 1994 for a critique).

    Finally, consider the explicatures of (6.29) in (6.30).

(6.29) Evidently, Frederick the Great entertained Voltaire at Sanssouci.
(6.30) a. It is evident that Frederick the Great entertained Voltaire at Sanssouci
       b. The speaker strongly believes that Frederick the Great entertained Voltaire at Sanssouci

Evidentials make clear the source or reliability of the evidence on which a statement is based, as shown by the use of *evidently* in (6.29). (6.30a) and (6.30b) may be the higher-level explicatures for (6.29).

Now see whether you can do Exercise 2 on p. 207.

6.2.3. Implicature

I turn next to what is taken as implicit content, or implicature, in relevance theory, defined as a communicated assumption derivable solely via pragmatic inference. The recovery of an implicature differs from that of an explicature in that while the latter involves both decoding and inference, the former involves only inference (Sperber and Wilson 1986, 1995). Let us call implicatures in the relevance-theoretic sense **r-implicatures**, in the hope that no confusion will arise with Grice's notion of (conversational) implicatures.

There are two kinds of r-implicature in relevance theory: (i) **implicated premises** and (ii) **implicated conclusions**. The former is a contextual assumption intended by the speaker and supplied by the addressee, and the latter is a contextual implication communicated by the speaker. By way of illustration, take (6.31).

(6.31)   Car salesman: Are you interested in test-driving a Rolls Royce?
          John: I'm afraid I'm not interested in test-driving any expensive car.

John's reply may yield the following r-implicatures:

(6.32)   a. A Rolls Royce is an expensive car
          b. John isn't interested in test-driving a Rolls Royce

Here, (6.32a) is an implicated premise, and (6.32b) is an implicated conclusion, of John's reply. (6.32b) follows deductively from (6.32a) combined with (6.31). However, this analysis is limited to the class of examples like (6.31) in the relevance theory literature, and more generally, is applicable only to what is treated as a particularized conversational implicature in the Gricean and neo-Gricean framework (see Chapter 2). How it can be applied to a generalized conversational implicature in the Gricean sense is, to say the least, unclear. For example, it is not clear what the implicated premise is in (6.33) (but see Sperber and Wilson 1995: 276–8 and Carston 1998 for a relevance-theoretic analysis of generalized conversational implicatures in the Gricean sense).[10]

(6.33)   Some of John's friends are vegans.

(6.34)   a. Implicated premise: ?
          b. Implicated conclusion: Not all of John's friends are vegans

---

[10] On Recanati's (2004a: 48) view, implicated premises are not implicatures. The reason is that they are not part of what the speaker means. Rather, they are part of what he or she takes for granted or presupposes (see Chapter 3) and expects the addressee to take for granted.

To sum up, in an overall, relevance-theoretic comprehension process, three subtasks are involved (Sperber and Wilson 1995, Wilson and Sperber 2004).

(6.35)   Subtasks in the overall comprehension process
   a. Constructing an appropriate hypothesis about explicit content (explicatures) via decoding, disambiguation, reference resolution, and other pragmatic enrichment processes.
   b. Constructing an appropriate hypothesis about the intended contextual assumptions (implicated premises).
   c. Constructing an appropriate hypothesis about the intended contextual implications (implicated conclusions).

By now you should be able to do Exercise 3 on p. 207.

A second dichotomy relating to r-implicatures is that between **strong** and **weak r-implicatures**. Following Grice's idea that implicatures may sometimes be indeterminate (see note 11 in Chapter 2), Sperber and Wilson (1986, 1995) posited that they may be more or less strong. In other words, the strength of an r-implicature may vary along a continuum. Simply put, strong r-implicatures are those r-implicatures whose recovery is essential to understand the speaker's intended meaning. By contrast, weak r-implicatures are those r-implicatures whose recovery is not essential, because the r-implicatures may be one of a wide array of equally possible r-implicatures engendered by an utterance. As an illustrating example, consider (6.36), taken from Wilson and Sperber (2004).

(6.36)   Peter: Did John pay back the money he owed you?
         Mary: No. He forgot to go to the bank.
(6.37)   a. John was unable to repay Mary the money he owes because he forgot to go to the financial institution
         b. John may repay Mary the money he owes when he next goes to the financial institution
         c. ...

Mary's reply in (6.36) may give rise to a range of r-implicatures, as in (6.37). Of these r-implicatures, (6.37a) is a strong r-implicature. Otherwise, Mary's reply would not be relevant. On the other hand, Mary's reply may encourage the addressee to derive further r-implicatures such as (6.37b). But (6.37b) is a weak r-implicature because it is indeterminate and its recovery is not essential (Wilson and Sperber 2004).

Turn to p. 207 and try your hand at Exercise 4.

It should be emphasized at this point that the recovery of both explicatures and r-implicatures is guided by the communicative principle of relevance. Moreover, the first satisfactory interpretation discovered by the use of the relevance-theoretic comprehension procedure is the only satisfactory one. This interpretation is the one that the addressee should select (Deirdre Wilson personal communication).

6.2.4. Conceptual versus procedural meaning

We come finally to the dichotomy between conceptual and procedural meaning in relevance theory, a dichotomy developed largely by Blakemore (1987, 2002, 2004). On Blakemore's view, **conceptual meaning** contributes concepts to the logical form of a sentence, that is, it enters into the semantic representation. In other words, in conceptual encoding, linguistic forms encode conceptual information. For example, *lion*, *eat*, and *happy* are lexical items which encode conceptual information. By contrast, **procedural meaning** does not contribute any concept but rather provides a constraint on, or indication of the way in which certain aspects of pragmatic inference should proceed, that is to say, it indicates particular computational processes. Another way of putting it is that in procedural encoding, linguistic forms encode procedural information (but see Bach 1999b for a dissenting view). Discourse markers or connectives like *after all*, *but*, and *so* (which are treated as triggers of conventional implicatures in the Gricean framework) are examples of linguistic expressions which encode procedural meaning. Consider, for instance, (6.38).

(6.38)   We want peace but they want war.

Here, the discourse marker *but* functions as a pointer to the pragmatic inference the addressee is to work out. More specifically, it instructs the addressee to interpret the clause that follows it as contradicting and eliminating a proposition which is most likely derived from the preceding clause, thus generating a denial of the expected interpretation. Stated thus, *but* encodes only procedural information (Blakemore 2002, see also Blass 1990 on Sisaala).

In Blakemore (1987), it was suggested that whereas conceptual encodings contribute to explicatures, procedural encodings constrain only pragmatic inferences which yield r-implicatures. This position, however, was called into question by Sperber and Wilson (1993). On Sperber and Wilson's view, procedural encodings play an important role not only on the implicit but also on the explicit side of communication. More specifically, Sperber and Wilson proposed that pronouns, demonstratives, and even mood, tense, and inverted word order encode information about the inferential computations in which basic and higher-level explicatures are derived (see also Blakemore 2004).

6.3. From Fodorian 'central process' to submodule of 'theory of mind'

6.3.1. Fodorian theory of cognitive modularity

Let us start with the question whether or not there is a **pragmatics module** in the mind—or, put in a more precise way, whether utterance comprehension is a specialized cognitive domain with its own innately specified principles and mechanisms. In order to provide an answer to this question, we need first to take a look at the Fodorian theory of cognitive modularity.

One of the currently most influential theories of mind is the one put forward by Fodor (1983), inspired in part by Chomsky's view of language and linguistics.[11] The central thesis of the now classical Fodorian theory of cognitive modularity is the claim that the mental architecture of *homo*

---

[11] Another is **connectionism**—also frequently called **parallel distributed models** or **neural networks**. The main thesis of connectionist models is that human cognition operates through the interactions of numerous simple units. The processing is highly distributed throughout the entire system. There are, for example, no specialized modules in the Fodorian sense. See Bechtel and Abrahamson (1991) and Horgan and Tienson (1996) for an introduction to connectionism. In the late 1980s and early 1990s, there was an intense debate about the architecture of cognition between connectionists and symbolists in cognitive science and cognitive linguistics. See, for example, the exchanges between Fodor and Pylyshyn (1988) and Chalmers (1993).

sapiens is divided roughly into a basic dichotomy between a **central processor** and a number of distinct **cognitive systems**. These specialized cognitive systems, called **modules**, have a number of relatively well-defined characteristics: they are **domain-specific** (they are specialized for particular domains), **primary** (they are not 'assembled', that is, they are not composed of other more elementary mechanisms), **computationally autonomous** (they do not share mental resources, such as memory, with other cognitive systems), **fast** and **mandatory** (for example, we have no choice but to hear sounds we are exposed to), **innately specified** (their structure and function are not determined by some learning process only), and **informationally encapsulated** (they have no access to information of a certain kind, and operate without interference from central control). The five senses—sight, hearing, smell, taste, and touch—are such cognitive systems, each of which constitutes one module or a cluster of modules. Language is taken to be another module or a cluster of modules. These modules feed into the central system, which is neither domain-specific nor informationally encapsulated. The central system is responsible for general mental capacities such as rational thought formation, problem solving, and belief fixation. Furthermore, whereas not restricted exclusively to this role, one of the major functions of a module is to provide 'input' to the central system. Hence Fodor considered language as a dedicated input system, analogous to those devoted to the five senses[12] (e.g., Fodor 1983, Huang 2001a, and Smith 2004).[13]

[12] The characterization of language as an input system was, however, challenged by Chomsky (1986: 18). On Chomsky's view, the language faculty is a cognitive system of knowledge rather than an input or output system. See Smith (2004) for discussion of further differences between Fodor and Chomsky.

[13] See also Atlas's (1997) comments from a philosophical perspective. On Atlas's view, speech is both modular and hermeneutic. It is modular in the sense that sounds are first translated algorithmically into semantic information; it is hermeneutic in the sense that the speaker's intention behind the propositional content is then interpreted.

One of the anonymous referees of this book pointed out that modularity, as espoused by Fodor, plays no role in processing accounts of how language is produced and understood. In fact, much of the recent research in neuroscience has shown that linguistic, for example, lexical and syntactic, information is processed in parallel.

6.3.2. Sperber and Wilson's earlier position: pragmatics as Fodorian 'central process'

Given the distinctive properties of modules, mentioned above, the question presents itself whether pragmatics or utterance comprehension is a module in the classic Fodorian sense. The answer provided by the earlier Sperber and Wilson is that it is not (see Sperber and Wilson 1986 and Wilson and Sperber 1986). As an alternative, Sperber and Wilson argued that like scientific theorizing—a paradigmatic case of a non-modular process in the Fodorian sense—pragmatics is part of the Fodorian central, inferential process, albeit a spontaneous, intuitive rather than a conscious, reflective one. Furthermore, they hypothesized that the Fodorian central system is a non-demonstrative inference process which works in such a way as to tend to maximize relevance. The main difference is that while Fodor conceded that the central processor operates in a mysterious way along non-deductive lines, and is therefore essentially unstructured and putatively uninvestigable, Sperber and Wilson (1986) took the central processor as an inference-generating system with a strong deductive component.

6.3.3. Sperber and Wilson's current position: pragmatics as submodule of 'theory of mind'

On Sperber and Wilson's view, in recent years there has been a general tendency in cognitive science to shift away from Fodor's basic dichotomy between the relatively undifferentiated central system and the specialized modules towards an increasingly modular concept of the human mind.[14] Against this background, Sperber and Wilson have abandoned their earlier position of treating pragmatics or utterance comprehension as a Fodorian central, inferential process (Sperber and Wilson 2002, Wilson and Sperber 2004). Instead, they are now of the view that utterance comprehension involves a more modular ability for **mind-reading**, or '**theory of mind**', which

[14] This is strongly disputed by the same anonymous referee, who said that contrary to Sperber and Wilson's claim, in cognitive science there is in fact increasingly compelling evidence for immense plasticity and connectivity during development, and for parallel processing in dealing with language. For recent accounts of the acquisition process, see e.g., Clark (2003, 2004) and Tomasello (2003).

involves the more general metapsychological ability to inferentially attribute mental states or intentions to others on the basis of their behaviour (e.g., Davies and Stone 1995, Carruthers and Smith 1996). Furthermore, Sperber and Wilson argued that, contrary to the popular assumption that a submodule is not needed to handle pragmatic abilities in mind-reading (e.g., Bloom 2000, 2002), utterance comprehension is subject to a distinct interpretation submodule of the 'theory of mind', that is, a specialized, automatic computational device with its own special principles and mechanisms. The workings of this comprehension submodule of the 'theory of mind' are underpinned by the communicative principle of relevance, and contain the relevance-theoretic comprehension procedure as a basic component. Given the relevance-theoretic comprehension procedure, which is a dedicated domain-specific inferential apparatus, the addressee will be able to infer what the speaker means on the basis of the evidence provided (Sperber and Wilson 2002, Wilson and Sperber 2004).

6.4. Relevance theory compared with classical/ neo-Gricean theory

What are the main differences between relevance theory and classical/neo-Gricean theory? The first difference concerns whether an inferential theory of human communication should be based on the study of usage principles or cognitive principles. One of the central issues of any pragmatic theory is to explain how the addressee works out the speaker's intended meaning on the basis of the evidence available. The answer provided by Grice is that utterances automatically raise certain expectations, and these expectations guide the addressee towards what the speaker intends (but see Bach 1999a, Saul 2002; see also note 16 below). More specifically, Grice put forward an account of these expectations in terms of a co-operative principle and a set of attendant maxims of conversation. The Gricean co-operative principle and its associated maxims of conversation are essentially usage principles based on the rational nature of human communication, and indeed of any goal-oriented (human) activity (Grice 1989: 28). In other words, they are general communicative norms recognized jointly, though tacitly, by the speaker and the addressee in order to communicate effectively and efficiently. Where do the co-operative principle and its attendant maxims of conversation come from, and how do the speaker and the addressee come to know them? Whereas Grice was non-committed on the source of these inferential principles and their place in our overall cognitive architecture, one possible answer provided by him is that they are likely to be learned. To quote him: 'it is just a well-recognized empirical fact that people do behave in these ways; they learned to do so in childhood and have not lost the habit of doing so; and, indeed, it would involve a good deal of effort to make a radical departure from the habit' (Grice 1989: 29).

Relevance theory, on the other hand, is an attempt 'to shift the whole centre of gravity of pragmatic theorizing away from the study of usage principles to the study of cognitive principles' (Levinson 1989). In the relevance-theoretic framework, pragmatics is reduced to a single notion of relevance, which is realized in two principles of relevance. But unlike Grice's co-operative principle and its attendant maxims, the principles of relevance are not a maxim addressed to the speaker, known by the addressee, and obeyed or exploited in communication. Rather, grounded in a general view of human cognition, they are an automatic reflex of the human mental capacity that works without the communicators having any overt knowledge of it. How do the speaker and the addressee follow the principles of relevance? They do not. According to Sperber and Wilson (1987), '[c]ommunicators and audience need no more know the principle of relevance to communicate than they need to know the principles of genetics to reproduce ... Communicators do not "follow" the principle of relevance; and they could not violate it even if they wanted to. The principle of relevance applies without exception: every act of ostensive communication communicates a presumption of relevance'. Relevance is thus a form of unconscious inference. Put in a slightly different way, the principles of relevance are governing cognitive principles that are not themselves an object of processing. This raises the larger issue of whether relevance theory can be falsified or not. Given that relevance is an exceptionless generalization, it is likely to be immune from any possible counterexamples (e.g., Levinson 1989, Huang 1991, 1994, 2000a, 2001a, but see Wilson and Sperber 2004 for counterarguments).[15]

---

[15] One of the minimal Popperian criteria for a scientific theory is falsifiability, which dictates that empirically based theories (under which linguistics falls) can only be refuted, but not proved true (e.g., Popper 1973).

In the second place, relevance theory and classical/neo-Gricean theory differ in whether or not separate notions of explicature and implicature are needed in the recovery of explicit and implicit content, respectively. As already noted in Section 6.2.1, on Grice's view the propositional content of what is said is not fully worked out until reference is identified, deixis is interpreted, and ambiguity is resolved. How can all this be done? Grice (1989: 25) seemed to take the recovery of the explicit propositional content as largely the outcome of linguistic and contextual decoding. This led Sperber and Wilson to their criticism that in the Gricean paradigm, only the recovery of implicit context (implicature) is taken to be properly pragmatic, and that as a result, the key part pragmatics plays in computing explicit content is overlooked. Consequently, Sperber and Wilson put forward their notion of explicature. Explicature plays an extremely important role in relevance theory, and as a result, many types of implicature in the Gricean sense are reduced to explicature. This, for example, is the case for 'conjunction buttressing', 'bridging-cross reference' (see Chapter 2), and many others.

By contrast, in the neo-Gricean pragmatic framework, the explicit–implicit distinction is rejected (e.g., Levinson 2000: 195–6). Levinson argued that so-called explicatures result from the same pragmatic apparatus that engenders what is conversationally implicated. Therefore, they are largely the same beast as implicatures. This in turn gives rise to a problem known as **Grice's circle**, namely, how what is conversationally implicated can be defined in contrast to and calculated on the basis of what is said, given that what is said seems to both determine and to be determined by what is conversationally implicated (e.g., Levinson 2000, Huang 2001a). Levinson's proposal was that one should reject the 'received' view of the pragmatics–semantics interface, namely, the view that the output of semantics is the input to pragmatics, and allow implicatures to play a systematic role in 'pre'-semantics, that is, to help determine the truth-conditional content of an utterance (Levinson 2000, see also Huang 2001, 2003, 2004b).

Thirdly, there is the difference relating to whether an inferential theory of human communication should contain two levels or three levels. Building on the Gricean generalized versus particularized implicature dichotomy, Levinson (1995, 2000) developed a theory of presumptive meaning. On a traditional, standard view, there are only two levels of meaning to a theory of communication: a level of sentence-meaning versus a level of speaker-meaning, or, to make use of Lyons's (1977: 13–18) distinction between type and token, a level of **sentence-type-meaning** versus a level of **utterance-token-meaning**. But Levinson (2000: 23) argued that such a view 'is surely inadequate, indeed potentially pernicious, because it underestimates the regularity, recurrence, and systematicity of many kinds of pragmatic inferences'. He proposed to add a third level—**utterance-type-meaning**—to the two generally accepted levels of sentence-type-meaning and utterance-token-meaning. This third layer is the level of generalized, preferred or default interpretation, which is dependent not upon direct computations about speaker-intentions but rather upon expectations about how language is characteristically used. Generalized conversational implicatures, Levinson argued, should be included on this layer, as these pragmatic inferences have an expectable, stable, and even standardized or conventionalized interpretation (see also Bach 2004, Noveck 2001, Bezuidenhout 2002, Hamblin and Gibbs 2003, Papafragou and Musolino 2003, Bezuidenhout and Morris 2004, Breheny, Katsos, and Williams to appear). Stated in this way, a neo-Gricean pragmatic theory of conversational implicature, which is largely concerned with generalized rather than particularized implicature, is essentially a theory of utterance-type-meaning on a level intermediate between sentence-type-meaning on the one hand and utterance-token-meaning on the other. In other words, it is ultimately a theory of presumptive meaning—pragmatic inference that is generalized, default, and presumed (see also Jaszczolt 2002, 2005).

However, as pointed out by Levinson (2000), this middle-layer of utterance-type-meaning has been constantly subject to attempts to reduce it on the one hand to the upper layer of sentence-type-meaning, as in, for example Kamp's Discourse Representation Theory (DRT) (e.g., Kamp and Reyle 1993), and on the other to the lower layer of utterance-token-meaning, as in relevance theory, Thomason's (1990) accommodation account and certain artificial intelligence 'local pragmatics' analyses. In my view, such reductionist efforts, though highly desirable given the metatheoretical principle known as 'Occam's razor' discussed in Chapter 1, cannot be successful. The reason they will fail is this: on the one hand, generalized conversational implicatures are defeasible, thus not code-like, as claimed by Sperber and Wilson (2002). This will make it difficult for them to be semanticized. On the other hand, other things being equal, a theory about types is in principle better than a theory about tokens in that the former enjoys more predictive and explanatory power. Therefore, any attempts to reduce generalized conversational implicatures to context-induced, 'nonce' or 'once-off' inferences should be resisted (but see Reboul 2004). If these arguments are correct, a three-tiered theory of communication with a layer of default but defeasible interpretation sitting midway is in principle to be preferred over a two-levelled one without such an intermediate layer (Huang 1991, 1994, 2000a, 2003, 2004b, 2006b).

Finally, somewhat related to the difference concerning communication theory levels above is the difference with respect to the distinction in conversational implicature type or context type. In the Gricean framework, there are two types of conversational implicature: generalized and particularized. Alternatively, one can argue that there is only one type of conversational implicature but two types of context: default and specific. In relevance theory, by contrast, there is no distinction either in conversational implicature type or in context type. As noted already, all conversational implicatures are reduced to a kind of context-induced, 'nonce' or 'once-off' inference, namely, what I have called r-implicatures (Levinson 1989, Huang 1991, 1994, 2000a, 2001a, 2003, 2004b, 2006b).[16] I shall return to some of the issues discussed here in the next chapter.

6.5. Summary

In this chapter, I have considered the interface between pragmatics and cognition, focusing on Sperber and Wilson's relevance theory. Section 6.1 looked first at the cognitive and then at the communicative principles of relevance. Section 6.2 considered the concepts of explicature, implicature, and conceptual versus procedural distinction in relevance theory. The topic

---

[16] Cf. Saul (2002), who is of the view that relevance theory and classical/neo-Gricean theory are not as incompatible as they may appear. This is because while Grice's main goal is to develop a theory of speaker-meaning, or utterance production, Sperber and Wilson are primarily concerned with the construction of a cognitive, psychological theory of utterance comprehension (see also Horn 2004). When there are meaning discrepancies between utterance production and comprehension, one has what Saul (2002) calls an audience-implicature (see Thomas 1995: 58–61 and Gibbs 1999: 5–6 for exemplification). This view is echoed by Bach (1999a), who argued that utterance interpretation is a problem not for pragmatics but for cognitive and social psychology (but see Levinson 2004). Both Saul and Bach think that relevance theory has misunderstood this main goal of Grice's thinking.

of Section 6.3 was the recent relevance-theoretic shift from treating pragmatics or utterance comprehension as a Fodorian central, inferential process to the view that it is a submodule of the 'theory of mind'. Finally, in
Section 6.4, relevance theory was compared and contrasted with classical
and neo-Gricean pragmatic theory.

Key concepts

relevance
cognitive principle of relevance
communicative principle of relevance
cognitive/contextual effect
processing effort
code model versus inferential model of communication
ostensive-inferential communication
explicature
saturation
free enrichment
ad hoc concept construction
loose use
higher-level/order explicature
r-implicature
implicated premise versus implicated conclusion
strong versus weak r-implicature
conceptual versus procedural meaning
module
central processor
mind-reading
Grice's circle
two versus three levels in a theory of communication
sentence-type-meaning
utterance-type-meaning
utterance-token-meaning

Exercises and essay questions

1. What are the explicatures of the following?
   I've visited the Great Wall in China.
   (ii) The thieves have stolen everything.
   (iii) 'Much of the Walled Garden at the Botanic Garden is made up of rectangular botanical family borders.' *The University of Oxford, Botanic Garden Living Library*
   (iv) The oven is hot enough.
   (v) Jane has found a mole.
   (vi) Nobody understood the professor's talk on genetic engineering.
   (vii) The building collapsed some time after the bomb went off.
   (viii) Little Johnny ate the chocolate heart on the cake.
   (ix) John told Steve that he had won the prize.
   (x) I haven't shaved.
   (xi) They went to a pizza restaurant. The Italian waiter was handsome.
   (xii) The children are coming.

2. What are the higher-order explicatures of the following?
   (i) Frankly, I don't fancy him.
   (ii) Father to son: Please pick up the books on the floor.
   (iii) Their European patent has been granted.
   (iv) John to wife: I shan't drink heavily any more.

3. In the following exchanges, what are the implicated premises and the implicated conclusions?
   (i) John: Let's go and watch *The Last Emperor* directed by Bernardo Bertolucci.
   Mary: Period epics are tedious.
   (ii) Guest: I'm afraid I'm late. Am I still in time for dinner?
   Receptionist: I'm afraid, Sir, the kitchen has already closed.
   (iii) John: Has Steve's paper been accepted for presentation at the conference?
   Mary: His was one of the best papers submitted.
   (iv) John: Lucy doesn't seem to have a boyfriend these days.
   Mary: She's been paying a lot of visits to London lately.
   (v) John: How about going out to play football?
   Mary: It's snowing heavily.
   (vi) John: I've run out of soy sauce.
   Mary: There's a small Chinese supermarket just around the corner.

4. What are the strong implicatures, and what are the possible weak implicatures, of the following?
   (i) John: Would you like any beef, or pork perhaps?
   Mary: I'm a vegetarian.

5. What is cognitive effect, and what is processing effort? How can they be measured?
6. What is the cognitive principle of relevance? What is the communicative principle of relevance? What is the relationship between them?
7. In which main areas does pragmatics play an important role in enriching the incomplete logical form of an utterance into an explicature?
8. What are the essential properties of the Fodorian modules?
9. What is the recent relevance-theoretic shift regarding the place of utterance comprehension in the overall architecture of the human mind?
10. What are the main differences between relevance theory and classical/neo-Gricean theory?

Further readings

Sperber and Wilson (1995).
Wilson and Sperber (2004).
Carston (2002). Chapters 1 and 2.

7

Pragmatics and semantics

In the previous chapter, I looked at the interface between pragmatics and cognition with special reference to relevance theory. In this chapter, I turn my attention to the **pragmatics–semantics interface**.

Semantics and pragmatics are the two subdisciplines of linguistics which are concerned with the study of meaning. That much is largely accepted. However, what constitutes the domain of semantics, and what constitutes that of pragmatics? Can semantics and pragmatics be distinguished? Are they autonomous, or do they overlap with each other? To what extent and how do they interact with each other? These are some of the questions that have puzzled, and are still puzzling, linguists and philosophers of language. In this chapter, I present a critical survey of some recent attempts at providing more satisfactory answers to these questions by both linguists and philosophers of language.

The structure of this chapter is as follows. In Section 7.1, I identify two main theoretical positions with regard to the relationship between semantics and pragmatics. The focus of Section 7.2 is then on a number of influential ways in which the semantics–pragmatics distinction has been drawn. Finally, in Section 7.3, I concentrate on the issue of pragmatic intrusion into the classical Gricean concept of what is said, which has recently become the centre of intense debate among both linguists and philosophers of language, and among both semanticists and pragmaticists. The discussion in this section will focus on Grice's characterization of what is said versus what is conversationally implicated (7.3.1), the relevance theorists' notion of explicature (7.3.2), Recanati's idea of the pragmatically enriched said (7.3.3), Bach's concept of conversational impliciture (7.3.4), and Levinson's argument that the pragmatic inference under consideration is nothing but a neo-Gricean conversational implicature (7.3.6). In between (7.3.4) and (7.3.6) I consider the question of whether explicature/the pragmatically enriched said/impliciture can be distinguished from conversational implicature (7.3.5). The section will end with a brief comparison of Grice's, the relevance theorists', Recanati's, Bach's, and Levinson's analyses (7.3.7).

7.1. Reductionism versus complementarism

Regarding the relationship between semantics and pragmatics, two main theoretical positions can be isolated: (i) **reductionism** and (ii) **complementarism**[1] (e.g., Huang 2001a). According to the first view, the putative distinction between semantics and pragmatics should be abolished (e.g., Lakoff 1972, 1987, Jackendoff 1983: 105–6, 1990: 18, 1992: 32, Langacker 1987: 154; see also Matthews 1995)—a position Levinson (2000) dubbed '**pragmantics**'. This reductionist camp can further be divided into two subcamps: (i) those taking the view that pragmatics should be entirely reduced to semantics, to be called **semantic reductionism**; and (ii) those holding the position that semantics is wholly included in pragmatics, as represented, for example, by what Recanati (2004b) called the speech act theoretical view. This can be labelled **pragmatic reductionism** (Huang 2001a).[2] This reductionist approach, however, runs counter to the fact that there are

---

[1] The term 'complementarism' is borrowed from Leech (1983: 6).

[2] Leech (1983: 6) called the two extreme positions 'semanticism' and 'pragmaticism'. Posner's (1980) terms were 'monism of meaning' and 'monism of use', and Dascal (1981) labelled them 'radical literalism' and 'radical contextualism'. See Turner (1997) for further discussion of Posner (1980) and Dascal (1981).

linguistic phenomena such as entailment (see Chapter 1) which are relatively uncontroversially semantic, and there are also linguistic phenomena such as conversational implicature (see Chapter 2), which are relatively uncontroversially pragmatic.

In contrast to the reductionist position, on a complementarist view, the division between semantics and pragmatics—a distinction that was first introduced by philosophers in the ideal language tradition (e.g., Frege 1897, Morris 1938, Carnap 1942) (see Chapter 1)—can in principle be retained. Within complementarism, a further distinction can be made between what may be called **radical semantics** and **radical pragmatics**. Whilst radical semanticists (such as philosophers in the ideal language tradition and generative semanticists in the 1970s) have argued that much of the study of meaning should be attributed to semantics, radical pragmatics (such as philosophers in the ordinary language tradition) have attempted to assimilate as much of the study of meaning as possible to pragmatics.[3] The complementarist viewpoint, which sees semantics and pragmatics as complementary though distinct subdisciplines of linguistics, shedding light on different aspects of meaning, is more widely accepted.

7.2. Drawing the semantics–pragmatics distinction

The distinction between semantics and pragmatics has been formulated in a variety of different ways. Lyons (1987), for example, attempted to explain it in terms of the following dichotomies: (i) meaning versus use, (ii) conventional versus non-conventional meaning, (iii) truth-conditional versus non-truth-conditional meaning, (iv) context independence versus context dependence, (v) literal versus non-literal meaning, (vi) sentence (or proposition) versus utterance, (vii) rule versus principle, and (viii) competence versus perform-

---

[3] In Posner's (1980) terminology, these two intermediate positions are occupied by his 'meaning-maximalist' and 'meaning-minimalist' categories, respectively. Dascal (1981) dubbed the two intermediate positions 'moderate literalism' and 'moderate contextualism'. More recently, Recanati (2004a: 83–6) has called the various extreme and intermediate positions 'literalism', 'indexicalism', 'the syncretic view' (or 'syncretism'), 'quasi-contextualism', and 'contextualism'. He has also put them on the above ordered scale, with the first three lying on the literalist side, and the last two on the contextualist side.

ance. To these, one may add: (i) type versus token, (ii) content versus force, (iii) linguistic meaning versus speaker's meaning, (iv) saying versus implicating, (v) linguistically encoded versus non-linguistically encoded meaning, (vi) compositionality versus non-compositionality, and (vii) intention dependence versus intention independence (see, e.g., Levinson 1983, Bach 1999a, Nemo 1999, Szabó 2005a).[4] Of these formulations, three, according to Bach (1999a, 2004), are particularly influential. They are (i) truth-conditional versus non-truth-conditional meaning, (ii) conventional versus non-conventional meaning, and (iii) context independence versus context dependence. Let us take a look at them in turn.

7.2.1. Truth-conditional versus non-truth-conditional meaning

In the first place, the semantics–pragmatics distinction has been characterized in terms of truth-conditional versus non-truth-conditional meaning. According to this formulation, semantics deals with truth-conditional meaning, or in Recanati's (2004b) terminology, words–world relations; pragmatics has to do with non-truth-conditional meaning. This characterization of pragmatics is captured in a well-known Gazdarian formula: pragmatics = meaning − truth conditions (Gazdar 1979: 2).

There are, however, a number of problems at the very core of this approach to the semantics-pragmatics division, which Recanati (2004b) called the Carnapian approach. First of all, there are linguistic forms that do not denote anything and therefore do not make any contribution to truth-conditional content. Paradigmatic cases include greetings like *Good morning!*, conventional implicature triggers like *but*, and syntactic constructions like imperatives. Secondly and more importantly, as noted in Chapters 1 and 6, and as will be discussed in detail in Section 7.3 below, the linguistically coded meaning of a sentence does not always fully determine its truth conditions (i.e., the linguistic underdeterminacy thesis discussed in Chapter 1) (e.g., Austin 1962, Atlas 1977, 1989, 2005, Searle 1979, 1992, 1996, Nunberg 1979, Travis 1981, 1997, Sperber and Wilson 1986, 1995, Recanati 1989, 1994, 2004a, 2004b, Bach 1999a, 2004, Levinson 2000,

---

[4] See also Nemo and Cadiot (1997), which listed more than thirty ways in which the boundary between semantics and pragmatics can be drawn, and the papers collected in Turner (1999), Bianchi (2004a), and Szabó (2005b), respectively.

Carston 2002, Horn 2004; but see Borg 2004 and Cappelen amd Lepore 2004 for dissent). Furthermore, there is often pragmatic intrusion into the truth-conditional content of a sentence uttered. Following the lead from earlier work by Cohen (1971), Wilson (1975), Atlas (1977), and Gazdar (1979), Levinson (2000), for example, showed that neo-Gricean conversational implicatures can intrude on to (i.e., contribute to) the truth conditions of a sentence uttered. All this has led Recanati (1993, 2004b) to dub part of pragmatics 'truth-conditional pragmatics'. If this is correct, one has to conclude that the truth-condition constraint cannot itself distinguish semantics from pragmatics in a principled way. I shall return to the issue of pragmatic intrusion into truth-conditional content in Section 7.3 below.

7.2.2. Conventional versus non-conventional meaning

Secondly, the demarcation line between semantics and pragmatics has been defined in terms of conventional versus non-conventional meaning.[5] On this view, which has remained influential since Katz (1977), semantics studies the conventional aspects of meaning; pragmatics concerns the non-conventional aspects of meaning. Consequently, while a semantic interpretation, being conventional in nature, cannot be cancelled, a pragmatic inference, which is non-conventional in character, can.

But, as pointed out by Bach (1999a, 2004), among others, this way of invoking the semantics–pragmatics division runs into trouble with the fact that there are linguistic expressions whose conventional meaning is closely associated with use. A case in point is discourse deictic expressions. As we saw in Chapter 5, a major function of discourse deictic expressions such as *anyway*, *after all*, *beside*s, *by the way*, and *in conclusion* is to indicate that there is a relation between the utterance that contains them and some portion of the prior discourse (Levinson 1983: 87–8). In other words, 'the only way to specify their semantic contribution (when they occur initially or are otherwise set off) is to specify how they are to be used' (Bach 1999a: 71). A further point to note is that the conventionality of a linguistic phenomenon may be a matter of more or less rather than a matter of yes

---

[5] It should be pointed out here that conventional meaning is meaning of linguistic expressions and non-conventional meaning is not. I am grateful to Kent Bach for clarifying this for me.

or no. For example, as observed by Jaszczolt (2002: 225–6) drawing on work by Levinson (2000), of the three types of implicature identified by Grice (1989) (see Chapter 2), conventional implicature is the most conventional, hence the most 'semantic' and the least 'pragmatic' (but see below); particularized conversational implicature is the least conventional, hence the least 'semantic' and the most 'pragmatic', with generalized conversational implicature lying somewhere in between.[6] In other words, the three types of implicature form a semantics–pragmatics continuum whose borderline is difficult to mark. From facts like these, one can arrive at the conclusion that there is not a neat correlation between the semantics–pragmatics distinction and the conventional–non-conventional meaning distinction (if in the meantime, the semantics–pragmatics distinction is also grounded in the meaning–use distinction).[7]

Notice next that a particular linguistic phenomenon can sometimes be categorized as part of the domain of either semantics or pragmatics, depending on how the semantics–pragmatics distinction is defined. This is the case with conventional implicature. If semantics is taken to be concerned with those aspects of meaning that affect truth conditions, then the investigation of conventional implicature falls on the pragmatic side of the divide rather than on the semantic side, since, as noted in Chapter 2, conventional implicature does not make any contribution to truth conditions (but see Bach 1999b). On the other hand, if pragmatics is conceived of as dealing with those inferences that are non-conventional, hence cancellable, then conventional implicature falls within the province of semantics but outside that of pragmatics, since it cannot be defeated (Horn 1988, Huang 2001a).

7.2.3. Context independence versus context dependence

Finally, the semantics–pragmatics distinction has been equated with context independence versus context dependence. According to this formulation, if a linguistic phenomenon is invariant with respect to context, then it

---

[6] But see Bach (1995), who was of the view that generalized conversational implicatures are not conventional but standardized.

[7] I am grateful to Recanati (personal communication) for pointing this out to me.

is the concern of semantics. By contrast, if a linguistic phenomenon is sensitive to context, then it is a topic within pragmatics.

This characterization of the semantics–pragmatics distinction, however, rests on a mistaken assumption that context has no role to play in semantics. Contrary to this assumption, according to Bach (1999a), in the case of deictics and demonstratives, especially what philosophers of language call pure indexicals (e.g., Kaplan 1989), such as *I*, *here*, and *now*, it is on the semantic side of the ledger that content varies with context. Consequently, Bach postulated two types of context: (i) **narrow context** and (ii) **broad context**. Narrow context denotes any contextual information that is relevant to the determination of the content of, or the assignment of the semantic values to, variables such as those concerning who speaks to whom, when, and where. Narrow context thus defined is semantic in nature. In contrast, broad context is taken to be any contextual information that is relevant to the working out of what the speaker overtly intends to mean. It is also relevant to the successful and felicitous performance of speech acts (see Chapter 2). Hence it is pragmatic in nature. Needless to say, narrow context is much more restricted in scope and much more limited in role than broad context (see also Recanati 2004b). Given that context plays a role in both semantics and pragmatics, the semantics–pragmatics distinction cannot correspond to the context independence–dependence distinction, either.

To sum up, the semantics–pragmatics distinction does not *systematically* coincide with any of the distinctions between truth-conditional versus non-truth-conditional meaning, conventional versus non-conventional meaning, and context independence versus context dependence. But this does not necessarily mean that semantics and pragmatics do not have their own characteristics. Recanati (2004b) isolated three essential features of a pragmatic interpretation. The first is **charity**. By charity is meant that a pragmatic interpretation is possible only if we presuppose that the interlocutors are rational. Secondly, there is **non-monotonicity**. This amounts to saying that a pragmatic interpretation is defeasible or cancellable. The third and final property identified by Recanati is **holism**. Given the feature of defeasibility or cancellability of a pragmatic interpretation, there is virtually no limit to the amount of contextual information that can in principle affect such an interpretation. Combined together, the three properties form what Recanati called the **hermeneutic** character of a pragmatic interpretation. This hermeneutic character of a pragmatic interpretation presents a striking contrast with the algorithmic, mechanical character of a semantic interpretation.

7.3. Pragmatic intrusion into what is said and the semantics–pragmatics interface

In recent years there has been an intense debate about the division of labour between, and interaction of, semantics and pragmatics among both linguists (e.g., Sperber and Wilson 1986, 1995, Levinson 2000, Carston 2002) and philosophers of language (e.g., Travis 1981, 1985, 1991, Recanati 1989, 1993, 2004a, 2004b, 2005, Bach 1994a, 1994b, 2004, 2005), and among both semanticists (e.g., Stanley and Szabó 2000a, Berg 2002, Borg 2004, Cappelen and Lepore 2005, King and Stanley 2005) and pragmaticists (e.g., Bach, Carston, Levinson, Recanati, Sperber and Wilson). Much of this debate has centred around pragmatic intrusion into the classical Gricean notion of what is said. In this section, I examine the four most influential pragmatic proposals, made by the relevance theorists, Recanati, Bach, and Levinson.

7.3.1. Grice: what is said versus what is implicated revisited

As mentioned in Chapters 2 and 6, on a classical Gricean account a distinction is made between what is said and what is conversationally implicated (e.g., Grice 1989: 25). However, as pointed out by Levinson (2000), Grice's characterization of what is said is rather complex and by no means straightforward, though it may roughly be presented as follows (Levinson 2000: 170):

(7.1)   Grice's concept of what is said
    U said that p by uttering x if and only if:
    a. x conventionally means p
    b. U speaker meant p
    c. p is the conventional meaning of x minus any conventional implicature

where U stands for the utterer, p for a proposition, and x for a linguistic expression. Given this definition, what is said is generally taken to be (i) the conventional meaning of the sentence uttered with the exclusion of any conventional implicature, and (ii) the truth-conditional propositional content of the sentence uttered (e.g., Grice 1989: 25, Levinson 1983: 97, 2000: 170, Neale 1992: 520–1, Clark 1996: 141, Carston 2002: 114–15).[8] However, according to Grice (1989: 25), before one works out what is said, one has (i) reference to identify, as in (6.5) in Chapter 6 and (7.2) below; (ii) deixis to fix, as in (6.11) in Chapter 6 and (7.3) below; and (iii) ambiguity and ambivalences to resolve, as in (6.12)–(6.14) in Chapter 6 and (7.4) below.

(7.2) (Chinese, Huang 2000a)[9]
   a. Chen Xiansheng renwei Liu Xiansheng tai   kuangwang, Ø
      Chen Mr   think   Liu   Mr   too   arrogant
      zongshi   kanbuqi   ziji.
      always   look down upon   self
      'Mr Chen₁ thinks that Mr Liu₂ is too arrogant, and (he₂) always looks down upon self₁'
   b. Chen Xiansheng renwei Liu Xiansheng tai   zibei, Ø
      Chen Mr   think   Liu   Mr   too   self-abased
      zongshi   kanbuqi   ziji.
      always   look down upon   self
      'Mr Chen₁ thinks that Mr Liu₂ is too self-abased, and (he₂) always looks down upon self₂'
(7.3) Mary: How do *I* look?
      John: *You* look really cool!
(7.4) (Levinson 2000: 174)
   a. The view could be improved by the addition of a plant out there.
      plant = living organism such as a flower, tree or vegetable
   b. The view would be destroyed by the addition of a plant out there.
      plant = factory

---

[8] Notice that the term 'what is said' is ambiguous in at least three distinct ways. In the first, 'what is said' is understood in 'a technical and artificially strict sense' (Salmon 1991). In the second, it is interpreted in an ordinary everyday sense of 'what is stated' (Levinson 2000: 194). Finally, in the third, 'what is said' is ambiguous between 'general content' in one, technical sense and 'contextually enriched content' in another, everyday sense (Berg 2002 crediting François Recanati; see also Recanati 1989, 1993, 2004a, 2005, Barker 2003). Other ambiguities of 'what is said' involve it in the 'locuationary' versus 'illocutionary sense' (e.g., Bach 1994a, 1994b, 2001, 2004, 2005, Szabó 2005a).

[9] Note that in (7.2a), the Chinese reflexive *ziji* has its antecedent outside its local clause. A reflexive thus used is called a 'long-distance reflexive'. In fact, many of the world's languages allow a reflexive to be used in a long-distance fashion (e.g., Huang 1994, 1996, 2000a). I shall discuss long-distance reflexivization in the next chapter.

To these, Levinson (2000, 172–86) added (iv) unpacking ellipsis, as in (7.5), and (v) narrowing generality, as in (7.6).

(7.5)   (Barton 1988)
          A: They won't visit Mary's parents.
          B: Old grudge.
(7.6)   I don't drink.

According to Bach (2004), the Gricean notion of what is said is needed in order to describe cases of three kinds. In the first, the speaker means what he or she says and something else as well, as in conversational implicatures and indirect speech acts. The second case is where the speaker says one thing and means something else instead, as in non-literal utterances such as metaphor, irony, and hyperbole. Finally, there is the case where the speaker says something and does not mean anything by it—for instance, when the speaker reads someone else's poems out loud (Kent Bach personal communication).[10, 11]

What is conversationally implicated is then defined in contrast to, and calculated on the basis of, what is said (and in the case of M-implicatures, together with how it is said). In simple terms, what is conversationally implicated can be defined along the following lines (Levinson 2000: 171).

(7.7)   Grice's concept of what is conversationally implicated:
          By saying p, U conversationally implicates q if:
          a. U is presumed to be following the maxims,
          b. the supposition of q is required to maintain (a),[12] and
          c. U thinks that the recipient will realize (b).

Stated in this way, what is said is supposed to provide input to what is conversationally implicated.

It turns out, however, that the determination of (7.2)–(7.6) involves pragmatic inference of some kind. In the context of (7.2a), *Chen Xiansheng*

---

[10] On the basis of the existence of the third case, Bach (personal communication) argued that (7.1b) should be dropped.

[11] Bach's third case apart, what is said can also be contrasted with **what is communicated/meant**, which is the sum of what is said and what is implicated (e.g., Levinson 2000, Carston 2002, Horn 2004). A further distinction between what is meant in the illocutionary sense and what is meant in the perlocutionary sense is also made in Szabó (2005a).

[12] Bach (personal communication) pointed out to me that 'the supposition of q' in (7.7b) should be replaced with 'the supposition that U means q'.

(Mr Chen) is the most likely choice for antecedent of the Chinese long-distance reflexive *ziji*, whereas in the context of (7.2b), *Liu Xiansheng* (Mr Liu) becomes the most likely candidate for antecedent of *ziji*. The Gricean maxim of Relation plays a role in interpreting the deictic expressions in (7.3). The disambiguation of the lexical item *plant* in (7.4) is crucially dependent on our real-world knowledge about what would most likely improve or destroy a view. Next, as Barton (1988) showed, the interpretation of the elided constituent in (7.5) requires a substantial amount of inference of the Gricean sort. Finally, the predicate *drink* in (7.6) has to be pragmatically narrowed down to 'drink alcohol'. Put another way, it is now generally acknowledged that in examples like (7.2)–(7.6), there is pragmatic intrusion of some sort, namely the pragmatically inferred content, into the conventional, truth-conditional content involved in working out what Grice called what is said (e.g., Levinson 2000, Huang 2004b).[13]

Two issues are of particular interest in the analysis of pragmatic intrusion into the classical Gricean characterization of what is said and beyond. The first is concerned with the question of what the pragmatic intrusion under consideration is. Secondly, there is the question of what is the best way to delimit the respective territories of semantics and pragmatics, taking pragmatic intrusion into account. Let us now take a look at some of the answers provided by linguists and philosophers of language.

7.3.2. Relevance theorists: explicature

As discussed in detail in the last chapter, in relevance theory, pragmatic intrusion into Grice's notion of what is said is analysed as explicature—an inferential development of one of the incomplete conceptual representations or logical forms encoded by an utterance. In other words, an explicature functions to flesh out the linguistically given incomplete logical form of the sentence uttered, yielding fully propositional content. It falls on the side of what is said rather than on the side of what is implicated, but in relevance theory the Gricean notion of what is said is abandoned. This has the consequence that in Sperber and Wilson's framework the explicit–implicit distinction, that is, the distinction between the explicit content

---

[13] Bach (personal communication) denied that there is any pragmatic intrusion into what is said.

and the implicit import of an utterance, is recast in terms of the relevance-theoretic notions of explicature and (r-)implicature (Sperber and Wilson 1986, 1995, Carston 1998, 2002, 2004).

7.3.3. Recanati: the pragmatically enriched said

Somewhat similar to the relevance-theoretic view is the position taken by Recanati (1989, 1993, 2001, 2002, 2004a, 2004b). According to Recanati, there are aspects of what is said that must be pragmatically enriched. In other words, on Recanati's view, what is said or the proposition associated with what is said necessarily involves **unarticulated constituents**.[14] More specifically, Recanati (2004b) postulated three types of **primary pragmatic processes**[15] to bridge the gap between linguistic (or sentence) meaning and what is said.[16] In the first place, there is what Recanati (1989, 1993: 243, 2002, 2004a: 23) called '**saturation**'. As already mentioned in Chapter 6, saturation is a pragmatic process whereby a given slot, position, or variable in the linguistically decoded logical form is contextually filled. In other words, in this type of pragmatic enrichment, a slot, position, or variable

[14] By unarticulated constituents is meant unarticulated propositional constituents. Recanati's view was shared by Searle (1979, 1980, 1983) and Travis (1981, 1985, 1991) among many others (but see Bach 2000 for a dissenting view). In recent years, the postulation of unarticulated constituents has become a centre of intense interest in the philosophy of language literature (see also, e.g., Perry 1998, Stanley 2000, Stanley and Szabó 2000a, 2000b, Taylor 2001).

[15] According to Recanati (1993: 260–1), primary pragmatic processes are ones that play a role in the very constitution of what is said. In other words, they pragmatically enrich what is said. By contrast, secondary pragmatic processes are ones that presuppose that something has been said or a proposition has been expressed. Implicatures in the relevance-theoretic sense (i.e., what I have called r-implicatures) fall in this category.

[16] While linguistic (or sentence) meaning in Recanati's sense corresponds roughly to Kaplan's (1989) notion of **character** and Perry's (1993) concept of **role**, what is said is roughly equivalent to Kaplan's notion of **content** (i.e., proposition) and Perry's notion of **value**. See also Braun (1995, 1996) for his reworking of Kaplan's notions of character and content. It has been argued by some scholars (e.g., Kaplan 1989, Stalnaker 1999) that '[w]hat semantics assigns to expression-types, independent of context, is not a fully-fledged content but a linguistic meaning or character that can be formally represented as a function from contexts to contents' (Recanati 2004b: 447).

must be contextually saturated for the utterance to express a complete proposition. Saturation is a typical linguistically mandated, 'bottom-up' process, that is, a process which is triggered by a linguistic expression in the utterance itself. Expressions that give rise to saturation include unspecified comparison sets, as in (7.8a); possessive constructions, as in (7.8b), and expressions with free variable slots, as in (7.8c) (Recanati 2004b).

(7.8)   a. Elizabeth is cleverer.
          b. I enjoyed reading John's book.
          c. John was late.
(7.8)   can be pragmatically saturated into, for example, (7.9).
(7.9)   a. Elizabeth is cleverer [than Naomi].
          b. I enjoyed reading the book [written by] John.
          c. John was late [for the seminar].

The second type of primary pragmatic process is what Recanati called **'free enrichment'**. We have already seen in Chapter 6 that in this case, although there does not seem to be either an overt indexical or a covert slot in the linguistically decoded logical form of the sentence uttered, the logical form nevertheless needs to be conceptually enriched. The process of free enrichment is 'free' because it is entirely pragmatic rather than linguistic. Free enrichment is a typical optional and contextually driven 'top-down' process (Recanati 2004a: 24–6).

Recanati identified two subtypes of free enrichment. First, there is the subtype of **strengthening** or logical enrichment. Strengthening takes a complete proposition resulting from saturation as input and yields as output a richer proposition which entails the original input proposition. By way of illustration, take (7.10).

(7.10) a. 'Some people are a bit surprised when they find out I've got a brain.'
              (Catherine McQueen)
          b. The Buddhist temples are some distance away.
          c. I have brushed my teeth.

The propositions expressed by the sentences in (7.10) are strengthened into the propositions expressed by the sentences in (7.11). As the reader can verify for him- or herself, the enriched propositions expressed by the sentences in (7.11) entail the original input propositions in (7.10).[17]

---

[17] But on Bach's (1994a) view, entailment does not play a role in strengthening. This is because if the sentences in (7.10) are negated, the relevant entailments will go the other way, and yet the pragmatic enrichments will be the same.

(7.11)   a. 'Some people are a bit surprised when they find out I've got a [high-functioning] brain.'
b. The Buddhist temples are [a considerable] distance away.
c. I have brushed my teeth [this morning].

The second subtype of enrichment is **expansion**, *à la* Bach (1987). In this subtype, a contextually provided conceptual constituent needs to be added, but the output proposition yielded by the input one does not need to entail the original input proposition. This can be illustrated by a consideration of (7.12).

(7.12)   a. The windows are bullet-proof.
b. I have nothing to wear.

The propositions expressed by the sentences in (7.12) are expanded into the propositions expressed by the sentences in (7.13). But the enriched propositions in (7.13) do not entail the propositions in (7.12).[18]

(7.13)   a. The windows [of the president's limousine] are bullet-proof.
b. I have nothing [suitable] to wear [to John's wedding].

Finally, there is the third type of primary pragmatic process, namely, what Recanati (2004a: 26–7) termed **semantic transfer**, following Nunberg (1979, 1995, 2004) and Fauconnier (1985). In this type of primary pragmatic process, the output proposition is neither an enriched nor an impoverished version of the concept literally expressed by the input proposition. Rather, it represents a different concept, provided that there is a salient functional relation between the new concept and the old one encoded by the original input proposition. In short, it is a case in which one points *a* to refer to *b*. A few well-known examples of semantic transfer, due originally to Nunberg (1979) and Fauconnier (1985), are given in (7.14).

(7.14)   a. I am parked out back.
b. Shakespeare is on the top shelf.
c. The ham sandwich left without paying.

In (7.14a), the predicate *parked out back* literally denotes a property of a car when it is parked out back. As a result of semantic transfer, it carries a different sense, which comes to denote a property of the person (e.g., the

---

[18] Recanati (personal communication) pointed out to me that strengthening and expansion are two ways of construing enrichment rather than two distinct phenomena. He believed that a unitary notion can account for both of them.

owner or the driver) whose car is parked out back. In (7.14b), the proper name *Shakespeare*, which literally denotes a certain individual, is used to refer, through semantic transfer, to one or more books written by him. Finally, in (7.14c), *the ham sandwich* is employed to contribute, via semantic transfer, the derived property THE CUSTOMER WHO ORDERED THE HAM SANDWICH or simply THE HAM SANDWICH ORDERER (e.g., Nunberg 2004, Recanati 2004a; see also Pustejovsky 1995, Jackendoff 1997, Montalbetti 2003, and Cruse 2004 for further discussion).[19]

7.3.4. Bach: conversational impliciture

A third approach is due to Bach (1994a, 1994b, 1999a, 2001, 2004). On Bach's view, there is no pragmatic intrusion into what is said, because certain aspects of communicative content do not need to be recognized as either part of what is said or part of what is implicated. Rather, they constitute a middle ground between what is said and what is implicated. This middle level of speaker-meaning Bach called **conversational impliciture**.

What, then, is a conversational impliciture? Consider first (7.15).

(7.15)   a. John is ready.
         b. Steel is not strong enough.
         c. John has finished.
         d. John is too tired.
         e. John needs a boat.
         f. President Chirac has just arrived.

According to Bach, each of the sentences in (7.15) expresses an incomplete proposition. In other words, it is subpropositional. Consequently, it cannot be evaluated truth-conditionally. Bach dubbed propositional fragments of this kind **propositional radicals**, which need to be completed or filled in contextually to become fully propositional. The pragmatic process of **completion** will provide extra content to the propositional radicals in (7.15), resulting in the corresponding minimal but full propositions in (7.16). The full propositions in (7.16) can then be assigned a truth value.

---

[19] See Recanati (2004a: Chapter 3) for discussion of the differences between his theory and relevance theory.

(7.16)   a. John is ready [for the interview]
       b. Steel is not strong enough [for that part of the roof]
       c. John has finished [writing his MBA thesis]
       d. John is too tired [to carry the suitcase]
       e. John needs a boat [to cross the river]
       f. President Chirac has just arrived [at Buckingham Palace]

Next, let us move on to (7.17).

(7.17)   a. I have had a shower.
       b. She has nothing to wear.
       c. Everyone was touched by *Captain Corelli's Mandolin*.
       d. John and Mary are married.
       e. John has eaten a lot of oily fish recently and his blood cholesterol level has been lowered.
       f. You are not going to die.
       g. The little boy has had measles.
       h. There are nine thousand students in this university town.
       i. John and Mary did some groundbreaking research in climate change.
       j. Kelly Holmes won two gold medals at the 2004 Athens Olympic Games.

According to Bach, unlike in (7.15), each of the sentences in (7.17) expresses a minimal, though full proposition. But such a proposition falls short of what the speaker intends to mean. Consequently, it needs to be expanded. The pragmatic process of **expansion** will flesh out the proposition expressed by the sentence uttered and engender a richer proposition. The pragmatically enriched proposition will then be identical to what the speaker intentionally meant, thus allowing the assignment of an appropriate truth condition to it. The pragmatically expanded propositions of (7.17) are given in (7.18).

(7.18)   a. I have had a shower [this morning]
       b. She has nothing [appropriate] to wear [at tonight's party]
       c. Everyone [who went to see the film] was touched by *Captain Corelli's Mandolin*
       d. John and Mary are married [to each other]
       e. John has eaten a lot of oily fish recently and [as a result] his blood cholesterol level has been lowered
       f. You are not going to die [from the injury]
       g. The little boy has had measles [before]
       h. There are [approximately] nine thousand students in this university town

> i. John and Mary did some groundbreaking research on climate change [together]
> j. Kelly Holmes won [exactly/precisely] two gold medals at the 2004 Athens Olympic Games

Clearly, in both (7.16) and (7.18), each of the bracketed elements of meaning contributes to what is communicated. Bach called the vehicle of such a pragmatically enriched proposition an impliciture, because it is implicit in what is said. More specifically, an impliciture is an implicit strengthening, weakening, or specification of what is said. As Bach (1994b: 273) remarks:

Implicitures go beyond what is said, but unlike implicatures, which are additional propositions external to what is said, implicitures are built out of what is said.

Stated in this way, impliciture represents a third category of communicated content—a category that is intermediate between Grice's what is said and what is implicated. As Horn (2004) told us, impliciture cannot be constitutive of what is said, because it can be felicitously cancelled, as can be seen in (7.19); neither can it be derived as a conversational implicature, because it is truth-conditionally relevant (but see Section 7.3.6 below; see also Vincente 2002 for a critique of Bach's notion of impliciture largely from a relevance-theoretical point of view).

(7.19) a. I have had a shower, but not this morning.
        b. John and Mary are married, but not to each other. Also:
           The title of a country song (Horn 1989: 390)
           When you are married, but not to each other.
        c. John has eaten a lot of oily fish recently and his blood cholesterol level has been lowered, but the latter is not necessarily the result of the former.

Begin work in this chapter by having a go at Exercise 1 on p. 243.

7.3.5. *Can explicature/the pragmatically enriched said/ impliciture be distinguished from implicature?*

In the last three subsections I discussed the relevance theorists', Recanati's, and Bach's accounts of pragmatic intrusion into the classical Gricean concept of what is said (but see note 13 above). Given the relevance theorists' analysis of the pragmatic inference under discussion as explicature,

Recanati's account of it as the pragmatically enriched aspect of what is said, and Bach's analysis of it as impliciture, one important question arises: can explicature/the pragmatically enriched said/impliciture be discriminated from conversational implicature? In other words, how can a pragmatically determined aspect of an utterance be recognized as explicature/part of what is said/impliciture rather than part of what is conversationally implicated? Recanati (1993) provided two answers to this question, neither of which, however, is unproblematic.

In the first place, Recanati claimed that the distinction between explicature/the pragmatically augmented said/impliciture and conversational implicature can be delineated on an intuitive basis. This is embodied in his **availability principle**.

(7.20)   Recanati's (1993) availability principle
In deciding whether a pragmatically determined aspect of utterance meaning is part of what is said, that is, in making a decision concerning what is said, we should always try to preserve our pre-theoretical intuition on the matter.

What the availability principle basically says is this: the pragmatically enriched aspect of what is said is consciously available to the speaker and the addressee. As a case in point, consider (7.21).

(7.21)   a. Mary has broken a leg.
b. Mary has broken a leg, either her own or someone else's
c. Mary has broken her own leg

On a standard Gricean account, what is said in (7.21a) is represented in (7.21b). But this pragmatically determined interpretation seems to run contrary to our pre-theoretical intuition. Consequently, according to Recanati's availability test, (7.21b) is rejected as what is said. By contrast, given our pre-theoretical intuition, the pragmatically amplified interpretation in (7.21c) is part of what is said. It follows therefore that, by the availability principle, this pragmatically determined aspect is considered to be part of what is said rather than part of what is conversationally implicated. However, as pointed out by Richard (1990), Horn (1992b), Bach (1994a: 137–9, 2002), Levinson (2000: 197), and Carston (2002), given the fact that our pre-theoretical intuition tends not to be very reliable in many cases, Recanati's availability test has to be taken with great caution.[20]

---

[20] Gibbs and Moise (1997) presented an off-line experimental investigation of the Gricean dichotomy between what is said and what is implicated. Across a range

The second test put forward by Recanati for drawing the division between explicature/the pragmatically enriched said/impliciture and conversational implicature is the **scope principle**, essentially following an earlier proposal by Cohen (1971).

(7.22)   The Cohen–Recanati scope principle
         A pragmatically determined aspect of meaning is part of what is said (and, therefore, not a conversational implicature) if—and, perhaps, only if—it falls within the scope of logical operators.[21]

Cohen (1971) was perhaps the first to present a serious challenge to Grice's analysis of *and* in English. On a standard Gricean account, (7.23a) and (7.23b) have exactly the same truth-conditional content, even though they differ in the temporal sequentiality of events. This difference in conveyed meaning, which was also observed by, for example, Strawson

of experimental conditions, their subjects are overwhelmingly in favour of the pragmatically enriched over the non-pragmatically enriched, minimal interpretation as best reflecting what a speaker says. On the basis of this evidence, Gibbs and Moise concluded that (i) people have clear intuitions about the distinction between what is said and what is implicated, (ii) they take what is said to correspond to the pragmatically enriched rather than the non-pragmatically enriched, minimal proposition, and (iii) the results lend support to Recanati's availability principle (see also Bezuidenhout and Cutting 2002, Gibbs 2002). However, in a later psychopragmatic study, by replicating some of Gibbs and Moise's experiments, Nicolle and Clark (1999) reported that some of their subjects tend to opt for a conversational implicature rather than a pragmatically enriched said or a non-pragmatically enriched, minimal interpretation. This led Nicolle and Clark to conclude that there is no experimental support either for people's intuitions about what is said versus what is implicated or for Recanati's availability principle. See Gibbs (1999) for a reply to Nicolle and Clark (1999), and see also Carston (2002: 167–8) and Huang (2004b). To the best of my knowledge, at present there is no experimental work in pragmatics that can distinguish alleged different types of pragmatic inference such as explicature, the pragmatically enriched said, impliciture, and implicature. For other recent psychopragmatic experimental work, see the papers collected in Noveck and Sperber (2004).

[21] The Cohen–Recanati scope principle is explicitly endorsed by the relevance theorists (see, e.g., Carston 2002: 191–5). I think that in principle it can also be used to differentiate implicitures from conversational implicatures with the addition indicated in italics: 'A pragmatically determined aspect of meaning is part of what is said *or what is implicit* (and, therefore, not a conversational implicature) if—and, perhaps, only if—it falls within the scope of logical operators.'

(1952), Ryle (1954), and Urmson (1956), is accounted for in terms of generalized conversational implicature, as in (7.24a) and (7.24b).

(7.23)   (Cohen 1971)
       a. The old king has died of a heart attack and a republic has been declared.
       b. A republic has been declared and the old king has died of a heart attack.
(7.24)   a. The old king has died of a heart attack [first] and [then] a republic has been declared.
       b. A republic has been declared [first] and [then] the old king has died of a heart attack.

On Cohen's view, this analysis of Grice's is untenable. If (7.23a) and (7.23b) really have the same truth-conditional content and differ only in conversational implicatures, then when they are embedded in the antecedent of a conditional, as in (7.25a) and (7.25b), given Grice's analysis of *if*, they should also have the same truth-conditional content.

(7.25)   a. If the old king has died of a heart attack and a republic has been declared, then Tom will be quite content.
       b. If a republic has been declared and the old king has died of a heart attack, then Tom will be quite content.

But (7.25a) and (7.25b) are not truth-conditionally equivalent. The pragmatically inferred temporal relation which holds between the conjuncts in (7.23a) and (7.23b) is an integral part of the antecedents of the conditionals in (7.25a) and (7.25b). With one temporal sequence of events, Tom will be happy; with the other temporal sequence of events, Tom will be unhappy (see also Cohen 1977). This indicates that the pragmatically inferred temporal relation falls within the scope of the conditional—a logical operator. By the same token, the temporal relation also falls within the scope of other logical operators such as negation, disjunction, and comparative. If this is the case, argues Recanati (1993), then the pragmatically derived temporal relation is not a genuine conversational implicature, but an explicature/a pragmatic constituent of what is said/an impliciture.

At first glance, the scope test appears to provide a good basis for the distinction between explicature/the pragmatically enriched said and conversational implicature. As an example, take (7.8b), repeated here as (7.26a) for convenience.

(7.26)   a. I enjoyed reading John's book.
       b. I enjoyed reading the book [written by] John.

When (7.26a) is negated, as in (7.27a), what is saturated is retained, as can be shown by (7.27b).

(7.27)   a. I didn't enjoy reading John's book.
        b. I didn't enjoy reading the book [written by] John.

In other words, the pragmatically determined element of meaning in (7.27a) falls within the scope of negation. By the Cohen–Recanati scope criterion, it is an explicature/a pragmatic constituent of what is said/an impliciture rather than a conversational implicature.

By contrast, let us now look at a case of what I called r-implicature in the last chapter. Mary's reply in (7.28) has the pragmatic inference in (7.29). But this pragmatically inferred element of meaning does not fall within the scope of the conditional, as can be seen in (7.30).

(7.28)   John: Has Steve's paper been accepted for presentation at the conference?
        Mary: His is one of the best papers submitted.
(7.29)   Steve's paper has been accepted for presentation at the conference.
(7.30)   If Steve's is one of the best papers submitted, it has the chance to win a prize.

The reason is that the consequent of (7.30) is not dependent on the paper being accepted for presentation at the conference. The pragmatic inference under consideration is therefore not an explicature/the pragmatically enriched part of what is said/an impliciture. Rather, it is a genuine conversational implicature.

There is, however, a serious problem attaching to the Cohen–Recanati scope test. As pointed out by Recanati himself, the problem concerns metalinguistic negation. We have already seen in Chapter 2 that metalinguistic negation is a device for rejecting a previous utterance on any grounds whatever, including its morphosyntactic form, its phonetic realization, its style or register, and/or the implicatures it potentially engenders. In addition to the examples listed in Chapter 2, some further exemplification is given below.

(7.31)   a. John isn't overweight, he's downright obese.
        b. Mary won't give you a [vaːz], she'll give you a [veiːz].
        c. I don't use elevators, I use lifts.

Of these examples, (7.31a) is of particular relevance to our discussion here. But before proceeding to discuss it, let us first take a look at (7.32). As noted in Chapter 2, the uttering of (7.32) gives rise to the now familiar Q_{scalar} implicature in (7.33).

(7.32)   <obese, overweight>
      John's overweight.

(7.33)   John's not obese, *or*
      John is no more than overweight

Notice that when (7.32) is negated descriptively, as in (7.34), the original Q-scalar implicature is preserved. In other words, the implicature falls within the scope of negation. Given the Cohen–Recanati scope test, the pragmatic inference cannot be an implicature. Rather, it is taken to be an explicature or a pragmatic constituent of what is said.

(7.34)   John isn't overweight, he's quite slim.

This analysis has consequences for the relevance theorists, Recanati, and Bach. For the relevance theorists, it may force them to treat Q-scalar implicatures as explicatures, which are currently taken to be conversational implicatures. Within both the Recanatian and the Bachian frameworks, most cases of neo-Gricean generalized conversational implicatures will be reduced to pragmatic constituents of what is said or implicitures.[22]

Returning next to (7.31a), where (7.32) is negated in a metalinguistic way, the speaker does not deny that John is overweight, because that is entailed by what the speaker asserts, namely that John is downright obese. What is rejected here is nothing but the very same Q-scalar implicature. Put another way, in (7.31a) the implicature falls outside the scope of negation. By virtue of the Cohen–Recanati scope criterion, the pragmatic inference here has to be considered as a genuine conversational implicature. The contrast shown by (7.32) and (7.31a) gives rise to a puzzle, namely, why the same Q-scalar implicature may or may not fall within the scope of negation, hence may or may not be a genuine conversational implicature (see also

---

[22] Given that both presupposition and conventional implicature fall within the scope of negation, as shown in (i) and (ii) below, within the relevance-theoretic, the Recanatian, and the Bachian frameworks they have to be treated as explicature, the pragmatically enriched said, and impliciture, respectively.

(i)   a. The boy cried wolf again.
     b. The boy didn't cry wolf again.
     >> The boy cried wolf before

(ii)   John is poor but he is honest.
     It is not the case that John is poor but he is honest.
     +>> There is a contrast between poverty and honesty

Levinson 2000). The solution proposed by Recanati to tackle the problem is to appeal to our pre-theoretical intuition to decide on when a logical operator is or is not used metalinguistically. It is considerations of this kind that have led Recanati to the view that the availability principle is of a more fundamental character than the scope principle. All this indicates that explicatures/the pragmatically enriched said/impliciures may not be distinguished from conversational implicatures on a principled basis.

7.3.6. Levinson: conversational implicature

We finally come to Levinson's (2000) analysis of pragmatic intrusion into what is said as conversational implicature. On Levinson's view, pragmatic intrusion into what is said is neither an explicature, nor the pragmatically enriched said, nor an implicture. Rather, it is nothing but a neo-Gricean conversational implicature. The reason for this is twofold. First of all, pragmatic intrusion into what is said is engendered by the same Gricean inferential mechanism that yields a conversational implicature. Secondly, as we saw in the last section, currently there is no reliable test that can be employed to distinguish alleged explicature/the pragmatically enriched said/impliciure from conversational implicature on a principled basis.

Following in the footsteps of Cohen (1971), Wilson (1975), Atlas (1977), and Gazdar (1979), Levinson (2000) argued that contrary to Grice, conversational implicatures can intrude upon truth-conditional content. This has already been evidenced by temporally and causally asymmetric conjunctions in (7.23) and conditionals in (7.25), which were used by Cohen (1971) to argue against Grice's analysis of the truth-functionality of *and* and *if*.

Levinson extended this classic Cohen–Wilson argument into the working out of what is said or how propositions are literally expressed. His focus of attention is on how neo-Gricean conversational implicatures are involved in the determination of indexicalilty and related phenomena.

Reference resolution
Consider (7.35).

(7.35)   (Levinson 2000: 218, 227)
         (Context: Two men are clearly visible; one has two children near him and the other has three children near him. The first is the speaker's brother, the second his brother-in-law.)

The man with two children near him is my brother; the man with three children near him is my brother-in-law.

What is said by the speaker in (7.35) corresponds to (7.36).

(7.36)   The man with *at least* two children near him is my brother; the man with *at least* three children near him is my brother-in-law.

This has the consequence that the referential expression *the man with two children near him* refers equally to the speaker's brother and to his brother-in-law. Thus, on any purely semantic theory of definite description, the referential expression will render (7.35) either false (Russell 1905) or truth-valueless (Strawson 1950). But this is intuitively wrong; the definite expression neither makes (7.35) false nor fails to denote. On the contrary, it denotes felicitously and refers successfully. How can this be possible? According to Levinson, it is because the individual referents are picked up by a Q-scalar implicature enriching *the man with two children near him* to 'the man with exactly two children near him' and *the man with three children near him* to 'the man with exactly three children near him' (see Chapters 1 and 2). This is represented in (7.37).[23]

(7.37)   The man with [exactly] two children near him is my brother; the man with [exactly] three children near him is my brother-in-law.

Next, we turn to (7.38).

(7.38)   a. John said that he won the ten metres platform diving yesterday.
         b. John said that the young man won the ten metres platform diving yesterday.

(7.38) involves anaphoric reference. Intuitively, while the pronoun *he* in (7.38a) is preferably coreferential with *John*, the definite description *the young man* is disjoint in reference with *John*. As shown by Huang (1991, 1994, 2000a, 2004a, 2006c) and Levinson (1987a, 1987b, 1991, 2000), this contrast can be accounted for in terms of the interaction between the I and M-implicatures. The preferred coreferential interpretation between *he* and *John* in (7.38a) is due to the working of the I-principle (you use a

---

[23] See Levinson (2000: Section 3.4.1) for the argument that implicaturally determined definite reference cannot be reduced either to Donnellan's (1966) referential versus attributive distinction or to Kripke's (1977) distinction between semantic-reference and speaker-reference.

semantically general anaphoric expression *he*, I get a semantically more specific interpretation *he = John*); the disjoint reference interpretation in (7.38b) is the outcome of the operation of the M-principle (you use a marked, more prolix anaphoric expression *the young man*, I get a marked interpretation *the young man ≠ John*). All this indicates that neo-Gricean conversational implicatures contribute to the resolution of both definite and anaphoric reference. I shall return to the discussion of the pragmatics of anaphoric reference in the next chapter.

Deixis fixing

Consider the interpretation of the time deictic expression *Sunday* in (7.39).

(7.39)   We'll go to church on Sunday.

As noted in Chapter 5, the use of time deictic expressions like *yesterday*, *today*, and *tomorrow* pre-empts the use of the calendrical terms for the relevant days. Thus, *Sunday* said on a Saturday will engender the Q-scalar implicature to the effect that the Sunday in question is not tomorrow, as is indicated in (7.40).

(7.40)   (Said on a Saturday)
          <tomorrow, Sunday>
          We'll go to church on Sunday.
          Sunday +> ~ tomorrow

The reason is this: if the Sunday under consideration were tomorrow, the speaker would have used the semantically more informative deictic expression *tomorrow*, since there are many Sundays, but only one tomorrow for a given today. There is thus evidence in support of Levinson's argument that neo-Gricean conversational implicatures play a role in fixing deictic or indexical parameters.

Disambiguation

Consider how the syntactic structures of (7.41) are disambiguated by generalized Q-scalar implicatures.

(7.41)   (Levinson 2000: 175).
          John is an indiscriminate dog-lover: he likes some cats and dogs.
          a. John likes [some cats] and dogs
              John likes some cats and dogs in general
          b. John likes [some [cats and dogs]]
              John likes some cats and some dogs

Notice that the second clause in (7.41) is structurally ambiguous. It can be understood in the manner of (7.41a) or in the manner of (7.41b). Now, given the syntactic structure of (7.41a), the use of the clause creates the generalized Q-scalar implicature that John does not like all cats. This implicature is in keeping with the semantic content of the first clause. By contrast, given the syntactic structure of (7.41b), the uttering of the clause gives rise to the generalized Q-scalar implicature that John does not like all cats and all dogs. But such an interpretation is incompatible with the semantic content of the first clause. Consequently, in order for the whole sentence in (7.41) not to be contradictory, the syntactic structure of (7.41a) is allowed but that of (7.41b) is excluded. This shows that neo-Gricean conversational implicatures intrude on the disambiguation of the syntactic structures of examples like (7.41).

Ellipsis unpacking

As pointed out in Huang (2000a: 133, 147), the resolution of VP-ellipsis sometimes has to be effected pragmatically. As an illustrative example, take (7.42).

(7.42)   (Huang 2000a: 133)
         I will, if you will.

The interpretation of the elided element in (7.42) is contextually dependent. That is to say, the elided constituent will be supplied from the surrounding physical context. This can be achieved via the I-implicature, together with a particularized conversational implicature due to Grice's maxim of Relation. One contextually derived interpretation might be the one in (7.43).

(7.43)   (By a swimming pool)
         I will jump into the swimming pool, if you will jump into the swimming pool.

Generality narrowing

Finally, the same story can be said to hold for generality narrowing. Here, generality narrowing can be classified into two groups: (i) Q-implicature-based, as in (7.44), and (ii) I-implicature-based, as in (7.45).

(7.44)   a. The soup is warm.
         b. John cut a finger.
         c. John folded the newspaper neatly into a rectangle.

(7.45)   a. She had two eggs for breakfast this morning.
         b. The FBI agent is talking to his secretary.
         c. The watermelon is red.

The utterances in (7.44) are Q-narrowed to the propositions expressed in (7.46).

(7.46)   a. The soup is[n't hot].
         b. John [didn't] cut a [thumb].
         c. John [didn't] fold the newspaper neatly into a [square].

The utterances in (7.45) are I-narrowed to the proposition expressed in (7.47).

(7.47)   a. She had two [hen's] eggs for breakfast this morning.
         b. The FBI agent is talking to his [female] secretary.
         c. The watermelon is red [in its inside flesh].

There is thus the conclusion that neo-Gricean conversational implicatures are also involved in generality narrowing.

Furthermore, Levinson argued that the classic Cohen–Wilson argument can also be extended into other logical connective constructions such as comparatives, disjunctions, and *because*-clauses. This is illustrated in (7.48)–(7.50).

(7.48)   Comparatives
         Brushing your teeth and going to bed is better than going to bed and brushing your teeth.
(7.49)   Disjunctions
         Susan either suffered a heart attack and underwent quadruple by-pass surgery, or underwent quadruple by-pass surgery and suffered a heart attack; but I don't know which.
(7.50)   *Because*-clauses
         Because some of her Ph.D. students came to her talk, Professor Heim was unhappy.

Together with conditionals, these constructions are labelled '**intrusive constructions**' by Levinson. The reason is that in these constructions, 'the truth conditions of the whole depend in part on the implicatures of the parts' (Levinson 2000: 198).[24] The truth-conditional content of the comparative

---

[24] See also Green's (1998) **embedded implicature hypothesis**, which runs as follows: 'If assertion of a sentence S conveys the implicatu[re] that p with nearly

(7.48) is dependent crucially on the generalized I-implicature stemming from the use of *and* to mean 'and then', as in (7.51). Otherwise, (7.48) would be contradictory. The same I-implicature intrusion is found in the disjunction (7.49). Without *and* being I-strengthened to 'and then', as in (7.52), the two disjuncts would have the same semantic content. This would render the speaker's assertion of ignorance over the two possibilities inconsistent or anomalous. Finally, the quantifier *some* in the *because*-clause (7.50) has to be Q-implicated to 'some but not all', as in (7.53). Otherwise, Professor Heim's unhappiness would be left unexplained (but see Horn 2004 for a different view of the *because*-clauses; see also King and Stanley 2005). Once again, there is no avoiding the conclusion that the truth condition of the complex construction has to be calculated taking into account the implicature of its part.

(7.51)   Brushing your teeth and [then] going to bed is better than going to bed and [then] brushing your teeth.
(7.52)   Susan either suffered a heart attack and [then] underwent quadruple by-pass surgery, or underwent quadruple by-pass surgery and [then] suffered a heart attack; but the speaker doesn't know which.
(7.53)   Because some [but not all] of her Ph.D. students came to her talk, Professor Heim was unhappy.

If neo-Gricean conversational implicatures can intrude on to truth-conditional content, argued Levinson (2000), then one has to reject the 'received' view of the semantics–pragmatics interface, according to which the output of semantics provides input to pragmatics, which then maps literal meaning to speaker meaning. Rather, one should allow Gricean pragmatics to play a systematic role in 'pre'-semantics, that is, to help determine the truth-conditional content of the sentence uttered (see also Taylor 2001). As Levinson (2000: 242) told us: 'There is every reason to try and reconstrue the interaction between semantics and pragmatics as the intimate interlocking of distinct processes, rather than, as traditionally, in terms of the output of one being the input to the other'. Such a radical proposal amounts to saying that the whole architecture of the theory of meaning needs to be radically reconstructed.

Now see whether you are ready to do Exercise 2 on pp. 243–4.

universal regularity, then when S is embedded the content that is usually understood to be embedded for semantic purposes is the proposition (S & p).'

7.3.7. The five analyses compared

Grice

Grice's concept of what is said is largely semantic. It constitutes semantic representations or linguistic meanings of a sentence, together with a set of preconditions on the determination of the proposition expressed: (i) identifying reference, (ii) completing deixis, and (iii) disambiguating expressions. What is said in the Gricean sense is minimally yet fully propositional. By contrast, what is conversationally implicated, as articulated by Grice, is intended to handle both enriched and additional propositions, in the terminology of Levinson (2000: 195). Consequently, within the classical Gricean paradigm, while semantic representations and minimal propositions fall under semantics, enriched and additional propositions are the concern of pragmatics. It is unclear where the pragmatic resolution of reference, deixis, and ambiguities should fall for Grice.

Relevance theorists

The relevance theorists have adopted a broader, more pragmatic notion of what is said, though they do not use the term 'what is said'. What is said in the relevance-theoretic sense can be roughly divided into two parts: semantic representations and explicatures. Explicatures are responsible for the pragmatically enriched level of what Sperber and Wilson (1986, 1995) call explicit content. They cover both pragmatic resolution of indexicals and ambiguities, and minimal and enriched propositions. On the other hand, r-implicatures account for additional propositions. It follows, therefore, that semantic representations fall in the domain of semantics; both explicatures and r-implicatures belong to pragmatics.

Recanati

Like the relevance theorists, Recanati has also endorsed a wider, more pragmatic conception of what is said. Both the relevance theorists' and Recanati's notion of what is said, in what Levinson (2000) labels the 'everyday sense of what is stated', constitutes what Berg (2002) calls 'contextually enriched content'. On Recanati's view, what is said has a semantic part, i.e., semantic representation or sentence meaning, and a pragmatic part, i.e., the pragmatically enriched said (e.g., Recanati 2004a: 6). The semantic part corresponds roughly to what Recanati (2000) calls **i-content** (intuitive truth-conditional content of utterance) and what Recanati (2001) dubs '**what is said**$_{min}$'. The pragmatic part, meanwhile, corresponds to what Recanati (2000) labels **c-content** (compositionally articulated content of utterance) and what Recanati (2001) calls '**what is said**$_{max}$'. Reference assignment, deixis identification, disambiguation, and minimal and expanded propositions all belong to the pragmatically enriched what is said. Only additional propositions are the output of conversational implicatures.

Bach

In contrast to the relevance theorists and Recanati, Bach has opted for a notion of what is said that is even narrower than the original minimal Gricean concept. Following Grice (1989), Bach (1994a, 2001, 2004) was of the view that what is said should be 'closely related to the conventional meaning of the ... sentence ... uttered' and must correspond to 'the elements of [the sentence], their order and their syntactic character' (Grice 1989: 87). He called this narrower criterion for what is said the '**syntactic correlation constraint**' (but see Carston 2002: 172–3, 181 for qualification). What is said thus understood is closely linked with both the conventional, semantic content and the syntactic structure of the sentence uttered.[25] This locutionary sense of what is said is roughly equivalent to Berg's (2002) characterization of what is said as being general content, as

---

[25] Elsewhere, in an attempt to dispense with Grice's notion of conventional implicature, Bach (1999b) postulated an **Indirect Quotation test** or **IQ test**.

(i) Bach's IQ test
An element of a sentence contributes to what is said in an utterance of that sentence if and only if it can be an accurate and complete indirect quotation of the utterance (in the same language) which includes that element, or a corresponding element, in the 'that'-clause that specifies what is said.

According to this test, *but*, *still*, and *even* are part of what is said because they can be straightforwardly embedded in an indirect quotation, as in (ii). By contrast, *in other words*, *frankly*, and *nevertheless* are not constitutive of what is said, because they cannot pass the IQ test. This is illustrated in (iii).

(ii)   a. Mary is fast asleep, but Victoria is wide awake.
     b. John said that Mary is fast asleep, but Victoria is wide awake.
(iii) a. In other words, the patent should be granted in amended form.
     b. ?John said that in other words, the patent should be granted in amended form.

opposed to contextually enriched content. In addition, on Bach's account, reference resolution, deixis fixing, and disambiguation are also part of what is said. The semantic representation of what is said may be subpropositional. In other words, it can be in the form of what Bach called propositional radicals. Propositional radicals and minimal propositions undergo a process of expansion and completion respectively to be transformed into what is implicit, i.e., implicitures. Implicitures then provide input to the classical Gricean inferential mechanism (the co-operative principle and its component maxims), yielding conversational implicatures as output. Thus, in Bach's theory, the traditional Gricean dichotomy between what is said and what is implicated is replaced by a trichotomy between what is said, what is implicit, and what is implicated. Whereas what is said falls within the province of semantics, both what is implicit and what is implicated are the concerns of pragmatics.

One of the main attractions of Bach's model is that, as pointed out by Horn (2004), the classical Gricean semantic conception of what is said, along with a post-semantic orthodox Gricean characterization of what is implicated, is retained in a neo-classical way. But a drawback of the model (if it is a drawback) is that this is achieved only at the expense of postulating a further representational level between what is said and what is implicated.

Levinson

Levinson has retained the classical Gricean characterization of what is said. As mentioned above, the Gricean semantic notion of what is said consists of semantic representations, a set of preconditions for determining the propositions expressed, and minimal propositions. But unlike Grice, Levinson allows conversational implicatures to intrude on to the assignment of truth-conditional content. In other words, on Levinson's view, conversational implicatures are not only needed to account for additional propositions

---

There are, however, problems with this test. For example, on Bach's view, *frankly* should not contribute to what is said. But it does seem to pass the IQ test, as the following example from Carston (2002: 176) shows. The same can be said of Chinese (Feng 2006).

(iv)   Beth said that frankly she'd had enough of John's lies.

For a recent debate between Bach and Recanati about whether what is said is constrained by syntax or pre-theoretical intuition, see, for example, Bach (2001) and Recanati (2001).

'post'-semantically, but they are also required pre-semantically to account for reference determination, deictic resolution, disambiguation, ellipsis unpacking, and generality-narrowing, as well as to affect truth conditions in complex constructions such as comparatives, conditionals, and *because*-clauses. Thus, within the Levinsonian neo-Gricean framework, only semantic representations are categorized as the proper domain of semantics. All the rest is dealt with in pragmatics.

As noted in the last chapter, Levinson's argument that conversational implicature can contribute to propositional content gives rise to the problem known as Grice's circle, namely, how what is implicated can be defined in contrast to and calculated on the basis of what is said, given that what is said seems to both determine and be determined by what is implicated (e.g., Levinson 2000, Huang 2001a). The suggestion put forward by Levinson to deal with the problem is that one should give up the traditional, 'received' view that semantics and pragmatics are autonomous with respect to each other, and the output of semantics is input to pragmatics. Rather, one should treat semantics and pragmatics as two overlapping and interrelated fields of study.

Conclusion
The semantics–pragmatics distinction as reflected in the five analyses discussed above can be set out as in (7.54).

(7.54)   The semantics–pragmatics interface (adapted from Levinson 2000: 195)

To sum up, as can be seen from (7.54), what everyone agrees on is that there is a level of semantic representation, or the linguistic meaning of a sentence, and this level belongs to semantics. Next, what the relevance theorists, Recanati, Bach, and Levinson have in common is the viewpoint that at least part of the original Gricean notion of what is said has to be understood as involving much more of a pragmatic contribution than Grice has acknowledged. But what they cannot agree on are two points. In the first place, while the relevance theorists, Recanati, and Levinson believe that there is substantial pragmatic intrusion into what is said, Bach denies that there is such an intrusion, and posits a level intermediate between what is said and what is implicated. Secondly, the disagreement concerns the nature of the pragmatic inference under consideration. For the relevance theorists, Recanati, and Bach, the pragmatic inference in question is of a special kind, which differs from conversational implicature;

Author	Semantic representation	Dectic and reference resolution	Minimal proposition	Enriched proposition	Additional proposition
Grice	What	is	said	Implicature	
Relevance theorists		Explicature			Implicature
Recanati		Pragmatically enriched said			Implicature
Bach	What is said			Impliciture	Implicature
Levinson	What is said				
	Implicature				

Semantics

Pragmatics

for Levinson, it is the same beast as conversational implicature. This difference certainly has implications for the domain of semantics and that of pragmatics, for the interface between semantics and pragmatics, and indeed for the theory of meaning as a whole. Other things being equal, given the metatheoretical principle known as 'Occam's razor' ('theoretical entities are not to be multiplied beyond necessity'; see Chapter 1), Levinson's model is theoretically and methodologically preferable, because it postulates fewer representational levels in the interpretation of an utterance than its competitors.

7.4. Summary

This chapter has been concerned with the interface and division of labour between pragmatics and semantics. In Section 7.1, I discussed two theoretical positions with regard to the relationship between semantics and pragmatics, namely, reductionism and complementarism. Section 7.2 then examined the three influential ways in which the boundary between semantics and pragmatics has been drawn, and showed that there does not seem to be a clear-cut demarcation between these two core components of linguistics. Finally, in Section 7.3, I focused my attention on pragmatic intrusion into the classical Gricean characterization of what is said—an issue that has been, and is still being, vigorously debated by both linguists and philosophers of language, and by both semanticists and pragmaticists. In particular, I concentrated on the proposals put forward by the relevance theorists, Recanati, Bach, and Levinson. The general conclusion that can be reached seems to be that semantics and pragmatics constitute two distinct domains of inquiry, but they are inextricably intertwined in such a manner that the boundary between them is not easy to draw in a neat and systematic way.[26] Echoing a rather pessimistic remark made by Lyons almost twenty years ago that 'current presentations of the distinction between semantics and pragmatics tend to be riddled with inconsistencies and unjustified assumptions' (Lyons 1987: 155), Recanati (2004b) concluded:

[I]t is futile to insist on providing an answer to the twin questions: What is the principled basis for the semantics/pragmatics distinction? Where does the boundary lie? Answers to these questions can still be given, but they have to be rely on stipulation.

Key concepts

pragmatics–semantics interface
reductionism
semantic reductionism
pragmatic reductionism
complementarism
radical semantics
radical pragmatics
narrow context versus broad context
charity
non-monotonicity
holism
what is said
what is communicated/meant

[26] There are also linguistic phenomena that straddle the semantics–pragmatics boundary. One such phenomenon is presupposition. Another is deixis.

pragmatic intrusion
unarticulated (propositional) constituent
primary pragmatic process
saturation
free enrichment
strengthening
expansion
semantic transfer
availability principle
scope principle
(conversational) impliciture
propositional radical
completion
intrusive construction
Indirect Quotation or IQ test

Exercises and essay questions

1. Of the following propositions, which need saturation (Recanati) or completion (Bach), which need free enrichment (Recanati) or expansion (Bach), which need semantic transfer, and which need loosening? Can you saturate/complete, freely enrich/expand, loosen or 'transfer' them accordingly?
   (i) I haven't been to Australia.
   (ii) Christmas is some time away.
   (iii) Mary is not slim enough.
   (iv) The tram is full.
   (v) In all probability John is going to marry the pretty face.
   (vi) The university campus is some distance from the rail station.
   (vii) Peter and Susan drove to LA. Their car broke down half way.
   (viii) This laptop is cheaper.
   (ix) Confucius is on the top shelf. It's bound in leather.
   (x) She's a real beauty with brains.
   (xi) The children stood in a circle around the Christmas tree.
   (xii) The semantics/pragmatics conference starts at nine.
   (xiii) Susan lost everything.
   (xiv) People say that he owns a van Gogh.
2. Is there any pragmatic intrusion into the following constructions? Can you identify what type of conversational implicature is involved in each case?
   (i) It's better to be faithful to your wife than to be not unfaithful to her.

(ii)   If some of his children oppose the government's immigration policy, the minister will not resign,—but if all of them do, he will.

(iii) Helen either had a baby and got married or got married and had a baby, but I don't know which.

(iv)   Living in a not undemocratic country is worse than living in a democratic one.

(v)   Because a mathematician and an economist wrote the monograph, it sold well.

(vi)   It's better to stop your car than to cause it to stop.

(vii) John persuaded Catherine to marry the man who loves her, but not the man who likes her.

3. What are the main differences between reductionism and complementarism regarding the relationship between semantics and pragmatics?

4. Why can semantics and pragmatics not be distinguished systematically on the basis of the distinction between truth conditions versus non-truth conditions, conventional versus non-conventional meaning, or context independence versus context dependence?

5. Can explicature/the pragmatically enriched said/impliciture be distinguished from conversational implicature on a principled basis? If yes, how; if no, why not?

6. What is the main evidence adduced by Levinson in support of his argument that conversational implicatures intrude on to the determination of the truth conditions of the intrusive constructions?

7. Compare and contrast any two of the analyses of pragmatic intrusion into what is said discussed in this chapter. Bach's theory of impliciture may be one of them, though he denies that there is any such intrusion.

8. What is your view about the interaction and division of labour between semantics and pragmatics?

Further readings

Bach (1994a).
Levinson (2000). Chapter 3.
Recanati (2004b).
Carston (2002). Chapter 2.

8

Pragmatics and syntax

In the last chapter I discussed the pragmatics–semantics interface. In this chapter I shall consider the **pragmatics–syntax interface**, focusing on anaphora and binding.[1]

Anaphora can in general be defined as a relation between two linguistic elements, in which the interpretation of one (called an **anaphoric expression**) is in some way determined by the interpretation of the other (called an **antecedent**) (e.g., Huang 2000a: 1, 2004a, 2006c). In terms of syntactic category, anaphora falls into two main groups: (i) **NP-**, including **N-bar, anaphora**, and (ii) **VP-anaphora**.[2] In an NP-anaphoric relation, both the anaphoric expression and its antecedent are NPs. This is illustrated in (8.1).

(8.1)   Mike₁ said that he₁ almost lost his₁ life to cancer.

---

[1] For a discussion of some other topics in the pragmatics–syntax interface such as passivization, extraposition, and negative transportation, see, for example, Green (2004).

[2] I shall not discuss VP-anaphora in this chapter. The interested reader is referred to Huang (2000a, 2006c).

In (8.1), *he* and *his* are anaphoric expressions, and *Mike* is their antecedent. *He*, *his life*, and *Mike* are all NPs. In an N-bar-anaphoric relation, by contrast, both the anaphoric expression and its antecedent are N-bars rather than NPs. An example of N-bar-anaphora is given in (8.2).

(8.2)   John's sister is a nursery teacher, and Bill's Ø is a policewoman.

In (8.2), the empty category or gap represented by Ø is the anaphoric expression, and *sister* is its antecedent. Neither the anaphoric expression nor its antecedent is a full NP. In this chapter I concentrate on that type of NP-anaphora known in the generative syntax literature as binding.

As pointed out in Huang (e.g., 1991, 1994, 2000a, 2004a, 2006c), anaphora is at the centre of research on the interface between syntax, semantics, and pragmatics in linguistic theory. It is also a key concern of psycho- and computational linguistics, and of work in the philosophy of language and on the linguistic component of cognitive science. It has aroused this interest for a number of reasons. In the first place, anaphora represents one of the most complex phenomena of natural language, and is a source of fascinating problems in its own right. Second, anaphora has long been regarded as one of the few 'extremely good probes' (Chomsky 1982: 23) in furthering our understanding of the nature of the human mind, and thus in facilitating an answer to what Chomsky (e.g., 1981, 1995) considered to be the fundamental problem of linguistics, namely, the logical problem of language acquisition. In particular, certain aspects of anaphora have repeatedly been claimed by Chomsky (e.g., 1981) to present evidence for the argument that human beings are born equipped with some internal, unconscious knowledge of language, known as the language faculty (to be elaborated below). Third, anaphora has been shown to interact with syntactic, semantic, and pragmatic factors. Consequently, it has provided a testing ground for competing hypotheses concerning the relationship between syntax, semantics, and pragmatics in linguistic theory.

This chapter is organized as follows. First, I summarize Chomsky's views about language and linguistics in Section 8.1. Section 8.2 outlines Chomsky's binding theory, and Section 8.3 goes on to discuss the problems for Chomsky's binding theory. In Section 8.4, I present a revised neo-Gricean pragmatic theory of anaphora as developed in Huang (2000a, 2000b, 2004a, 2006c) (see also Levinson 1987a, 1987b, 1991, 2000, and Huang 1991, 1994). Finally, in Section 8.5, I briefly discuss the theoretical implications of our pragmatic approach for the interface between pragmatics and syntax.

8.1. Chomsky's views about language and linguistics

In Chomsky's (1986, 1995) view, linguistics is essentially concerned with the nature of the human mind/brain. The central issue of linguistics is **knowledge of language**: its nature (what constitutes knowledge of language), origin (how knowledge of language is acquired), and use (how knowledge of language is put to use). The ultimate goal of **generative grammar** is to provide an answer to what Chomsky considers to be the fundamental problem of linguistics, namely, the **logical problem of language acquisition**, that is, how it is possible for the child, on the basis of insufficient evidence about or severely limited experience of his or her language, to rapidly acquire the abstract and complex underlying system that represents his or her knowledge of language. This problem is taken to be a special case of what is known as **Plato-Russell's problem**, namely, to explain how we know so much given that the evidence available to us is so meagre. The answer provided by Chomsky to the logical problem of language acquisition is the **innateness hypothesis**—roughly, the argument that human beings are born equipped with some internal, unconscious knowledge of language, known as the **language faculty**. The initial state of the language faculty, being a component or module of the human mind/brain, is subject to a theory of **Universal Grammar (UG)**. Somewhat related to the innateness hypothesis is also the assumption that the underlying system of knowledge of language is much simpler than it superficially appears (e.g., Chomsky 1986, 1995). The development of generative grammar in the last fifty years is largely concerned with these fundamental problems of children's learnability, innateness, and universals. One topic of inquiry that has been at the very heart of Chomsky's generative grammar is the type of NP-anaphora known in the generative syntax literature as binding.

8.2. Chomsky's binding theory

As already mentioned in Chapter 1, within the **principles-and-parameters theory** and its **minimalist descendant**,[3] Chomsky (1981, 1995) distinguished

---

[3] The minimalist programme is the most recent orthodox version of Chomsky's generative grammar, which grew out of Chomsky's government and binding (GB) version of the principles-and-parameters approach. While there is not yet a fully

two types of abstract feature for NPs: anaphors and pronominals. An **anaphor** is a feature representation of an NP which must be referentially dependent and which must be bound within an appropriately defined minimal syntactic domain; a **pronominal** is a feature representation of an NP which may be referentially dependent but which must be free within such a domain. Interpreting anaphors and pronominals as two independent binary features, Chomsky hypothesized that one ideally expects to find four types of NP in a language—both overt and non-overt (i.e., empty).

(8.3)   Chomsky's (1995: 41) typology of NPs

		Overt	*Empty*
a.	[+anaphor, −pronominal]	lexical anaphor	NP-trace
b.	[−anaphor, +pronominal]	pronoun	*pro*
c.	[+anaphor, +pronominal]	–	PRO
d.	[−anaphor, −pronominal]	name	*wh*-trace/variable

Putting aside the four types of empty category (see note 3 in Chapter 1 for exemplification; see, e.g., Huang 1992, 1994, 1995, 2000a for comments), the three lexically realized types of overt NP can be illustrated in (8.4).

(8.4)   Overt NPs
  a. Lexical anaphors
    The anti-war campaigners congratulated *themselves/each other*.
  b. Pronouns
    He was killed by 'friendly fire' in Iraq.

fledged theory of minimalism, the minimalist programme may be presented in a nutshell as follows. In the minimalist framework, the set of four levels of representation is reduced to two interface levels: Logical Form (LF) and Phonological Form (PF). LF provides an input to the semantic-conceptual system, and PF provides an input to the articulatory-perceptual system. This reflects Chomsky's belief known as 'conceptual necessity': since language is a mapping between sound and meaning, all else being equal, language will deploy only those mechanisms needed to connect, on the one hand, to the physical world of sound, and on the other, to the mental world of cognition. In addition to a lexicon, syntax—what Chomsky now calls the computational system—stands between the two interfaces. There are two generalized transformations, Merge and Move, and one non-transformation, Spell-out, which regulate derivation. Furthermore, a number of principles of economy are postulated. Both derivation and representation are subject to these principles (Chomsky 1995; Hornstein, Nunes, and Grohmann 2005; see Seuren 2004 for a critique; see also notes 16 and 17 below).

    c. Names/definite descriptions
      John/the section head bitterly regretted last month's attack on his boss.

Of the three types of overt NP listed in (8.4), anaphors, pronominals, and
r[eferential]-expressions are subject to **binding conditions A**, **B**, and **C**
respectively (see also Chomsky 1995: 211 for the interpretative version of
these conditions within the minimalist framework).

(8.5)   Chomsky's (1995: 96) binding conditions
     A. An anaphor must be bound in a local domain.
     B. A pronominal must be free in a local domain.
     C. An r-expression must be free.

The definition of **binding** is given in (8.6) (Chomsky 1981, 1995: 93).

(8.6) α binds β if and only if
     (i) α is in an A-position,
     (ii) α c-commands β, and
     (iii) α and β are coindexed.

Note that given (i) of (8.6), the binding conditions specified in (8.5) apply
to A-binding (i.e., binding by a category in an argument position) but not
to non-A-binding (i.e., binding by a category in a non-argument position).
C-command is commonly defined as follows:

(8.7) α c-commands β if and only if
     (i) α does not dominate β,
     (ii) β does not dominate α, and
     (iii) the first branching node dominating α also β dominates β.

Finally, the notion of local binding domain is standardly defined in terms
of **governing category (GC)** or complete functional complex (CFC). One
common version of GC is given in (8.8).

(8.8) α is a GC for β if and only if α is the minimal category
     (i.e. the smallest NP or S) containing β, a governor of β, and a SUBJECT
     accessible to β.

The paradigmatic patterns for binding are illustrated from English in (8.9).

(8.9)   a. Bach_1 adored himself_1.
     b. Bach_1 adored him_2.
     c. Bach_1 adored Bach_2.

In (8.9a), *himself* is a reflexive and therefore an anaphor in the Chomskyan
sense. As such, it falls under binding condition A, according to which it

must be bound to its local antecedent *Bach*. Next, in (8.9b), *him*, being a pronominal, is subject to binding condition B. Given binding condition B, it cannot be bound in its local domain, and there is thus disjoint reference between it and *Bach*. Finally in (8.9c), both *Bach*s are r-repressions. By binding condition C, the second *Bach* cannot be co-indexed with the first one. From examples like these, Chomsky concluded that the syntactic distribution of anaphors, pronominals, and r-expressions is accounted for by binding conditions A, B, and C.[4]

8.3. Problems for Chomsky's binding theory

8.3.1. Binding condition A

Cross-linguistically, Chomsky's binding theory is problematic. Let us take the binding condition A pattern first. To begin with, many languages in the world systematically allow **long-distance reflexives**—reflexives that are bound outside their local syntactic domain, and even across sentence boundaries into discourse. These include most East, South, and Southeast Asian languages (e.g., Chinese, Kannada, and Malay), some mainland and insular Scandinavian languages (e.g., Norwegian, Swedish, and Icelandic), some Germanic (other than Scandinavian) and Romance languages (e.g., Dutch, Italian, and Old Provençal), some Slavonic languages (e.g., Czech, Polish, and Russian), and languages such as Modern Greek, KiNande, and Northern Pomo. Following is an example from Chinese.

(8.10) (Chinese)

Xiaoming$_1$	shuo	Xiaohua$_2$	kanbuqi	ziji$_{1/2}$.
Xiaoming	say	Xiaohua	look down upon	self

'Xiaoming$_1$ says that Xiaohua$_2$ looks down upon him$_1$/himself$_2$.'

---

[4] Chomsky's approach is essentially a syntactic or 'geometric' approach, in which binding is formulated predominantly in configurational terms, appealing to purely structural concepts like c-command, government, and locality. In contrast to this syntactically based approach is the semantic or argument structure approach, which is represented by Reinhart and Reuland's (1993) theory of reflexivity. The semantically oriented approach attempts to give an account of binding primarily in argument-structure terms. See Huang (2000a, 2004a) for detailed discussion of the semantic approach.

Given (8.8), the local binding domain of the Chinese morphologically simplex reflexive/anaphor *ziji* (self) is the embedded clause. However, contrary to the prediction of binding condition A, the reflexive *ziji* can be bound by the matrix subject *Xiaoming*, which is outside its local binding domain.[5]

A second type of counterevidence to Chomsky's binding condition A is presented by the distribution of certain morphologically simplex reflexives in languages such as Dutch and Norwegian. It has been observed by, for example, Reinhart and Reuland (1993) that there is a contrast in the use of this type of reflexive in intrinsic (i.e., self-directed) and extrinsic (i.e., other-directed) reflexivization contexts. By intrinsic or self-directed is meant that the action denoted by the predicate is typically performed by a human agent on him- or herself, whereas in the case of extrinsic or other-directed, the action denoted by the predicate is typically directed against others. The contrast is that whereas a morphologically simplex reflexive can be locally bound in the former, as in (8.11a), it cannot be locally bound in the latter, as in (8.11b).

(8.11)   (Dutch)

a. Rint   schaamt   zich.
    Rint   shames   self
    'Rint is ashamed.'

b. *Rint   veracht   zich.
    Rint   despises   self
    'Rint despises himself.'

In (8.11a) the predicate is self-directed, and the Dutch morphologically simplex reflexive/anaphor *zich* (self) is allowed. However, in (8.11b) the predicate is other-directed, and *zich* is not permitted. Since *zich* is an anaphor in the Chomskyan sense, why is it not allowed in its local binding domain in (8.11b)?

There is thus evidence that cross-linguistically, the distribution of reflexives/anaphors violates Chomsky's binding condition A in both directions: on the one hand, a reflexive/anaphor can be bound outside its local domain, as in Chinese, and on the other, it may not be bound within its local domain, as in Dutch.

---

[5] In recent years there have been a number of generative strategies to tackle the locality problem posed by long-distance reflexivization for Chomsky's binding theory. However, as I have demonstrated in Huang (1996, 2000a), none of these proposals really works.

Turn to pp. 275–6 and try to do Exercises 1 and 2.

8.3.2. Binding condition B

We move next to the binding condition B pattern. Once again, evidence from various languages casts serious doubt on Chomsky's binding condition B. In the first place, many languages in the world have no reflexives and consequently utilize pronouns as one of the means to encode coreference. These include some Low West Germanic languages (e.g., Old and Middle Dutch, Old English, Old Frisian and perhaps West Flemish and Modern Frisian), Bamako Bambara, Biblical Hebrew, Isthmus Zapotec, the majority of Australian languages (e.g., Gumbaynggir, Jiwarli, and Nyawaygi), some Austronesian languages (e.g., Chamorro, Kilivila, and Tahitian), some Papuan languages (e.g., Harway), and many pidgin and creole languages (e.g., the Spanish-based Palenquero, and perhaps Bislama, Chinook Jargon, the French-based Guadeloupe, the Arabic-based KiNubi, Kriyol, Martinique Creole, and Negerhollands). An example from Fijian is given below.

(8.12)   (Fijian, cited in Levinson 2000)

Sa	va'a-.dodonu-. ta'ini	'ea	o	Mika.
ASP	correct	3SG-OBJ	ART	Mika

'Mike corrected himself/him.'

Secondly, there are languages that lack first- and/or second-person reflexives. In these languages, first- and second-person pronouns are instead used as bound anaphors. Some Germanic (e.g., Danish, Dutch, and Icelandic) and Romance (e.g., French and Italian) languages, for instance, belong to this type.

(8.13)   (Danish, cited in Huang 2000)

Jeg	barberede	mig.
I	shaved	me

'I shaved myself.'

(8.14)   (German)

Du	denkst	immer	nur	an	dich.
you	think	always	only	of	you

'You always think only of yourself.'

Thirdly, the use of a locally bound third-person pronoun in syntactic structures where its corresponding third-person reflexive is not available is attested in a range of languages. This can be illustrated from Piedmontese in (8.15). Similar examples can be found in, for example, Catalan, French, Galician, Portuguese, Rumanian, Russian, Sardinian, Spanish, and Tsaxur.

(8.15)   (Piedmontese, Burzio 1991)
      Giuanin   a parla   sempre   d'   chiel.
      Giuanin   CL-speak   always   of   him
      'Giuanin always talks about himself.'

All this shows that the use of a pronoun as an anaphor in the world's languages is not highly marked, as Reinhart and Reuland (1993) claimed. Consequently, Chomsky's binding condition B cannot be entirely correct. This is because given Chomsky's binding condition B, a pronominal is not allowed to be bound within its local domain. But, as we have already seen in (8.12)–(8.15) above, it is.

8.3.3. Complementarity between anaphors and pronominals

Next, given the standard formulation of Chomsky's binding conditions A and B, it is predicted that anaphors and pronominals should be in strict complementary distribution; that is, anaphors can occur only where pronominals cannot, and vice versa. This is because the two binding conditions are precise mirror-images of each other.

This predicted distributional complementarity between anaphors and pronominals, however, seems to be a generative syntactician's dream world. Even in a 'syntactic' language like English, it is not difficult to find syntactic environments where the complementarity breaks down. Well-known cases include (i) 'picture' NPs (8.16a), (ii) adjunct PPs (8.16b), (iii) possessive NPs (8.16c), and (iv) emphatic NPs (8.16d).

(8.16)   a. John Kerry$_1$ saw a picture of himself$_1$/him$_1$ in *The New York Times*.
      b. Steve$_1$ looked behind himself$_1$/him$_1$.
      c. [Pavarotti and Domingo]$_1$ adore [each other's]$_1$/their$_1$ performances.
      d. Pavarotti$_1$ said that tenors like himself$_1$/him$_1$ would not sing operas like that.

Worse still, when we take a look at a wider range of languages, we find that the total distributional complementarity entailed by Chomsky's binding conditions A and B stands on shakier ground. First, as I have remarked above, there are long-distance reflexivization languages—languages that systematically allow a reflexive to be bound outside its local domain. In these languages, there is a systematic syntactic distributional overlap between anaphors and pronominals, as can be exemplified in (8.17).

(8.17)   (Malay)
      Fatimah$_1$ mengadu   bahawa   Ali$_2$ mengecam   dirinya$_1$/nya$_1$.
      Fatimah   complain   that   Ali   criticize   self-3SG/3SG
      'Fatimah$_1$ complains that Ali$_2$ criticizes her$_1$/himself$_2$.'

Second, as suggested by Burzio (1996) and Huang (2002a), languages can be grouped into three types with respect to bound possessive anaphora: (i) those allowing anaphors but not pronominals (e.g., Basque, Chechen, Danish, Hindi/Urdu, Ingush, Kashimir, Norwegian, Latin, and Russian), (ii) those permitting pronominals but not anaphors (e.g., Arabic, Akan, German, Guugu Yimidhirr, and Spanish), and (iii) those permitting both anaphors and pronominals (e.g., Bangala, Chinese, Japanese, Korean, Malay, Malayalam, Marathi, Sinhala, Tamil, and Tuki) (see also Exercise 5 on pp. 276–7). In the first, 'reflexives only' type, the possessive and the antecedent are 'near' enough to allow only a reflexive but not a pronoun to encode coreferentiality, as in (8.18).

(8.18)   (Gimira, cited in Huang 2002)
      ba/yi   dor   gotue.
      3-REFL/his   sheep   sold-3-M-FIN
      'He$_1$ sold his self's$_1$/his$_2$ sheep.'

In the second, 'pronouns only' type, because either there is no possessive reflexive in the language or the possessive reflexive cannot be used, only a pronoun is permitted, as in (8.19).

(8.19)   John$_1$ loves his$_{1/2}$ wife.

Finally, in the third, 'both reflexives and pronouns' type, the possessive and the antecedent are both 'close' enough to allow a reflexive and at the same time 'distant' enough to permit a pronoun as well, as in (8.20).[6]

---

[6] As noted in Huang (2002a), there may be a mixture of types within a single language. For example, Mundani is a 'reflexives only' language in third-person

(8.20)   (Oriya, Ray 2000)
     raama$_1$ nija$_1$/taa$_1$ bahi   paDhilaa.
     Rama   self's his   book   read
     'Rama$_1$ read selfs$_1$/his$_1$ book.'

While Chomsky's binding conditions A and B make correct predications for the distribution of bound possessive anaphora in 'reflexives only' and perhaps also in 'pronouns only' languages depending on how the local binding domain is defined, they certainly make wrong predictions for 'both reflexives and pronouns' languages.

Third, still another type of distributional overlap is found cross-linguistically. This involves certain emphatic contexts. Morphologically, emphatic expressions can be either simplex or complex. Morphologically complex emphatic expressions are usually in the form of 'pronoun/reflexive + adjunct/modifier', with the adjunct/modifier having the meaning of 'self', 'same', 'body', 'head', 'eye', 'soul', 'marrow', 'seed', or—in the case of possessives—'own' (e.g., Levinson 1991, Baker 1995, König and Siemund 2000). These morphologically complex emphatic expressions can alternate with pronouns.

(8.21)   Pronoun versus pronoun + 'self'
     Mary thinks that her son is more musical than her/herself.
(8.22)   Pronoun versus pronoun + 'same'
     (French)
     François pense   que Viviane aime   Pierre   plus
     François believes that Viviane loves Pierre more
     que lui/lui-même.
     than him/him-same
     'François believes that Viviane loves Pierre more than him/himself.'
(8.23)   Pronoun versus pronoun + 'own'
     The little boy is struggling with his/his own shoe laces.

singular, but a 'pronouns only' language in third-person plural, as can be seen from the following examples (data from Parker 1986).
  (i)   ta$_1$ dzi   akende   a-zi$_1$/to$_2$.
      3SG   eat   banana   self's/his
      ' He$_1$ has eaten selfs$_1$/his$_2$ banana.'
  (ii) bɔ$_1$ le   ni   eghi   bɔb$_{1/2}$.
      they   3PL   take   things   their
      'They$_1$ took their$_{1/2}$ things.'

We can thus conclude that the strict distributional complementarity between anaphors and pronominals dictated by Chomsky's binding conditions A and B cannot be maintained.

8.3.4. Binding condition C

We come finally to the binding condition C pattern. Following Chomsky (1981), Lasnik (1989) argued that binding condition C be split into two subconditions, to be called **binding conditions C_1 and C_2**.

(8.24)   Lasnik's binding condition C (my phrasing)
C_1 An r-expression is r-expression-free everywhere.
C_2 An r-expression is pronoun-free everywhere.

What binding condition C_1 says is that an r-expression cannot be bound by another r-expression anywhere in the sentence, and what binding condition C_2 dictates is that an r-expression cannot be bound by a pronoun anywhere in the sentence. Furthermore, Lasnik claimed that while binding condition C_1 is subject to parametric variation, binding condition C_2 is universal.

But this way of looking at binding condition C is not tenable. Take binding condition C_1 first. Counterexamples can easily be demonstrated cross-linguistically, especially in some East, South and Southeast Asian languages such as Chinese, Bangala, Hindi/Urdu, Japanese, Malayalam, Sinhala, Vietnamese, and Thai.

(8.25)   (Thai)
Cɔɔn₁   chɔɔp   Cɔɔn₁.
John   likes   John
'John₁ likes John₁.'

Next arises the question of whether or not binding condition C_2 can be maintained universally. The answer is again negative, as the following classic example from English (Evans 1980) shows.

(8.26)   Everyone has finally realized that Oscar₁ is incompetent.
Even he₁ has finally realized that Oscar₁ is incompetent.

In (8.26), the r-expression in the second sentence is preceded and c-commanded by the pronoun in the matrix clause of the same sentence, yet it is bound by the pronoun, *contra* binding condition C_2.[7] There is thus no avoiding the conclusion that binding condition C_2 can also be falsified.

Now have a look at Exercise 3 on p. 276.

8.4. A revised neo-Gricean pragmatic theory of anaphora

In the previous section I showed that Chomsky's binding conditions are not adequate in accounting for cross-linguistic binding patterns. In this section, I shall present a revised neo-Gricean pragmatic theory of anaphora, based on Huang (2000a, 2000b, 2001b, 2001c, 2001d, 2002b, 2004a, 2006c, 2006d; see also Levinson 1987b, 1991, 2000 and Huang 1991, 1994, 1995, 1996).[8] As I have emphasized in, for example, Huang (1991, 1994, 2000a: 212–214, 2004a), the pragmatic theory of anaphora I have been advancing does not deny the existence of distinct syntactic, semantic, and pragmatic levels and modes of explanation in linguistic theory. On the contrary, it presumes the independence of an irreducible grammatical stratum for pragmatically motivated constraints: calculation of pragmatic inferences of the Gricean sort has to be made over a level of independent syntactic structure and semantic representation. What I have been arguing is that pragmatics interacts with syntax to determine many of the anaphoric processes that are thought to be at the very heart of grammar. If this is the case, then a large portion of linguistic explanation concerning anaphora which is currently sought in grammatical terms may need to be shifted to pragmatics, hence the **interaction and division of labour between pragmatics and syntax**. This interface and division of labour between pragmatics and

[7] One proposal to accommodate counterexamples of this kind is to reinterpret binding theory as a theory of referential dependency, along the lines of Evans (1980). On this view, the reference of the pronoun in (8.26) has to be antecedently assigned in the previous sentence, and consequently, the pronoun can be accidentally coindexed with the relevant r-expression, thus in conformity with binding condition C_2. But, as pointed out in Huang (2000a, 2004a), such an escape mechanism both over- and under-generates, which indicates that Evans's proposal is not valid in explaining away counterexamples like (8.26).

[8] For a survey of some earlier neo-Gricean pragmatic analyses of anaphora, see Huang (1991, 1994, 2004a).

syntax may be summarized in a Kantian slogan: pragmatics without syntax is empty; syntax without pragmatics is blind (Huang 1994: 259, 2000a: 213).[9] What pragmatics does here is to provide a set of complementary, explanatory principles that constrains the production or interpretation of an utterance whose linguistic representation has already been antecedently cognized. But these are important and indispensable principles for linguistic explanation, for, as Horn (1988: 115) pointed out, 'a regimented account of language *use* facilitates a simpler and more elegant description of language *structure*'.

The central idea underlying our revised neo-Gricean pragmatic theory is that the interpretation of certain patterns of anaphora can be made utilizing pragmatic inference, dependent on the language user's knowledge of the range of options available in the grammar, and of the systematic use or avoidance of particular anaphoric expressions or structures on particular occasions. Put slightly differently, anaphoricity is a property not of specific lexical items (as can be seen by the fact that the binding conditions cannot be formulated as constraints on particular lexical items), but of the systematic use or avoidance of lexical items (see also Levinson 2000: 270). But before I turn to the theory itself, let us first take a look at the general pattern of anaphora.

8.4.1. The general pattern of anaphora

Consider the contrast pairs of the following kind.

(8.27)   a. Verdi$_1$ liked his$_{1/2}$ operas.
         b. He$_1$ liked Verdi's$_2$ operas.
(8.28)   a. Mary$_1$ said that she$_{1/2}$ was an animal rights activist.
         b. She$_1$ said that Mary$_2$ was an animal rights activist.
(8.29)   a. The rose$_1$ on the windowsill has come into blossom. The flower$_1$ is beautiful.
         b. The flower$_1$ on the windowsill has come into blossom. The rose$_2$ is beautiful.

---

[9] Cf. Kant's original apothegm from his *Critique of pure reason*: 'Concepts without percepts are empty; percepts without concepts are blind' (75 B, the Norman Kemp Smith translation).

There is a clear pattern here: the use of a reduced, semantically general anaphoric expression tends to indicate a locally coreferential interpretation, as shown by the a sentences of (8.27)–(8.29), whereas the use of a full, semantically specific anaphoric expression tends to mark a locally non-coreferential interpretation, as indicated by the b sentences of (8.27)–(8.29).[10] Following Levinson (1987b, 1991, 2000), let us call this the **general pattern of anaphora**.

(8.30) The general pattern of anaphora
    Reduced, semantically general anaphoric expressions tend to favour locally coreferential interpretations; full, semantically specific anaphoric expressions tend to favour locally non-coreferential interpretations.

8.4.2. A revised neo-Gricean pragmatic apparatus for anaphora

Now, assuming that the general pattern of anaphora is largely an instantiation, in the realm of linguistic reference, of the systematic interaction of the three Levinsonian neo-Gricean pragmatic principles discussed in Chapter 2, the question to be raised next is how it can be given an account in terms of the operation of these principles.

Applying the Q-, I-, and M-principles to the domain of anaphoric reference, one can derive a **revised neo-Gricean pragmatic apparatus** for the interpretation of various types of anaphoric expression. Assuming the **hierarchy of referentiality for different kinds of anaphoric expression** in (8.31), along the lines of Burzio (1991, 1996), Levinson (1991, 2000), and Huang (1991, 1994, 2000a), this pragmatic apparatus for anaphora can be presented in (8.32), with a **revised disjoint reference presumption (RDRP)** given in (8.33).

(8.31) A hierarchy of referentiality for deferent types of anaphoric expression
    Anaphors < pronominals < r-expressions
    (Anaphors are less referential than pronominals, and pronominals are less referential than r-expressions.)[11]

---

[10] Cf. the binding condition B pattern, as exemplified in (8.9b), where the use of a reduced, semantically specific anaphoric expression indicates a locally disjoint reference interpretation. But as we shall see in a moment, this is exactly what is predicted by our revised pragmatic theory of anaphora.

[11] Regarding the referentiality of empty categories or gaps, some can be grouped with anaphors, and others with pronominals.

(8.32)   A revised neo-Gricean pragmatic apparatus for anaphora (Huang 2000a, 2004a)
    (a) Interpretation principles
       (i) The use of an anaphoric expression x I-implicates a locally coreferential interpretation, unless (ii) or (iii).
      (ii) There is an anaphoric Q/Horn-scale $<x, y>$, where informally x is semantically stronger than y, in which case, the use of y Q-implicates the complement of the I-implicature associated with the use of x, in terms of reference.
     (iii) There is an anaphoric M-scale $\{x, y\}$, where informally x is unmarked with respect to or simpler than y, in which case, the use of y M-implicates the complement of the I-implicature associated with the use of x, in terms of either reference or expectedness.
    (b) Consistency constraints
       Any interpretation implicated by (a) is subject to the requirement of consistency with
       (i) The RDRP (see (8.33) below).
      (ii) Information saliency, so that
         (a) implicatures due to matrix constructions may take precedence over implicatures due to subordinate constructions, and
         (b) implicatures to coreference may be preferred according to the saliency of antecedent in line with the hierarchy topic > subject > object, etc.; and
     (iii) General implicature constraints, namely,
         (a) background assumptions,
         (b) contextual factors
         (c) meaning$_{nn}$, and
         (d) semantic entailments.

(8.33)   A revised disjoint reference presumption (RDRP) (Huang 2000a, 2004a)
    The co-arguments of a predicate are intended to be disjoint, unless one of them is reflexive-marked.[12]

At this point, it is useful to draw the reader's attention to the distinction of whether or not an anaphoric expression and its antecedent are the co-arguments of a single predicate. If they are, then the predicate may be reflexive-marked, to use Reinhart and Reuland's term. As pointed out in Huang (2000a: 163–4, 216–18, 2004a), a predicate can in general be reflexive-

---

[12] The disjoint reference presumption (DRP) was first put forward by Farmer and Harnish (1987). It goes thus: the arguments of a predicate are intended to be disjoint, unless marked otherwise.

marked in three distinct ways. In the first place, it can be reflexive-marked lexically by the use of an inherently reflexive verb, as in (8.11a) above and (8.34) below.

(8.34) a. On that occasion, the boys behaved (themselves) badly.
      b. *On that occasion, the boys behaved the girls badly.

Here, the English verb *behave* is an inherently reflexive verb. This can be seen by the fact that it cannot be used as a transitive verb, as shown by the ungrammaticality of (8.34b) (see Huang 2000a: 216–17 for detailed analysis of the use of inherently reflexive verbs). Second, a predicate can be reflexive-marked morphologically by the employment of a reflexive affix attached to the verb. This is the case in (8.35).

(8.35) (Chinese)
      Lao Xie zisha   le.
      Lao Xie self-kill PAR
      'Lao Xie killed himself.'

In (8.35) the attachment of the Chinese reflexive prefix *zi* reflexive-marks the predicate.

    Finally, a predicate can be reflexive-marked syntactically by the use of a reflexive pronoun, as in (8.9a) above and (8.36) below, or by a grammaticalized or standardized lexeme typically denoting human body parts including body itself, as in (8.37).

(8.36) (Lithuanian, cited in Huang 2000)
      Jis   gerbia   save.
      he   respects   self
      'He respects himself.'
(8.37) (Kabuverdiano, Schladt 2000)
      Manel   feri   se   cabeca.
      Manuel   hurt   3SG-POSS   head
      'Manuel hurt himself.'

In (8.36), the predicate is reflexive-marked by the Lithuanian morphologically simplex reflexive pronoun in the overt syntax. In (8.37), it is reflexive-marked by the Kabuverdiano grammaticalized lexeme *cabeca*. While the latter device is attested in a wide variety of languages including Abkhaz, Basque, Biblical Hebrew, Georgian, Lisu, Malagasy, Mojave, and Tamazight, it seems to be particular popular among African languages (see Huang 2000a: 162–3, 218–19 for detailed discussion).

Furthermore, the choice of one particular reflexivizing strategy over another in a language is in part determined by the semantics/pragmatics of the predicate in question. As already mentioned, the meaning of the predicate can roughly be divided into two types here: self-directed and other-directed. By self-directed is meant that the action denoted by the predicate is typically performed by a human agent on him- or herself, whereas in the case of other-directed, the action denoted by the predicate is typically directed against others. Events such as grooming, change of body posture, and some emotions such as being ashamed, frightened, or proud are typical examples of self-directed actions or attitudes. By contrast, communication, violent actions, and emotions such as love, hatred, anger, jealousy, or being pleased standardly fall in the category of other-directed actions or attitudes (e.g., König and Siemund 2000, see also Haiman 1985a: 120–30, 168–74).

It is particularly interesting that if one takes a careful look at the relationship between the meaning of a predicate and the various reflexivizing devices a language has, a cross-linguistic, iconic correlation emerges (adapted from König and Siemund 2000):

(8.38)   The predicate meaning/reflexivizing strategy correlation
         The more 'marked' a reflexivizing situation (e.g., other-directed) is, the more 'marked' (i.e., more complex) a reflexivizing strategy will be used to encode it.

What the **predicate meaning/reflexivizing strategy correlation** in (8.38) basically states is this: if a language has more than one reflexivizing strategy or form, one would expect the simplex ones to be employed for inherently reflexive predicates and other self-directed situations, and the complex ones to be utilized for other-directed situations. Different languages, of course, may afford their speakers different means to conform to this correlation. In some languages (e.g., Modern Hebrew, Russian, and Turkish) one finds a choice between verbal and nominal strategies; in others (e.g., English, Kannada, and Spanish) the opposition is between zero and non-zero anaphoric expressions; in yet others (e.g., Dutch, Norwegian, and Swedish) there is a contrast between morphologically simplex and complex reflexives, or the opposition is between the morphologically simplex pronouns and morphologically complex reflexives, as in Frisian. Finally, the choice may be between the use of a single versus a non-single emphatic expression (e.g., Lezgian, Tsakhur, and Turkish) (Huang 2000a: 219–20, König and Siemund 2000). An example in support of this correlation is given below. (See Huang 2000a, 2004a for further exemplification.)

(8.39) (Norwegian)
  a. Edward   skammer   seg.
     Edward   shames   self
     'Edward is ashamed.'
  b. Edward   foraktet   segselv.
     Edward   despises   self self
     'Edward despises himself.'

In Norwegian, the marking of reflexivity can be accomplished by either the morphologically simplex reflexive *seg* or the morphologically complex reflexive *segselv*. When the predicate denotes a self-directed action, as in (8.39a), the morphologically simplex *seg* is used. On the other hand, when the predicate denotes an other-directed action, as in (8.39b), the morphologically complex *seg selv* is employed—precisely as is predicted by the predicate meaning/reflexivizing strategy correlation in (8.38). This correlation is explicable in terms of the interaction between our I- and M-principles: to convey an unmarked message, use an unmarked linguistic expression, and to convey a marked one, use a marked linguistic expression.

See whether you can tackle Exercise 4 on p. 276.

8.4.3. The binding patterns

With all this in place, I can now give a revised neo-Gricean pragmatic account of intrasentential anaphora. I shall begin with cases where the anaphoric expression and its antecedent are the co-arguments of the same predicate. Consider the paradigmatic binding patterns in (8.9), repeated here as (8.40).

(8.40) a. Bach$_1$ adored himself$_1$.
       b. Bach$_1$ adored him$_2$.
       c. Bach$_1$ adored Bach$_2$.

  In (8.40a), since reflexivity is marked by a reflexive in the overt syntax, the RDRP is not applicable. Consequently, given (8.32a (i)), the interpretation of the reflexive is subject to the I-principle ('the speaker uses a semantically general term, and the addressee gets a semantically more specific interpretation'), which induces a locally coreferential interpretation.[13] Next, the binding condition B effect of (8.40b) can be obtained by the operation of both the Q-principle and the RDRP. By the referentiality hierarchy in (8.31) and the I-principle, a reflexive will be chosen if coreference is intended, because the reflexive is referentially the most economic anaphoric expression for encoding reflexivity. This has the consequence that if the reflexive is not employed but a pronoun is used instead, a Q-implicature will arise; namely, no coreference is intended. In other words, we have a Q/Horn-scale <reflexive, pronoun> here, such that the use of the semantically weaker pronoun Q-implicates that the use of the semantically stronger reflexive cannot be truthfully entertained, that is, the coreferential reading which is associated with the use of the reflexive should be avoided (see (8.32a (ii))). Reflexives are semantically stronger than pronouns in that (i) syntactically, they typically need to be bound in some domain; and (ii) semantically, they are normally referentially depen-dent. For example, they cannot in general be used as deictic expressions. In the meantime, since the pronoun encodes a co-argument of a predicate which is not reflexive-marked, it is also subject to the RDRP. Thus, the potential, locally coreferential interpretation between the pronoun and the local subject encouraged by the I-principle is ruled out twice, first by the rival Q-principle (Q > I) and then by the RDRP. Finally, in the case of (8.40c), for the same reasoning, the r-expression, being semantically weaker than reflexives, will again be read first by the Q-principle and then by the RDRP as preferably being disjoint in reference with the local subject.

Unlike Chomsky's binding condition B, our pragmatic theory can also accommodate those binding patterns where a pronoun is happily bound in its local binding domain. This is the case with (8.12)–(8.15) above, and (8.41) below.

(8.41)   (French)
        Pierre$_1$ a   honte   de   lui$_1$.
        Pierre   has   shame   of   him
        'Pierre is ashamed of himself.'

Here, the French reflexive *soi* cannot be used. Given the referentiality hierarchy (8.31), the pronoun *lui* becomes the next most favoured choice for encoding reflexivity. Since the RDRP is not at work here, because reflexivity is marked by the pronoun in the overt syntax, by (8.32a (i)) the

---

[13] A pragmatically less radical alternative is to retain binding condition A as a grammatically stipulated rule, as in Levinson (1991, 2000).

preference for a locally coreferential interpretation induced by the I-principle will go through unblocked. Exactly the same analysis can be applied to (8.12)–(8.15) above. Thus, unlike Chomsky's binding condition B, our analysis allows reflexivity to be marked by a lower-ranked anaphoric expression (such as a pronoun) if its immediately higher-ranked counterpart (such as a reflexive) is not available—an account that is empirically more accurate.

8.4.4. Beyond the binding patterns

What is even more interesting, from a pragmatic point of view, is the interpretation of cases where an anaphoric expression and its antecedent are not the co-arguments of a predicate, about which Chomsky's binding theory says nothing. Regarding the reflexive/pronoun distribution in these cases, three patterns can be identified: (i) those permitting reflexives but not pronouns for a coreferential interpretation, as in (8.42), (ii) those allowing pronouns but not reflexives, as in (8.43), and (iii) those warranting both reflexives and pronouns, as in (8.17) above and (8.44) below.

(8.42) (Russian, cited in Burzio 1996)

   | On_1 | dal | ej | umyt' | $sebj_1/ego_{*1/2}$. |
   | he | let | her | wash | self/him |

   'He_1 let her wash $him_{1/2}$.'

(8.43) $John_1$ said that *$heself_1$/he_1 wanted to further his research in nano-technology.

(8.44) (Icelandic, cited in Huang 2000)

   | Jon_1 | segir | að | Maria | elski | $sig_1/hann_1$. |
   | John | says | that | Maria | loves-SBJV | self/him |

   '$John_1$ says that Maria loves him_1.'

Note that in all these cases, the RDRP is irrelevant, the anaphoric expression and its antecedent being non-co-arguments of the same predicate. Now, in the case of (8.42), the interpretation of the reflexive falls under the I-principle, which gives rise to a locally coreferential reading. The interpretation of the pronoun is then due to the working of the Q-principle. The use of a semantically weaker pronoun where a semantically stronger reflexive could occur solicits a classical Q-implicature, to the effect that a locally coreferential interpretation is not available. The same can be said of the 'reflexives only' cases of possessive anaphora in (8.18) above. Next, in the case of (8.43), because no reflexive is available as a possible candidate to indicate coreferentiality, in accordance with the referentiality hierarchy (8.31) a pronoun is used instead. Consequently, there is no Q/Horn-scale <reflexive, pronoun> to prevent the pronoun going under the I-principle, which gives rise to a locally coreferential interpretation. The same is just as true of the 'pronouns only' cases of possessive anaphora in (8.19).

Finally, of particular interest to us is (8.44), where there is a distributional overlap between the reflexive and the pronoun. Given the referentiality hierarchy (8.31), one question arises: why should there be such an overlap? One plausible view, due to Burzio (1996), is that this may be the result of a conflict between the 'anaphors first' condition (induced by the I-principle in our theory), which favours the use of a reflexive, and the locality condition, which goes against the use of a reflexive and therefore indirectly facilitates the use of a pronoun. Regardless of whether or not this explanation is on the right track, within the proposed revised neo-Gricean pragmatic framework, (8.44) can be interpreted along the following lines. For reference, both the reflexive and the pronoun are subject to the I-implicated coreference. However, since the grammar allows the unmarked pronoun to be used to encode coreference, the speaker will employ it if such an interpretation is intended. This gives rise to the question as to why the marked reflexive can also be used. Put another way, a question may be raised as to whether or not there is any systematic semantic/pragmatic contrast between the reflexive on the one hand, and the pronoun on the other. The answer is certainly yes. Intuitively, the use of a reflexive in these locations indicates some sort of **unexpectedness** (Edmondson and Plank 1978). Examined in a more careful way, this unexpectedness turns out to be mainly of two types: (i) logophoricity and (ii) emphaticness/contrastiveness.

Now try to do Exercise 5 on pp. 276–7.

8.4.5. Logophoricity and emphaticness/contrastiveness

Logophoricity
Logophoricity refers to the phenomenon in which the perspective or point of view of an internal protagonist of a sentence or discourse, as opposed to that of the current, external speaker, is reported by some morphological

and/or syntactic means. The term 'perspective' or 'point of view' is used here in a technical sense and is intended to encompass words, thoughts, knowledge, emotion, perception, and space-location (Huang 1994, 2000a, 2001c, 2002b, 2004a). The concept of logophoricity was first introduced in the analysis of African languages like Aghem, Efik, and Tuburi, where a separate paradigm of logophoric pronouns is employed. By way of illustration, consider (8.45).

(8.45)   (Donno Sɔ, Culy 1994)
    a. Oumar Anta   inyemeñ   waa   be   gi.
       Oumar Anta   LOG-ACC   seen   AUX   said
      '$Oumar_1$ said that $Anta_2$ had seen him_1.'
    b. Oumar Anta   woñ   waa   be   gi.
       Oumar Anta   3SG-ACC   seen   AUX   said
      '$Oumar_1$ said that $Anta_2$ had seen him_3.'

In (8.45a), what Oumar has said is reported from the perspective of the internal protagonist Oumar, thus the use of the Donno Sɔ logophoric pronoun, which encodes a coreferential reading between it and the matrix subject *Oumar*. By contrast, in (8.45b) Oumar's words are reported from the perspective of the current, external speaker, hence the employment of the regular pronoun, which indicates a locally disjoint reference interpretation.

Cross-linguistically, logophoricity may be morphologically and/or syntactically expressed by one or more of the following mechanisms: (i) logophoric pronouns (e.g., Babungo, Mundani, and Yulu), as in (8.45a); (ii) logophoric addressee pronouns (e.g., Angas, Mapun, and Tikar), as in (8.46); (iii) logophoric verbal affixes (e.g., Ekpeye, Gokana, and Ibibio), as in (8.47), and (iv) long-distance reflexives (e.g., Korean, Modern Greek, and Turkish), as in (8.44) above and (8.48) below (see Huang 2000a: 172–204, 2002b for detailed discussion of logophoricity; see also Sells 1987, Zribi-Hertz 1989, Stirling 1993, and Kuno 2004).

(8.46)   (Mapun, Frajzyngier 1985)
    n- sat n-wur   taji   gwar   dim n   Kaano.
    I   say BEN-3SG PROHB ADDR go PREP Kano
    'I told him_1 that he_1 may not go to Kano.'
(8.47)   (Gokana, Hyman and Comrie 1981)
    aè   kɔ   aè   dɔ-è.
    he   said   he   fell-LOG
    'He_1 said that he_1 fell.'
(8.48)   (Marathi, Wali and Subbarao 1991)

Lili$_1$	samajte	ki	aapan$_1$	libral	aahot.
Lili	think	that	self	liberal	is

'Lili$_1$ thinks that self$_1$ is liberal.'

The use of long-distance reflexives in examples like (8.44) and (8.48) can be accounted for in terms of our M-principle. Since the grammar allows the unmarked pronoun to be employed to encode coreference, the speaker will use it if such an interpretation is intended. On the other hand, if the unmarked pronoun is not used, but the marked long-distance reflexive is employed instead, then an M-implicature will be licensed, so that not only coreference but logophoricity as well is intended.

Emphaticness/contrastiveness
A second dimension of unexpectedness arising from the use of a long-distance reflexive involves **emphaticness/contrastiveness**. The use of an emphatic expression is subject to certain semantico-pragmatic conditions, such as those proposed by Baker (1995). Emphaticness typically produces a number of effects: (i) contrariety to expectation, (ii) availability of a natural negative gloss, of the sort 'and not anyone else', etc., (iii) inducing a particular anaphoric/referential interpretation, (iv) contrastive stress, and (v) giving rise to a particular scope reading (e.g., Edmondson and Plank 1978 and especially Levinson 1991). Witness, for example, (8.49).

(8.49)   (Chinese)

Zhuxi	zongshi	yiwei	ta/ziji/taziji		dui,
chairman	always	think	3SG/self/3SG-self		right
bieren	dou	bu	dui.		
other	all	not	right		

'The chairman$_1$ always thinks that he$_1$ is right, but others are all wrong.'

The use of the Chinese pronoun *bieren* 'other' is a clear indication that (8.49) conveys an emphatic/contrastive message. This seems to explain why intuitively, the use of *ziji* and *taziji* sound slightly more natural than *ta* on the indexed interpretation. Furthermore, *taziji* is intuitively felt to be more emphatic/contrastive than *ziji*. On our account, the emphaticness/contrastiveness associated with the use of a long-distance reflexive again falls out naturally from the M-principle: it is because the use of a reflexive in these contexts would carry an emphatic/contrastive message that would not be conveyed by the use of either a pronoun or a gap that it is chosen. Furthermore, the fact that the use of *taziji* is more emphatic/contrastive than that of *ziji* can also be explained by the M-principle. Given this principle, it is predicted that the use of a more prolix expression tends to give a more marked message, hence the more emphatic/contrastive reading for *taziji*.

Looked at from a slightly different vantage point, an iconicity principle is also in operation here, namely, the more coding material, the more emphatic/contrastive the message. This analysis can be extended to the use of the morphologically complex emphatics in (8.21)–(8.23) and the 'both reflexives and pronouns' cases of possessive anaphora in (8.20). Furthermore, the repetition of the r-expression in (8.25) may also be given a similar account, for it also seems to carry a contrastive, emphatic message '... but not anyone else'. All this indicates that our revised neo-Gricean pragmatic theory can account for a range of facts relating to intrasentential anaphora that have always puzzled and embarrassed Chomsky's binding conditions (see Huang 2000a, 2000b for an extension of this analysis to discourse anaphora).

Another main advantage of our theory is that conversational implicatures being cancellable, one can always arrive at an interpretation that is best in keeping with our knowledge about the world. One example may suffice to illustrate this point.

(8.50)   (Chinese)

    a. Bingren shuo yisheng zhidao Ø mingtian gei ta kaidao.
       patient say doctor know   tomorrow for 3SG operate
       'The patient$_1$ says that the surgeon$_2$ knows that (I/you/he$_{2/3}$/we/they ...) will operate on him$_1$ tomorrow.'

    b. Yisheng shuo bingren zhidao Ø mingtian gei ta kaidao.
       doctor say patient know   tomorrow for 3SG operate
       'The surgeon$_1$ says that the patient$_2$ knows that (I/you/he$_{1/3}$/we/they ...) will operate on him$_2$ tomorrow.'

Recollect that given our pragmatic apparatus in (8.32), the interpretation of an anaphoric expression is subject to the I-principle, unless there is either a Q- or an M-contrast set or both to prevent the applicability of the I-principle. What the I-principle does here is to invite a locally coreferential interpretation for the anaphoric expression. In fact, there appears to be a rigid I-heuristic here: a local subject is in general preferred to a local object; a non-split antecedent is in general favoured over a split one; and a c-commanding antecedent is in general preferred to a non-c-commanding one. If none of these NPs seems to qualify as a possible antecedent, the next, more remote clause will be examined for possibilities in the same order, and so on until the root clause is reached. Failure to find an intrasentential antecedent will lead to the search for a previous discourse antecedent, preferably a topic, or else to an 'arbitrary' interpretation. However, any anaphoric interpretation generated by our pragmatic apparatus must not run contrary to the RDRP, information saliency, and the general consistency constraints on conversational implicatures. The general consistency constraints include (i) background assumptions (or real-world knowledge), (ii) contextual information, (iii) meaning$_{nn}$, and (iv) semantic entailments. In other words, on our account, all anaphoric interpretations are subject to the requirement of consistency with background assumptions; no interpretation will arise if it is not in keeping with real-world knowledge.

Returning to (8.50), given the I-heuristic, the preferred antecedent for the zero anaphor or gap in (8.50a) is correctly predicted to be the subject of the intermediate clause *yisheng* (the surgeon). However, by the same mechanism, the zero anaphor or gap in (8.50b) would first be interpreted as being preferably coreferential with the subject of the intermediate clause *bingren* (the patient). But this interpretation clearly runs counter to our background assumption that it is stereotypically a surgeon who operates on a patient rather than vice versa. This has the immediate consequence that such an interpretation is ruled out as the preferred interpretation. As a result, the zero anaphor or gap under consideration is I-implicated to be preferably coreferential with the matrix subject *yisheng* (the surgeon) in (8.50b)—a correct consequence (see Huang 1991, 1994, 2000a for further discussion).

Have a look at Exercise 6 on p. 277.

8.5. Theoretical implications

In the previous section, I presented a revised neo-Gricean pragmatic theory of anaphora. In this section, I shall point out a number of important implications our pragmatic theory has for current linguistic theorizing.[14] One major implication is that the theory forces a radical rethink of some of the current claims about the nature of grammatical rules and the way in which they interact with pragmatic principles. In the first place, many grammatical rules underlying anaphoric universals such as Chomsky's binding conditions are general, violable tendencies rather than absolute, exceptionless restrictions. Second, these rules are not something *sui generis*, but rather have their origins in language use. In other words, they are best seen as, to use Levinson's (1987a) metaphor, 'frozen pragmatics'—the outcome of a gradual, diachronic process from utterance-token-meaning via utterance-type-meaning to sentence-type-meaning. This, of course, does not mean that these rules as they are today are not part of the grammar. On the contrary, they are, and as such they should be dealt with in the grammar. But the point is that if they are the result of a historical grammaticalization process, they can no longer be held as evidence for a biologically pre-programmed human linguistic faculty. Third, as already mentioned, pragmatics and syntax are interconnected in regulating anaphora and binding, though they are distinct levels and modes of linguistic explanation. The interface between pragmatics and syntax may in general be summarized in a Kantian apothegm: pragmatics without syntax is empty; syntax without pragmatics is blind. Furthermore, the extent to which pragmatics and syntax interact varies typologically. There exists a class of languages (such as Chinese, Japanese, and Korean) where pragmatics plays a central role which in familiar European languages (such as English, French, and German) has hitherto been alleged to be played by the grammar. In these pragmatic languages, many of the constraints on anaphora are primarily due to principles of language use rather than rules of grammatical structure (see Huang 1994, 2000a for more detailed arguments). From a diachronic viewpoint, languages seem to change from being more pragmatic to more syntactic; from a synchronic perspective, different languages may simply be at different stages of this evolution.

---

[14] In recent years this theory has generated a new industry of production of pragmatic analyses of anaphora. See for example, Kim (1993) on Korean, Blackwell (2003) on Spanish, and Chiou (in preparation) on Modern Greek. See also Demirci (2001) on the acquisition of binding of English reflexives by Turkish L2 learners.

A second major ramification of our pragmatic theory concerns current thinking about important issues such as universals, innateness, and learnability. While a pragmatic approach to anaphora such as ours does not entirely contradict Chomsky's innateness hypothesis, the fact that so many anaphoric processes in such a wide variety of geographically, genetically, and typologically distinct languages can be explained as learnable on the basis of language use does undermine Chomsky's claim for the universality of UG and decreases the plausibility of his innateness hypothesis.[15] This is because anaphora as such can no longer be taken to be mere instantiations of human mental templates. There are aspects of anaphoric universals which clearly are of a grammatical nature; there are also aspects of anaphoric universals which are equally clearly of a pragmatic nature. Put in a slightly different way, anaphoric universals are the product of both nature and nurture. The challenge before the linguist is to work out precisely what are the grammatical rules and what are the pragmatic principles, what is the relationship between them, and how they interact with each other.

It is encouraging that recent developments in generative grammar seem to be moving towards the view of the pragmatics–syntax interface being advocated in this chapter. In the case of Chomsky's minimalist programme, given that the syntax/computational system is neither a phonological nor a semantic component, a large amount of current syntactic explanation has to be shifted to the LF and PF interfaces. As a consequence, syntax has inevitably to interact with semantics and pragmatics in a much more extensive way to link it to the mental world of cognition (e.g., Chomsky 1995: 219–20). This holds, of course, for the study of anaphora.[16] Similarly, the basic notions of **Optimality-theoretic (OT)** syntax are very

[15] See Huang (2000a), which contains a rich collection of data drawn from a representative range of some 550 of the world's languages.

[16] Chomsky has never put forward any systematic pragmatic theory of anaphora. However, his work on binding contains occasional reference to pragmatic principles. One such principle is the 'avoid pronoun' principle (Chomsky 1981: 65). Another is the general discourse principle (Chomsky 1981: 227), which allows binding condition C_1 to be overridden given the appropriate context under certain circumstances, though the relevant conditions have never been spelled out by Chomsky.

In more recent work on the minimalist programme, Chomsky (1995: 138–43, 145–6, 150) argued that both derivation and representation are subject to a kind of 'least effort' guideline: there are no superfluous steps in derivation and there are no

much in the spirit of the revised neo-Gricean pragmatic theory I have advocated here.[17] In fact, some of the insights central to an OT syntactic analysis such as competition, hierarchy, and soft constraints (e.g., Legendre, Grimshaw, and Viker 2001, Blutner and Zeevat 2004) have already been independently developed in our pragmatic approach (see also Mattausch 2004 for an attempt to recast our analysis in term of bidirectional OT). All this, I hope, will open the way for a more interactive approach between the I[nternalized and intensional]- and E[externalized and extensional]-models of language study (Chomsky 1995: 15–17). It seems unlikely that we can provide a satisfactory answer to what Chomsky (1986) has referred to as Humboldt's problem and as (a special case of)

superfluous symbols in representation. The economy of derivation and representation is considered to be the functional driving force behind certain innate grammatical rules such as the last resort constraint on movement and the full interpretation principle. Furthermore, on a more global level, this principle is linked to some notion of cost in relation to UG principles and language-specific rules. UG principles are less costly than language-particular rules, so they obtain wherever possible, with language-specific rules being employed only if they are not applicable. Chomsky regarded the least-effort principle of this kind as specific to the human language faculty, but more compelling evidence is needed before such a claim can be substantiated (see also Huang 2000a for a critique of some minimalist analyses of anaphora).

[17] Optimality theory (OT) can best be seen as a revisionist or dissident version of Chomsky's generative grammar. From a cognitive point of view, while Chomsky's principles-and-parameters theory and its minimalist descendant are largely rooted in Fodor's modularity theory, OT is associated at least in part with connectionism (see note 11 of Chapter 6). Next, unlike in the principles-and-parameters theory and the minimalist programme, in OT, grammatical regularities are considered to be fundamentally representational and parallel rather than derivational and serial in nature. UG consists of a set of universal but soft (i.e., violable) constraints. The grammatical system contains (i) a lexicon, (ii) a set of constraints, (iii) a ranking of constraints, and (iv) two functions: a generator (GEN), which creates a candidate output for the input, and an evaluator (EVAL), which selects the best (or optimal) candidate for the given input from the candidate output produced by the generator. Thus, in OT, universals are expressed in universal but violable constraints. Language variation is accounted for in terms of alternative rankings of the universal constraints. Language acquisition is considered to be a process of constraints ranking and reranking within the limits set up by UG (see, e.g., Prince and Smolensky 1993, 2004, Archangeli and Langendoen 1997, and Blutner and Zeevat 2004; see also Huang 2000a for a discussion of OT analyses of anaphora).

Plato(-Russell)'s problem without even trying to tackle Descartes's problem. In other words, the full understanding of the nature and ontogeny of knowledge of language appears to be partially dependent on a better understanding of the (creative) use of that knowledge.

8.6. Summary

In this chapter, I have discussed the interface between pragmatics and syntax, focusing on anaphora and binding. Section 8.1 outlined Chomsky's views about language and linguistics. Then, Section 8.2 presented Chomsky's binding conditions, and Section 8.3 pointed out the problems for these conditions. After that, Section 8.4 provided a revised neo-Gricean pragmatic theory of anaphora. Finally, Section 8.5 considered some theoretical implications of the neo-Gricean pragmatic approach for current linguistic theorizing.

Key concepts

pragmatics–syntax interface
anaphora
anaphoric expression
antecedent
NP-anaphora
N-bar-anaphora
logical problem of language acquisition
innateness hypothesis
anaphor
pronominal
r[eferential]-expression
binding conditions A, B, and C
binding
c-command
government category (GC)
long-distance reflexive
binding conditions C_1 and C_2
general pattern of anaphora

revised neo-Gricean pragmatic theory of anaphora
referentiality hierarchy
revised disjoint reference presumption (RDRP)
predicate meaning/reflexivizing strategy correlation
logophoricity
emphaticness/contrastiveness

Exercises and essay questions

1. Of the following grammatical and ungrammatical sentences, which can, and
   which cannot, be accounted for by Chomsky's binding condition A?
   (i) $Susan_1$ hates $herself_1$.
   (ii) (Norwegian, cited in Huang 2000a)

*Jon_1	foraktet	seg_1.
Jon	despises	self

   'Jon despises himself.'
   (iii) *$Chopin_1$ thought that $Liszt_2$ adored $himself_1$
   (iv) (Marathi, Wali and Subbarao 1991)

$Lili_1$	samajate	ki	$Suši_2$	$aaplyaa-laa_1$	haste.
Lili	thinks	that	Susi	self-to	laughs

   '$Lili_1$ thinks that Susi laughs at $self_1$.'
   (v) *$Chopin_1$ believed that $himself_1$ was a poet of the piano.
   (vi) (Icelandic, cited in Huang 2000a)

$Hann_1$	sagði	að	sig_1	vantaði	hæfileika.
he	said	that	self	lacked-SBJV	ability

   'He said that self lacked ability.'

2. Of the following grammatical and ungrammatical sentences, which are, and
   which are not, accountable in terms of Chomsky's binding condition A, paying
   particular attention to c-command?
   (i) $Madonna's_1 mother_2$ admired $herself_2$.
   (ii) *$Madonna's_1 mother_2$ admired $herself_1$.
   (iii) (Chinese)

$Xiaoming_1$ de	cuxin	hai le	$ziji_1$.
Xiaoming POSS	carelessness harm PFV		self

   'Xiaoming's careless has brought harm to him.'
   (iv) (Zribi-Hertz 1995)

   $John's_1$ face turned red despite $himself_1$.
   (v) *$John's_1$ fortune saved $himself_1$.
   (vi) (Icelandic, cited in Huang 2000a)

Skoðun	Siggu$_1$er að	sig$_1$	vanti	hæfileika.
opinion	Sigga's isthat	self	lacks	talent

'Sigga's opinion is that self lacks talent.'

3. Of the following grammatical and ungrammatical sentences, which can, and which cannot, be accommodated by Lasnik's binding condition C_1 or C_2?

  (i) Blair$_1$ admired Blair$_2$

  (ii) *George W. Bush$_1$ thought that Tony Blair admired George W. Bush$_1$.

  (iii) (Vietnamese)

Ho Chi Minh$_1$	tin	Ho Chi Minh$_1$	sẽ	thăńg.
Ho Chi Minh	thinks	Ho Chi Minh	will	win

'Ho Chi Minh$_1$ thinks that Ho Chi Minh$_1$ will win.'

  (iv) Mikes$_1$ father disliked Mike$_1$.

  (v) Victoria and David Beckham$_1$ have one thing in common: she thinks that David$_1$ is a football genius and he$_1$ thinks that David$_1$ is a football genius.

  (vi) *He$_1$ admired Charles Darwin$_1$.

4. Can you explain the contrast between the (a) and (b) sentences in terms of the predicate meaning/reflexivizing strategy correlation?

  (i) (Dutch, adapted from Reinhart and Reuland 1993)

    a. Willem wast zich.

       Willem washes self

       'Willem washes (himself).'

    b. Willem bewondert zichzelf.

       Willem admires self self

       'Willem admires himself.'

  (ii) (Turkish, König and Siemund 2000, errors corrected)

    a. yaka-mak

       wash

       'wash'

    a'. 'yaka-n-mak

       wash-EMPH

       'wash oneself'

    b. vur-mak

       beat

       'beat'

    b'. (Ø) kendi kendi-si-ni vur-du.

       3SG self self-3SG-ACC beat-PAST-3SG

       'He beat himself.'

5. How can the following cases of possessive anaphora be accounted for in terms of the revised neo-Gricean pragmatic theory?

  (i) (Arabic)

As'ad$_1$	daxala	maktab-hu$_{1/2}$.
Asad	enter-PST-3MSG	office-his

'Asad$_1$ entered his$_{1/2}$ office.'

(ii) (Telugu, Subbarao and Lalitha Murthy 2000)

roojaa-ki$_1$ tana$_1$/atani$_2$ amma   anTee   iSTam.
Roja-DAT   self's/his   mother   means   liking
'Roja$_1$ likes selfs$_1$/his$_2$ mother.'

(iii) (Kannada, cited in Huang 2004a)

raama$_1$ tanna$_1$/avana$_1$ makkaLanna-   hoDedanu.
Rama   self's/his   children-ACC   beat
'Rama$_1$ beat selfs$_1$/his$_1$ children.'

6. Can you provide a neo-Gricean pragmatic analysis of the anaphoric patterns in each of the following sentences?

   (i) Kylie$_1$ liked herself$_1$.

   (ii) Kylie$_1$ liked her$_2$.

   (iii) Kylie$_1$ liked Kylie$_2$.

   (iv) Kylie$_1$ liked her$_2$ and she$_1$ gave her$_2$ a silk handkerchief.

   (v) Kylie$_1$ liked her$_2$ and the woman$_3$ gave her$_2$ a silk handkerchief.

   (vi) George W. Bush$_1$ said that he$_1$ would visit France in person.

   (vii) George W. Bush$_1$ said that the president$_1$ would visit France in person.

  (viii) (Korean)

Lee$_1$-un   caki$_1$/ku$_1$-ka   salang-ey   ppacyessta-ko   malhayssta.
Lee-TOP   self/he-NOM   love-in   fell-COMP   said
'Lee$_1$ said that self$_1$/he$_1$ was in love.'

7. What is Chomsky's view about language and linguistics?

8. Can the distributional complementarity between anaphors and pronominals dictated by Chomsky's binding conditions A and B be maintained?

9. What are the common ways of reflexive-marking a predicate? Illustrate with your own examples.

10. To what extent can Chomsky's binding conditions be reduced to pragmatics?

11. What is logophoricity? How is logophoricity grammaticalized cross-linguistically?

12. What are the theoretical implications of the revised neo-Gricean pragmatic analysis of anaphora for current linguistic theorizing?

Further readings

Huang 2000a. Sections 1.2.1, 2.1, 2.3, 3.3, 4.2.
Huang 2004a.
Levinson 2000. Chapter 4.

Glossary

ad hoc concept construction: the pragmatic adjustment of a lexical concept in the linguistically decoded logical form, the adjustment being a narrowing or strengthening, a broadening or weakening, or a combination of both.

anaphora: a relation between two linguistic elements, in which the interpretation of one (called an anaphoric expression) is in some way determined by the interpretation of the other (called an antecedent).

broad context: any contextual information that is relevant to the working out of what the speaker overtly intends to mean, and to the successful and felicitous performance of speech acts.

communicative principle of relevance: a pragmatic principle which states that every ostensive stimulus (e.g., an utterance) conveys a presumption of its own optimal relevance.

constancy under negation: a property of presupposition which dictates that a presupposition generated by the use of a lexical item or a syntactic structure remains the same when the sentence containing that lexical item or syntactic structure is negated.

constative: an utterance that is employed to make an assertion or a statement.

context: any relevant features of the dynamic setting or environment in which a linguistic unit is systematically used.

conventional implicature: a non-truth-conditional inference which is not deductive in any general, natural way from the saying of what is said, but arises solely because of the conventional features attached to particular lexical items and/or linguistic constructions.

conversational implicature: a set of non-logical inferences which contains conveyed messages which are meant without being part of what is said in the strict sense. It is derived from the saying of what is said via the co-operative principle and its component maxims of conversation.

conversational implicature$_F$: a conversational implicature that is generated by the speaker's deliberately flouting one or more of the maxims of conversation.

conversational implicature$_O$: a conversational implicature that is engendered by the speaker's directly observing the maxims of conversation.

conversational impliciture: a term coined by Kent Bach which refers to a third category of speaker-meaning—a category that is implicit in what is said, and that is intermediate between what is said and what is conversationally implicated.

co-operative principle: the overarching principle put forward by Grice in his theory of conversational implicature, which determines the way in which language is used most efficiently and effectively to achieve rational interaction in communication.

defeasibility or **cancellability**: the property that an inference can simply disappear in certain linguistic or non-linguistic contexts.

deictic expression: an expression that has the deictic usage as basic or central. Demonstratives, first- and second-person pronouns, tense markers, adverbs of time and space, and motion verbs are typical deictic expressions. By contrast, a non-deictic expression is an expression that does not have a deictic usage as basic or central. For example, third-person pronouns in English are not taken to be deictic expressions.

deixis: the phenomenon whereby features of context of utterance or speech event are encoded by lexical and/or grammatical means in a language.

direct speech act: a speech act whose illocutionary force and sentence type are directly matched. In addition, an explicit performative, which happens to be in the declarative form, is also taken to be a direct speech act, because it has its illocutionary force explicitly named by the performative verb in the main part (or 'matrix clause') of the sentence.

discourse, **text**, or **textual deixis**: the use of a linguistic expression within some utterance to point to the current, preceding, or following utterances in the same spoken or written discourse.

entailment: a semantic relation between propositions or sentences expressing propositions.

explicature: a term used in relevance theory which refers to an inferential development of one of the incomplete conceptual representations or logical forms encoded by an utterance. In other words, an explicature functions to flesh out the linguistically given incomplete logical form of the sentence uttered, yielding fully propositional content.

face: the public self-image that every member of a society claims for him- or herself.

felicity condition (on speech acts): a condition that the world must meet for a performative or speech act to be felicitous or appropriate.

free enrichment: a pragmatic process whereby the linguistically decoded logical form of the sentence uttered is conceptually enriched.

general pattern of anaphora: reduced, semantically general anaphoric expressions tend to favor locally coreferential interpretations; full, semantically specific anaphoric expressions tend to favour locally non-coreferential interpretations.

generalized conversational implicature: a conversational implicature which arises without requiring any particular contextual conditions.

Grice's circle: the problem of explaining how what is conversationally implicated can be defined in contrast to and calculated on the basis of what is said, given that what is said seems to both determine and to be determined by what is conversationally implicated.

I-principle: an upper-bounding pragmatic principle which may be (and systematically is) exploited to invite lower-bounding I-implicatures: a speaker, in saying '...p...', conversationally implicates that (for all he or she knows) '...more than p...'.

illocutionary act: an act or action intended to be performed by a speaker in uttering a linguistic expression, by virtue of the conventional force associated with it, either explicitly or implicitly.

indirect speech act: a speech act whose illocutionary force and sentence type are not directly matched.

intrusive construction: a construction in which the truth conditions of the whole depend to some extent on the conversational implicatures of the parts.

linguistic underdeterminacy thesis: the view that the linguistically encoded meaning of a sentence radically underdetermines the proposition the speaker expresses when he or she utters that sentence

locutionary act: an act of producing a meaningful linguistic expression.

logophoricity: the phenomenon in which the perspective or point of view of an internal protagonist of a sentence or discourse, as opposed to that of the current, external speaker, is reported by utilizing some morphological and/or syntactic means. The term 'perspective' or 'point of view', used here in a technical sense, is intended to encompass words, thoughts, knowledge, emotion, perception, and space-location.

long-distance reflexive: a reflexive that is bound outside its local syntactic domain, and in some cases, even crosses sentence boundaries into discourse.

M-principle: a pragmatic principle which operates primarily in terms of a set of alternates that contrast in form. The basic idea of the M-principle is that the use of a marked linguistic expression gives rise to an M-implicature that negates the interpretation associated with the use of an alternative, unmarked linguistic expression in the same set.

maxims of conversation: the term used by Grice for the nine subprinciples of his co-operative principle classified into four categories: Quality, Quantity, Relation, and Manner. The co-operative principle and its associate maxims of conversation enjoin the speaker to make a well-founded, appropriately informative, and relevant contribution to communication in a perspicuous manner.

metalinguistic negation: a device for rejecting a previous utterance on any grounds whatever, including its morphosyntactic form, its phonetic realization, its style or register, or the implicatures it potentially engenders.

narrow context: any contextual information that is relevant to the determination of the content of, or the assignment of the semantic values to, variables such as those concerning who speaks to whom, when, and where.

negative face: an individual's right to freedom of action and his or her need not to be imposed on by others. Negative politeness orients to maintaining the negative face of others. When one employs negative politeness, one tends to opt for the speech strategies that emphasize one's deference for the addressee.

Occam's eraser or **modified Occam's razor**: a particular version of Occam's razor which dictates that senses or dictionary entries must not proliferate.

Occam's razor: a metatheoretical principle which dictates that entities are not to be multiplied beyond necessity.

particularized conversational implicature: a conversational implicature whose generation requires particular contextual conditions.

performative: an utterance that is used not just to say things, but actively to do things or perform acts as well.

perlocutionary act: an act that produces consequences or effects on the audience through the uttering of a linguistic expression, such consequences or effects being special to the circumstances of the utterance.

person deixis: the identification of the interlocutors or participant-roles in a speech event.

positive face: an individual's desire to be accepted and liked by others. Positive politeness orients to preserving the positive face of others. When one uses positive politeness, one tends to choose the speech strategies that emphasize one's solidarity with the addressee.

pragmatic intrusion: the phenomenon whereby the pragmatically inferred content intrudes or enters into the conventional, truth-conditional content of what is said.

pragmatics: the systematic study of meaning by virtue of, or dependent on, the use of language. The central topics of inquiry of pragmatics include implicature, presupposition, speech acts, and deixis.

presupposition: an inference or proposition whose truth is taken for granted in the utterance of a sentence. The main function of presupposition is to act as a precondition of some sort for the appropriate use of the sentence. This background assumption will remain in force when the sentence that contains it is negated.

presupposition projection problem: the problem of stating and explaining the presuppositions of complex sentences (as 'wholes') in terms of the presuppositions of their component simple sentences (as 'parts').

presupposition trigger: a lexical item and/or linguistic construction that engenders a presupposition.

proposition: what is expressed by a sentence when that sentence is used to make a statement, that is, to say something, true or false, about some state of affairs in the outside world.

propositional radical: a propositional fragment that needs to be completed contextually to become fully propositional.

Q-principle: a lower-bounding pragmatic principle which may be (and characteristically is) exploited to engender upper-bounding Q-implicatures: a speaker, in saying '...p...', conversationally implicates that (for all he or she knows) '...at most p...'.

Q-scale or **Horn-scale**: a semantic scale in which the semantically strong linguistic expression entails the semantically weak one; both linguistic expressions are equally lexicalized, of the same word class, and from the same register; and they are from the same semantic field, e.g., <all, most, many, some>, <boiling, hot, warm>, and <identical, similar>. The use of the semantically weak linguistic expression in a Q- or Horn-scale gives rise to a Q-scalar implicature.

relevance theory: a cognitive-pragmatic theory developed by Dan Sperber and Deirdre Wilson. Grounded in a general view of human cognition, the central thesis of the theory is that the human cognitive system works in such a way as to tend to maximize relevance with respect to communication.

saturation: a pragmatic process whereby a given slot, position, or variable in the linguistically decoded logical form is contextually filled.

scope principle: a principle which states that a pragmatically determined aspect of meaning is part of what is said (and, therefore, not a conversational implicature) if—and perhaps only if—it falls within the scope of logical operators.

semantic transfer: a pragmatic process whereby the concept literally expressed by the input proposition is transferred into a different concept, provided that there is a salient functional relation between the old and the new concepts.

sentence: a well-formed string of words put together by the grammatical rules of a language. As a unit of the language system, it is an abstract entity or construct defined within a theory of grammar.

social deixis: the codification of the social status of the speaker, the addressee, or a third person or entity referred to, as well as of the social relationships between them.

space deixis: the specification of location in space relative to that of the participants at utterance time in a speech event. Other terms include place, spatial, local, and locational deixis.

speech act: the uttering of a linguistic expression whose function is not just to say things but actively to do things or to perform acts as well.

time deixis: concerned with the encoding of temporal points and spans relative to the time at which an utterance is produced in a speech event.

truth condition: a condition that the world must meet for a sentence to be true.

truth value: a notion that is associated with proposition. A proposition may be true or false, but the truth or falsity of a proposition may vary from utterance occasion to utterance occasion. However, on a particular occasion, a proposition has a definite truth value, that is, it is either true or false. It is true if and only if it corresponds to some state of affairs that obtains on that occasion, and it is false if and only if it does not.

unarticulated constituent: a propositional constituent that is not expressed linguistically.

utterance: the use of a particular piece of language—be it a word, a phrase, a sentence, or a sequence of sentences—by a particular speaker on a particular occasion.

References

ACHIBA, MACHIKO (2003). *Learning to request in a second language: a study of child interlanguage pragmatics*. Clevedon: Multilingual Matters.

AGHA, AZIF (1996). Schema and superposition in spatial deixis. *Anthropological Linguistics* 38: 643–82.

AGYEKUM, KOFI (2004). The socio-cultural concept of face in Akan communication. *Pragmatics and Cognition* 12: 71–92.

ALISEDA-LIERA, A., VAN GLABBEEK, R., and WESTERSTAHL, D. (eds.) (1998). *Computing natural language*. Stanford: CSLI.

ALLAN, KEITH (2001). *Natural language semantics*. Oxford: Blackwell.

ALLWOOD, JENS (2000). An activity-based approach to pragmatics. In Bunt, H. and Black, W. (eds.) 47–80.

ALPHER, B. (1987). Feminine as the unmarked grammatical gender: buffalo girls are no fools. *Australian Journal of Linguistics* 7: 169–88.

ALSTON, WILLIAM (1994). Illocutionary acts and linguistic meaning. In Tsohatzidis, S. L. (ed.) 29–49.

ANDERSON, STEPHEN R. and KEENAN, EDWARD L. (1985). Deixis. In Shopen, T. (ed.) 259–308.

ANNAMALAI, E. (2000). Lexical anaphors and pronouns in Tamil. In Lust, B. et al. (eds.) 169–216.

ANSCOMBRE, JEAN-CLAUDE and DUCROT, OSWALD (1977). Deux *mais* en français? *Lingua* 43: 23–40.

ARCHANGELI, DIANA and LANGENDOEN, D. TERENCE (eds.) (1997). *Optimality Theory: an overview*. Oxford: Blackwell.

ARIEL, MIRA (1990). *Assessing noun-phrase antecedents*. London: Routledge.

ARIEL, MIRA (2004). *Most. Language* 80: 658–706.

ASHER, NICHOLAS and LASCARIDES, ALEX (1998). The semantics and pragmatics of presupposition. *Journal of Semantics* 15: 215–38.

ATLAS, JAY D. (1975). Frege's polymorphous concept of presupposition and its role in a theory of meaning. *Semantikos* 1: 29–44.

ATLAS, JAY D. (1977). Negation, ambiguity, and presupposition. *Linguistics and Philosophy* 1: 321–36.

ATLAS, JAY D. (1989). *Philosophy without ambiguity: a logico-linguistic essay*. Oxford: Oxford University Press.

ATLAS, JAY D. (1993). The importance of being 'only': testing the neo-Gricean versus neo-entailment paradigms. *Journal of Semantics* 10: 301–18.

ATLAS, JAY D. (1997). On the modularity of sentence processing: semantic generality and the language of thought. In Nuyts, J. and Pederson, E. (eds.) *Language and conceptualization*. Cambridge: Cambridge University Press. 213–28.

ATLAS, JAY D. (2004). Presupposition. In Horn, L. R. and Ward, G. (eds.) 29–52.

ATLAS, JAY D. (2005). *Logic, meaning, and conversation: semantic underdeterminacy, implicature, and their interface*. Oxford: Oxford University Press.

ATLAS, JAY D. and LEVINSON, STEPHEN C. (1981). It-clefts, informativeness and logical form: radical pragmatics. In Cole, P. (ed.) 1–61.

AUSTIN, J. L. (1962). *How to do things with words*. Oxford: Oxford University Press.

AUSTIN, J. L. (1975). *How to do things with words*. 2nd edn. Oxford: Oxford University Press.

AUSTIN, PETER (1982). The deictic system of Diyari. In Weissenborn, J. and Klein, W. (eds.) 273–84.

BABA, JUNKO (1999). Interlanguage pragmatics: compliment responses by learners of Japanese and English as a second language. München: Lincom Europa.

BACH, KENT (1987). *Thought and reference*. Oxford: Clarendon Press.

BACH, KENT (1994a). Conversational impliciture. *Mind and Language* 9: 124–62.

BACH, KENT (1994b). Semantic slack: what is said and more. In Tsohatzidis, S. (ed.) 267–91.

BACH, KENT (1995). Standardization vs. conventionalization. *Linguistics and Philosophy* 18: 677–86.

BACH, KENT (1999a). The semantics–pragmatics distinction: what it is and why it matters. In Turner, K. (ed.) 65–84.

BACH, KENT (1999b). The myth of conventional implicature. *Linguistics and Philosophy* 22: 327–66.

BACH, KENT (2000). Quantification, qualification and context: a reply to Stanley and Szabó. *Mind and Language* 15: 262–83.

BACH, KENT (2001). You don't say? *Synthèse* 127: 11–31.

BACH, KENT (2002). Seemingly semantic institutions. In Campbell, J. K. et al. (eds.) 21–33.

BACH, KENT (2004). Pragmatics and the philosophy of language. In Horn, L. R. and Ward, G. (eds.) 463–87.

BACH, KENT (2005). Context *ex machina*. In Szabó, Z. G. (ed.) 15–44.

BACH, KENT and HARNISH, ROBERT M. (1979). *Linguistic communication and speech acts*. Cambridge, MA: MIT Press.

BAKER, C. L. (1995). Contrast, discourse prominence, and intensification, with special reference to locally free reflexives in British English. *Language* 71: 63–101.

BALLMER, THOMAS (1975). Einführung und Kontrolle von Diskurswelten. In Wunderlich, D. (ed.) *Linguistische Pragmatik*. Berlin: Athenäum-Verlag. 183–206.

BALLMER, THOMAS (1978). *Logical grammar: with special consideration of topics in context change*. Amsterdam: North-Holland.

BAR-HILLEL, YEHOSHNA (1954). Indexical expressions. *Mind* 63: 359–79.

BAR-HILLEL, YEHOSHUA (1971). Out of the pragmatic wastebasket. *Linguistic Inquiry* 2: 401–7.

BARKER, STEPHEN (1991). *Even, still* and counterfactuals. *Linguistics and Philosophy* 14: 1–38.

BARKER, STEPHEN (2000). Is value content a component of conventional implicature? *Analysis* 60: 268–79.

BARKER, STEPHEN (2003). Truth and conventional implicature. *Mind* 112: 1–34.

BARRON, ANNE (2003). *Acquisition in interlanguage pragmatics*. Amsterdam: John Benjamins.

BARSALOU, LAURENCE (1983). Ad hoc categories. *Memory and Cognition* 11: 211–27.

BARTON, ELLEN (1988). *Base-generated constituents: a theory of grammatical structure and pragmatic interpretation*. Amsterdam: John Benjamins.

BATORI, ISTVAN (1982). On verb deixis in Hungarian. In Weissenborn, J. and Klein, W. (eds.) 155–65.

BAUERLE, R., REYLE, U., and ZIMMERMAN, T. E. (2003). *Presuppositions and discourse: essays offered to Hans Kamp*. Oxford: Elsevier.

BAYRAKTAROGLU, ARIN (2001). Advice-giving in Turkish: 'superiority' or 'solidarity'? In Bayraktaroglu, A. and Sifianou, M. (eds.) 177–208.

BAYRAKTAROGLU, ARIN and SIFIANOU, MARIA (eds.) (2001). *Linguistic politeness across boundaries: the case of Greek and Turkish*. Amsterdam: John Benjamins.

BEAVER, DAVID I. (1997). Presupposition. In van Benthem, J. and ter Meulen, A. (eds.) *Handbook of logic and language*. Amsterdam: North-Holland. 939–1008.

BEAVER, DAVID I. (2001). *Presupposition and assertion in dynamic semantics*. Stanford: CSLI.

BECHTEL, WILLIAM and ABRAHAMSEN, ADELE (1991). *Connectionism and the mind: an introduction to parallel processing in networks*. Oxford: Blackwell.

BECKER, ANGELIKA and MARY, CARROL (1997). *The acquisition of spatial relations in a second language*. Amsterdam: John Benjamins.

BELNAP, NOEL (1969). Questions: their presuppositions, and how they can fail to arise. In Lambert, K. (ed.) *The logical way of doing things*. New Haven: Yale University Press.

BENZ, ANTON, JÄGER, GERHARD, and VAN ROOY, ROBERT (2006). *Game theory and pragmatics*. London: Palgrave Macmillan.

BERG, JONATHAN (2002). Is semantics still possible? *Journal of Pragmatics* 34: 349–59.

BERGMAN, MARC L. and KASPER, GABRIELE (1993). Perception and performance in native and non-native apology. In Kasper, G. and Blum-Kulka, S. (eds.) 82–107.

BERTOLET, ROD (1994). Are there indirect speech acts? In Tsohatzidis, S. (ed.) 335–49.

BEZUIDENHOUT, ANNE (2002). Generalized conversational implicatures and default pragmatic inferences. In Campbell, J. K. et al. (eds.) 257–83.

BEZUIDENHOUT, ANNE and CUTTING, C. (2002). Literal meaning, minimal propositions and pragmatic processing. *Journal of Pragmatics* 34: 433–56.

BEZUIDENHOUT, ANNE and MORRIS, ROBIN K. (2004). Implicature, relevance and default pragmatic inference. In Noveck, I. and Sperber, D. (eds.) 257–82.

BHAT, DARBHE (2004). *Pronouns.* Oxford: Oxford University Press.

BIANCHI, CLAUDIA (2004a). Semantics and pragmatics: the distinction reloaded. In Bianchi, C. (ed.) 1–11.

BIANCHI, CLAUDIA (ed.) (2004b). *The semantics/pragmatics distinction.* Stanford: CSLI.

BIRD, GRAHAM (1994). Relevance theory and speech acts. In Tsohatzidis, S. (ed.) 292–311.

BISHOP, D. (1997). *Uncommon understanding.* Hove: Psychology Press.

BLACKWELL, SARAH E. (2003). *Implicatures in discourse: the case of Spanish NP anaphora.* Amsterdam: John Benjamins.

BLAKEMORE, DIANE (1987). *Semantic constraints on relevance.* Oxford: Blackwell.

BLAKEMORE, DIANE (2000). Procedures and indicators: *nevertheless* and *but. Journal of Linguistics* 36: 463–86.

BLAKEMORE, DIANE (2002). *Relevance and linguistic meaning: the semantics and pragmatics of discourse markers.* Cambridge: Cambridge University Press.

BLAKEMORE, DIANE (2004). Discourse markers. In Horn, L. R. and Ward, G. (eds.) 221–40.

BLASS, REGINA (1990). *Relevance relations in discourse: a study with special reference to Sissala.* Cambridge: Cambridge University Press.

BLOOM, PAUL (2000). *How children learn the meanings of the words.* Cambridge, MA: MIT Press.

BLOOM, PAUL (2002). Mindreading, communication and the learning of names for things. *Mind and Language* 17: 37–54.

BLOOMFIELD, LEONARD (1962). *The Menomini language.* New Haven: Yale University Press.

BLUM-KULKA, SHOSHANA, HOUSE, JULIANE, and KASPER, GABRIELE (eds.) (1989). *Cross-cultural pragmatics: requests and apologies.* Norwood: Ablex.

BLUM-KULKA, SHOSHANA and OLSHTAIN, E. (1984). Requests and apologies: a cross-cultural study of speech act realization patterns (CCSARP). *Applied Linguistics*: 5: 196–213.

BLUTNER, REINHARD (1998). Lexical pragmatics. *Journal of Semantics* 15: 115–62.

BLUTNER, REINHARD (2004). Pragmatics and the lexicon. In Horn, L. R. and Ward, G. (eds.). 488–514.

BLUTNER, REINHARD and ZEEVAT, HENK (eds.) (2004). *Optimality theory and pragmatics.* New York: Palgrave Macmillan.

BOËR, STEVEN E. and LYCAN, WILLIAM G. (1976). *The myth of semantic presupposition.* Bloomington: Indiana University Linguistic Club.

BORG, EMMA (2004). *Minimal semantics.* Oxford: Clarendon Press.

BOTNE, ROBERT (2005). Cognitive schemas and motion verbs: COMING and GOING in Chindali (Eastern Bantu). *Cognitive Linguistics* 16: 43–80.

BRADLEY, RAYMOND and SWARTZ, NORMAN (1979). *Possible world: an introduction to logic and its philosophy*. Oxford: Blackwell.

BRAUN, DAVID (1995). What is character? *Journal of Philosophical Logic* 24: 227–40.

BRAUN, DAVID (1996). Demonstratives and their linguistic meanings. *Noûs* 30: 145–73.

BREHENY, RICHARD, KATSOS, NAPOLEON, and WILLIAMS, JOHN (forthcoming). Are scalar implicatures generated by default? *Cognition*.

BRIDGE, DEREK (1991). Computing presuppositions in an incremental natural language processing system. PhD dissertation. University of Cambridge.

BROWN, J. K. (1975). Iroquois women: an ethnohistoric note. In Reiter, R. (ed.) *Toward an anthropology of women*. New York: Monthly Review Press. 235–51.

BROWN, PENELOPE and LEVINSON, STEPHEN C. (1978). Politeness: some universals in language usage. In Goody, E. N. (ed.) *Questions and politeness*. Cambridge: Cambridge University Press. 56–310.

BROWN, PENELOPE and LEVINSON, STEPHEN C. (1987). *Politeness: some universals in language usage*. Cambridge: Cambridge University Press.

BROWN, ROGER W. and GILMAN, ALBERT (1960). The pronouns of power and solidarity. In Sebeok, T. A. (ed.) *Style in language*. Cambridge, MA: MIT Press. 253–76.

BÜHLER, KARL (1934). The deictic field of language and deictic words. In Jarvella, R. J. and Klein, W. (eds.) (1982) 9–30.

BUNT, HARRY and BLACK, WILLIAM (eds.) (2000). *Abduction, belief and context in dialogue: studies in computational pragmatics*. Amsterdam: John Benjamins.

BURQUEST, DONALD A. (1986). The pronoun system of some Chadic languages. In Wiesemann, U. (ed.) 70–102.

BURTON-ROBERTS, N. (1989). *The limits to debate*. Cambridge: Cambridge University Press.

BURTON-ROBERTS, N. (1999). Presupposition-cancellation and metalinguistic negation: a reply to Carston. *Journal of Linguistics* 35: 347–64.

BURZIO, LUIGI (1991). The morphological basis of anaphora. *Journal of Linguistics* 27: 81–105.

BURZIO, LUIGI (1996). The role of the antecedent in anaphoric relations. In Fredin, R. (ed.) *Current issues in comparative grammar*. Dordrecht: Kluwer. 1–45.

CAMPBELL, J. K., O'ROUILEE, M., and SHIET, D. (eds.) *Meaning and truth: Investigations in philosophical semantics*. New York: Seven Bridges Press.

CAPPELEN, HERMAN and LEPORE, ERNIE (2005). *Insensitive semantics*. Oxford: Blackwell.

CARNAP, RUDOLF (1942). *Introduction to semantics*. Cambridge, MA: Harvard University Press.

CARRUTHERS, PETER and SMITH, PETER (eds.) (1996). *Theories of theories of mind*. Cambridge: Cambridge University Press.

CARSTON, ROBYN (1988). Implicature, explicature, and truth-theoretic semantics. In Kempson, R. (ed.) *Mental representations*. Cambridge: Cambridge University Press. 155–81.

CARSTON, ROBYN (1998). Informativeness, relevance and scalar implicatures. In Carston, R. and Uchida, S. (eds.) *Relevance theory: applications and implications*. Amsterdam: John Benjamins. 179–236.

CARSTON, ROBYN (2002). *Thoughts and utterances: the pragmatics of explicit communication*. Oxford: Blackwell.

CARSTON, ROBYN (2004). Relevance theory and the saying/implicating distinction. In Horn, L. R. and Ward, G. (eds.) 633–56.

CERIA, VERÓNICA G. and SANDALO, FILOMENA (1995). A preliminary reconstruction of Proto-Waikurúan with special reference to pronominals and demonstratives. *Anthropological Linguistics* 37: 169–91.

CHALMERS, D. (1993). Connectionism and compositionality: why Fodor and Pylyshyn were wrong. *Philosophical Psychology* 6: 305–19.

CHAPMAN, SIOBHAN (2005). *Paul Grice: philosopher and linguist*. London: Palgrave Macmillan.

CHIERCHIA, GENNARO (2004). Scalar implicatures, polarity phenomena, and the syntax/pragmatics interface. In Belletti, A. (ed.) *Structures and beyond*. Oxford: Oxford University Press. 39–103.

CHIERCHIA, GENNARO and MCCONNELL-GINET, SALLY (2000). Meaning and grammar. 2nd edn. Cambridge, MA: MIT Press.

CHIOU, MICHAEL (in preparation). NP-anaphora in Modern Greek: a neo-Gricean pragmatic approach. PhD dissertation. University of Reading.

CHOMSKY, NOAM (1981). *Lectures on government and binding*. Dordrecht: Foris.

CHOMSKY, NOAM (1982). *On the generative enterprise*. Dordrecht: Foris.

CHOMSKY, NOAM (1986). *Knowledge of language: its nature, origin and use*. New York: Praeger.

CHOMSKY, NOAM (1995). *The minimalist program*. Cambridge, MA: MIT Press.

CLARK, EVE (2003). *First language acquisition*. Cambridge: Cambridge University Press.

CLARK, EVE V. (2004). Pragmatics and language acquisition. In Horn, L. R. and Ward, G. (eds.) 562–77.

CLARK, HERBERT H. (1996). *Using language*. Cambridge: Cambridge University Press.

COHEN, L. JONATHAN (1971). Some remarks on Grice's views about the logical particles of natural language. In Bar-Hillel, Y. (ed.) *Pragmatics of natural languages*. Dordrecht: Reidel. 50–68.

COHEN, L. JONATHAN (1977). Can the conversationalist hypothesis be defended? *Philosophical Studies* 31: 81–90.

COLARUSSO, JOHN (1989). East Circassian (Kabardian dialect). In Hewitt, B. G. (ed.) *The indigenous languages of the Caucasus* vol. 2. New York: Caravan Books. 261–355.

COLE, PETER (ed.) (1978). *Syntax and semantics 9: pragmatics*. London: Academic Press.

COLE, PETER (ed.) (1981). *Radical pragmatics*. London: Academic Press.

COLE, PETER and MORGAN, JERRY (eds.) (1975). *Syntax and semantics 3: speech acts*. London: Academic Press.

COMRIE, BERNARD (1976). Linguistic politeness axes: speaker-addressee, speaker-reference, speaker-bystander. Pragmatic microfiche 1.7: A3–B1.

COMRIE, BERNARD (1985). *Tense*. Cambridge: Cambridge University Press.

COMRIE, BERNARD (1989). Some general properties of reference-tracking system. In Arnold, D. et al. (eds.) *Essays on grammatical theory and universal grammar*. Oxford: Oxford University Press. 37–51.

CORBETT, GREVILLE G. (1991). *Gender*. Cambridge: Cambridge University Press.

CORBETT, GREVILLE G. (2000). *Number*. Cambridge: Cambridge University Press.

COULMAS, FLORIAN (1981). Poison to your soul: thanks and apologies contrastively viewed. In Coulmas, F. (ed.) *Conversational routine: explorations in standardized communication situations and prepatterned speech*. The Hague: Mouton. 131–48.

COULMAS, FLORIAN (1982). Some remarks on Japanese deictics. In Weissenborn, J. and Klein, W. (eds.) 209–21.

CROFT, WILLIAM (1994). Speech act classification, language typology and cognition. In Tsohatzidis, S. (ed.) 460–77.

CRUSE, D. ALLAN (2004). *Meaning in language: an introduction to semantics and pragmatics*. 2nd edn. Oxford: Oxford University Press.

CULY, CHRISTOPHER (1994). Aspects of logophoric marking. *Linguistics* 32: 1055–94.

CYSOUW, MICHAEL (2002). 'We' rules: the impact of an inclusive/exclusive opposition on the paradigmatic structure of person marking. In Simon, H. and Wiese, H. (eds.) 41–62.

CYSOUW, MICHAEL (2003). *The paradigmatic structure of person marking*. Oxford: Oxford University Press.

DAHL, ÖSTEN (1985). *Tense and aspect systems*. Oxford: Blackwell.

DASCAL, MARCELO (1981). Contextualism. In Parret, H. et al. (eds.) *Possibilities and limitations of pragmatics*. Amsterdam: John Benjamins. 153–77.

DASCAL, MARCELO (1994). Speech act theory and Gricean pragmatics: some differences of detail that make a difference. In Tsohatzidis, S. (ed.).

DAVIES, MARTIN and STONE, TONY (eds.) (1995). *Mental simulation: philosophical and psychological essays*. Oxford: Blackwell.

DAVIS, WAYNE A. (1998). *Implicature: intention, convention, and principle in the failure of Gricean theory*. Cambridge: Cambridge University Press.

DE SOUSA MELO, CANDIDA (2002). Possible directions of fit between mind, language and the world. In Vanderveken, D. and Kubo, S. (eds.) 109–17.

DEMIRCI, MAHIDE (2001). Acquisition of binding of English reflexives by Turkish L2 learners: a neo-Gricean pragmatic account. *Journal of Pragmatics* 33: 753–75.

DENNY, J. P. (1982). Semantics of the Inuktitut (Eskimo) spatial deictics. *International Journal of American Linguistics* 48: 359–84.

DIESSEL, HOLGER (1999). *Demonstratives: form, function and grammaticalization.* Amsterdam: John Benjamins.

DILLER, ANTHONY (1993). Diglossic grammaticality in Thai. In Foley, W. A. (ed.) 393–420.

DIXON, R. M. W. (1972). *The Dyirbal language of North Queensland.* Cambridge: Cambridge University Press.

DIXON, R. M. W. (1977). *A grammar of Yidin.* Cambridge: Cambridge University Press.

DIXON, R. M. W. (1980). *The languages of Australia.* Cambridge: Cambridge University Press.

DIXON, R. M. W. (2003). Demonstratives: a cross-linguistic typology. *Studies in Language* 27: 61–112.

DONNELLAN, KEITH (1966). Reference and definite descriptions. *Philosophical Review* 75: 281–304.

DREW, PAUL and WOOTON, ANTHONY (eds.) (1988). *Erving Goffman: exploring the interaction order.* Cambridge: Polity Press.

DUCROT, OSWALD (1972). *Dire et ne pas dire.* Paris: Hermann.

DUFON, MARGARET A., KASPER, GABRIELE, TAKAHASHI, SATOMI, and YOSHINAGA, NAOKO (1994). Bibliography on linguistic politeness. *Journal of Pragmatics* 21: 527–78.

DURANTI, ALESSANDRO (1992). Language in context and language as context: the Samoan respect vocabulary. In Duranti, A. and Goodwin, C. (eds.).

DURANTI, ALESSANDRO (1997). *Linguistic anthropology.* Cambridge: Cambridge University Press.

DURANTI, ALESSANDRO and GOODWIN, CHARLES (eds.) (1992). *Rethinking context.* Cambridge: Cambridge University Press.

EDMONDSON, JEROLD A. and PLANK, FRANS (1978). Great expectations: an intensive *self* analysis. *Linguistics and Philosophy* 2: 373–413.

EDMONDSON, WILLIS and HOUSE, JULIA (1991). Do learners talk too much? The waffle phenomenon in interlanguage pragmatics. In Philippson, R. et al. (eds.) *Foreign language pedagogy research.* Clevedon: Multilingual Matters.

EISENSTEIN, MIRIAM and BODMAN, JEAN (1993). Expressing gratitude in American English. In Kasper, G. and Blum-Kulka, S. (eds.) 64–81.

ELLIS, ROD (1994). *The study of second language acquisition.* Oxford: Oxford University Press.

EVANS, GARETH (1980). Pronouns. *Linguistic Inquiry* 11: 337–62.

EVANS, NICHOLAS (1993). Code, inference, placedness and ellipsis. In Foley, W. A. (ed.) 241–80.

FARMER, ANN K. and HARNISH, ROBERT M. (1987). Communicative reference with pronouns. In Verschueren, J. and Bertuccelli-Papi, M. (eds.) 547–65.

FARNCESCOTTI, R. M. (1995). *Even*: the conventional implicature approach reconsidered. *Linguistics and Philosophy* 18: 153–73.

FAUCONNIER, GILLES (1985). *Mental spaces*. Cambridge, MA: MIT Press.

FAUCONNIER, GILLES (2004). Pragmatics and cognitive linguistics. In Horn, L. R. and Ward, G. (eds.) 657–74.

FENG, GUANGWU (2006). Pragmatic markers in Chinese and a theory of conventional implicature. PhD dissertation. University of Reading.

FILLMORE, CHARLES J. (1971). *The Santa Cruz lectures on deixis*. Bloomington, IN: Indiana University Linguistic Club.

FILLMORE, CHARLES J. (1982). Towards a descriptive framework for spatial deixis. In Jarvella, R. J. and Klein, W. (eds.) 31–59.

FILLMORE, CHARLES J. (1997). *Lectures on deixis*. Stanford: CSLI.

FODOR, JERRY (1983). *The modularity of mind*. Cambridge, MA: MIT Press.

FODOR, JERRY (2001). Language, thought and compositionality. *Mind and Language* 16: 1–15.

FODOR, JERRY and PYLYSHYN, Z. (1988). Connectionism and cognitive architecture: a critical analysis. *Cognition* 28: 3–71.

FOLEY, WILLIAM A. (ed.) (1993). *The role of theory in language description*. Berlin: Mouton de Gruyter.

FORTESCUE, MICHAEL (1984). *West Greenlandic Eskimo*. London: Croom Helm.

FRAJZYNGIER, ZYGMUNT (1985). Logophoric systems in Chadic. *Journal of African Languages and Linguistics* 7: 23–37.

FRAJZYNGIER, ZYGMUNT and CURL, TRACI S. (eds.) (2000). *Reflexives: forms and functions*. Amsterdam: John Benjamins.

FRASER, BRUCE (1988). Motor oil is motor oil: an account of English nominal tautologies. *Journal of Pragmatics* 12: 215–20.

FRASER, BRUCE (1990). Perspectives on politeness. *Journal of Pragmatics* 14: 219–36.

FREGE, GOTTLOB (1892). Über Sinn and Bedeutung. *Zeitschrift für Philosophie und Philosophisch Kritik* 100: 25–50. Trans. as On sense and reference. In Geach, P. and Black, M. (eds.) (1952). *Translations from the philosophical writings of Gottlob Frege*. Oxford: Blackwell. 56–78.

FREGE, GOTTLOB (1897). *Logic*. In Hermes et al. (eds.) (1979), *Gottlob Frege: posthumous writings*. Oxford: Blackwell. 126–51.

FRETHEIM, THORSTEIN (1992). The effect of intonation on a type of scalar implicature. *Journal of Pragmatics* 18: 1–30.

FRITZ, THOMAS A. (2003). 'Look here, what I am saying!': speaker deixis and implicature as the basis of modality and future tense. In Lenz, F. (ed.) 135–51.

FUKUSHIMA, SAEKO (2002). *Requests and culture: politeness in British English and Japanese*. Bern: Peter Lang.

GANDOUR, JACKSON T. (1978). On the deictic use of verbs of motion *come* and *go* in Thai. *Anthropological Linguistics* 20: 381–94.

GASS, SUSAN M. and HOUCK, NOËL (2000). *Interlanguage refusals: a cross-cultural study of Japanese-English*. Berlin: Mouton de Gruyter.

GATHERCOLE, VIRGINIA C. (1977). A study of the comings and goings of the speakers of four languages: Spanish, Japanese, English and Turkish. *Kansas Working Papers in Linguistics* 2: 61–94.

GAUKER, CHRISTOPHER (2003). *Words without meaning*. Cambridge, MA: MIT Press.

GAZDAR, GERALD (1979). *Pragmatics: implicature, presupposition and logical form*. London: Academic Press.

GEURTS, BART (1998). Presuppositions and anaphors in attitude contexts. *Linguistics and Philosophy* 21: 545–601.

GEURTS, BART (1999). *Presuppositions and pronouns*. Oxford: Elsevier Science.

GIBBS, RAYMOND (1999). Speakers' intentions and pragmatic theory. *Cognition* 69: 355–9.

GIBBS, RAYMOND (2002). A new look at literal meaning in understanding what is said and what is implicated. *Journal of Pragmatics* 34: 457–86.

GIBBS, RAYMOND and MOISE, JESSICA (1997). Pragmatics in understanding what is said. *Cognition* 62: 51–74.

GODDARD, CLIFF (1998). *Semantic analysis: a practical introduction*. Oxford: Oxford University Press.

GOFFMAN, ERVING (1967). *Interaction ritual: essays on face to face behavior*. New York: Anchor Books.

GOFFMAN, ERVING (1979). Footing. *Semiotica* 25: 1–29.

GOLDBERG, ADELE E. (1995). *Constructions: a construction grammar approach to argument structure*. Chicago: University of Chicago Press.

GORDON, DAVID and LAKOFF, GEORGE (1975). Conversational postulates. In Cole, P. and Morgan, J. (eds.) 83–106.

GREEN, GEORGIA M. (1975). How to get people to do things with words: the whimperative question. In Cole, P. and Morgan, J. (eds.) 107–42.

GREEN, GEORGIA M. (1996). *Pragmatics and natural language understanding*. 2nd edn. Mahwah, NJ: Lawrence Erlbaum.

GREEN, GEORGIA M. (2004). Some interactions of pragmatics and grammar. In Horn, L. R. and Ward, G. (eds.) 407–26.

GREEN, MITCHELL (1995). Quantity, volubility and some varieties of discourse. *Linguistics and Philosophy* 18: 83–112.

GREEN, MITCHELL (1998). Direct reference and implicature. *Philosophical Studies* 91: 61–90.

GREENBERG, J. H. (ed.) (1963). *Universals of language*. Cambridge, MA: MIT Press.

GREENBERG, J. H. (1966). *Language universals*. The Hague: Mouton.

GREENBERG, J. H., FERGUSON, C. A., and MORAVCSIK, E. A. (eds.) (1978). *Universals of human language*, 4 vols. Stanford: Stanford University Press.

GRENOBLE, L. (1994). Discourse deixis and information tracking. *Proceedings of the Annual Meeting of the Berkeley Linguistics Society* 20: 208–19.

GRICE, H. P. (1957). Meaning. *Philosophical Review* 66: 377–88.

GRICE, H. P. (1961). The causal theory of perception. *The Aristotelian Society: Proceedings*, Supplementary Volume 35: 121–168.

GRICE, H. P. (1969). Utterer's meaning and intentions. *Philosophical Review* 78: 147–77.

GRICE, H. P. (1975). Logic and conversation. In Cole, P. and Morgan, J. (eds.) 41–58.

GRICE, H. P. (1978). Further notes on logic and conversation. In Cole, P. (ed.) 113–28.

GRICE, H. P. (1981). Presupposition and conversational implicature. In Cole, P. (ed.) 183–98.

GRICE, H. P. (1989). *Studies in the way of words*. Cambridge, MA: Harvard University Press.

GRUNDY, PETER (2000). *Doing pragmatics*. 2nd edn. London: Arnold.

GU, YUEGUO (1990). Politeness phenomena in Modern Chinese. *Journal of Pragmatics* 14: 237–57.

HAIMAN, JOHN (1985a). *Natural syntax*. Cambridge: Cambridge University Press.

HAIMAN, JOHN (ed.) (1985b). *Iconicity in syntax*. Amsterdam: John Benjamins.

HAMBLIN, J. L. and GIBBS, R. W. (2003). Processing the meanings of what speakers say and implicate. *Discourse Processes* 35: 59–80.

HANKS, W. F. (1992). The indexical ground of deictic reference. In Duranti, A. and Goodwin, C. (eds.) 43–76.

HARLEY, HEIDI and RITTER, ELIZABETH (2002). Person and number in pronouns: a feature-geometric analysis. *Language* 78: 482–526.

HARNISH, ROBERT M. (1976). Logical form and implicature. In Beaver, T., Katz, J., and Langendoen, D. T. (eds.) *An integrated theory of linguistic ability*. New York: Crowell. 313–92.

HARRIS, RANDY ALLEN (1993). *The linguistic wars*. Oxford: Oxford University Press.

HARRIS, STEPHEN G. (1984). *Culture and learning: tradition and education in northeast Arnhem Land*. Canberra: Australian Institute of Aboriginal Studies.

HARRISON, S. P. (1976). *Makilese reference grammar*. Honolulu: University of Hawaii Press.

HAUSER, MARC (1996). *The evolution of communication*. Cambridge, MA: MIT Press.

HAVILAND, JOHN B. (1979). Guugu Yimidhirr brother-in-law language. *Language in Society* 8: 365–93.

HAVILAND, JOHN B. (1997). Shouts, shrieks, and shots: untruly political conversations in indigenous Chiapas. *Pragmatics* 7: 547–74.

HAWKINS, JOHN A. (1991). On (in)definite articles: implicatures and (un)grammaticality prediction. *Journal of Linguistics* 27: 405–42.

HEATH, J. (1980). Nunggubuyu deixis, anaphora, and culture. *Papers from the Regional Meeting of the Chicago Linguistics Society*: 151–65.

HEESCHEN, VOLKER (1982). Some systems of spatial deixis in Papuan languages. In Weissenborn, J. and Klein, W. (eds.) 81–109.

HEIM, IRENE (1983). On the projection problem for presuppositions. *Proceedings of the West Coast Conference on Formal Linguistics* 2: 114–25.

HEIM, IRENE (1992). Presupposition projection and the semantics of attitude verbs. *Journal of Semantics* 9: 183–221.

HELMBRECHT, JOHANNES (2003). Politeness distinctions in second person pronouns. In Lenz, F. (ed.) 185–202.

HERRING, S. C. (1994). Discourse functions of demonstrative deixis in Tamil. *Proceedings of the Annual Meeting of the Berkeley Linguistics Society* 20: 246–59.

HILL, CLIFFORD (1982). Up/down, front/back, left/right: a contrastive study of Hausa and English. In Weissenborn, J. and Klein, W. (eds.)

HIMMELMANN, NIKOLAUS (1997). *Deiktikon, Artikel, Nominalphrase*. Tübingen: Niemeyer.

HIRSCHBERG, JULIA (1991). A theory of scalar implicature. New York: Garland.

HOBBS, JERRY R. (2004). *Abduction in natural language understanding*. In Horn, L. R. and Ward, G. (eds.) 724–41.

HOLDCROFT, DAVID (1994). Indirect speech acts and propositional content. In Tsohatzidis, S. (ed.) 350–64.

HONG, WEI (1998). *Request patterns in Chinese and German: a cross-cultural study*. München: Lincom Europa.

HOPPER, ROBIN (2002). Deixis and aspect: the Tokelanan directional particles *mai* and *atu*. *Studies in Language* 26: 283–313.

HORGAN, TERENCE and TIENSON, JOHN (1996). *Connectionism and the philosophy of psychology*. Cambridge, MA: MIT Press.

HORN, LAURENCE R. (1972). On the semantic properties of logical operators in English. Ph.D. dissertation. University of California at Los Angeles.

HORN, LAURENCE R. (1984). Toward a new taxonomy for pragmatic inference: Q-based and R-based implicature. In Schiffrin, D. (ed.) *Meaning, form, and use in context: linguistic applications*. Washington, DC: Georgetown University Press. 11–42.

HORN, LAURENCE R. (1985). Metalinguistic negation and pragmatic ambiguity. *Language* 61: 121–74.

HORN, LAURENCE R. (1988). Pragmatic theory. In Newmeyer, F. J. (ed.) *Linguistics: the Cambridge survey*, vol. 1: 113–45.

HORN, LAURENCE R. (1989). *A natural history of negation*. Chicago: University of Chicago Press.

HORN, LAURENCE R. (1996). Presupposition and implicature. In Lappin, S. (ed.) 299–320.

HORN, LAURENCE R. (2004). Implicature. In Horn, L. R. and Ward, G. (eds.) 3–28.

HORN, LAURENCE R. and BAYER, SAMUEL (1984). Short-circuited implicature: a negative contribution. *Linguistics and Philosophy* 7: 397–411.

HORN, LAURENCE R. and WARD, GREGORY (2004). Introduction. In Horn, L. R. and Ward, G. (eds.): xi–xix.

HORN, LAURENCE R. and WARD, GREGORY (eds.) (2004). *The handbook of pragmatics*. Oxford: Blackwell.

HORNSTEIN, NORBERT, NUNES, JAIRO, and GROHMANN, KLEANTHES (2005). *Understanding minimalism*. Cambridge: Cambridge University Press.

HOTTENROTH, PRISKA-MONIKA (1982). The system of local deixis in Spanish. In Weissenborn, J. and Klein, W. (eds.) 133–53.

HOUSE, JULIA (1988). 'Oh excuse me please': apologizing in a foreign language. In Kettemann, B. et al. (eds.) *Englisch als Zweitsprache*. Tübingen: Narr. 303–27.

HU, HSIEN CHIN (1944). The Chinese concept of 'face'. *American Anthropologists* 46: 45–64.

HUANG, YAN (1987). The preference organisation of adjacency pairs in English conversation (written in Chinese). *Xiandai Waiyu* 3: 10–18.

HUANG, YAN (1991). A neo-Gricean pragmatic theory of anaphora. *Journal of Linguistics* 27: 301–35.

HUANG, YAN (1992). Against Chomsky's typology of empty categories. *Journal of Pragmatics* 17: 1–29.

HUANG, YAN (1994). *The syntax and pragmatics of anaphora: a study with special reference to Chinese*. Cambridge: Cambridge University Press.

HUANG, YAN (1995). On null subjects and null objects in generative grammar. *Linguistics* 33: 1081–123.

HUANG, YAN (1996). A note on the head-movement analysis of long-distance reflexives. *Linguistics* 34: 833–40.

HUANG, YAN (2000a). *Anaphora: a cross-linguistic study*. Oxford: Oxford University Press.

HUANG, YAN (2000b). Discourse anaphora: four theoretical models. *Journal of Pragmatics* 32: 151–76.

HUANG, YAN (2001a). Reflections on theoretical pragmatics. *Waiguoyu* 131: 2–14.

HUANG, YAN (2001b). Anaphora. In Smelser, N. J. and Baltes, P. B. (eds.) *International encyclopedia of the social and behavioural sciences*, 26 vols. New York: Elsevier Science. Vol. 1: 486–90.

HUANG, YAN (2001c). Marking of logophoricity in West African, East and South Asian languages. In *Proceedings of the 6th International Conference on the Languages of East, Southeast Asia and West Africa*. St Petersburg: University of St Petersburg Oriental Press. 224–38.

HUANG, YAN (2001d). Anaphora and word order. In Palek, B. and Fujimura, O. (eds.) *Item order*. Prague: Charles University Press. 329–46.

HUANG, YAN (2002a). Typology of coreferential anaphora and neo-Gricean pragmatics: implications for a newly defined artificial language. *Journal of Universal Language* 3: 31–56.

HUANG, YAN (2002b). Logophoric marking in East Asian languages. In Güldemann, T. and von Roncador, M. (eds.) *Reported discourse*. Amsterdam: John Benjamins. 213–24.

HUANG, YAN (2003). On neo-Gricean pragmatics. *International Journal of Pragmatics* 13: 87–110.

HUANG, YAN (2004a). Anaphora and the pragmatics–syntax interface. In Horn, L. R. and Ward, G. (eds.) 288–314.

HUANG, YAN (2004b). Neo-Gricean pragmatic theory: looking back on the past; looking ahead to the future. *Waiguoyu* 149: 2–25.

HUANG, YAN (2005). Lexical narrowing in English. In Chen, Y. and Leung, Y. (eds.) *Selected papers from the Fourteenth International Symposium on English Teaching*. Taipei: Crane Publishers. 55–66.

HUANG, YAN (2006a). Speech acts. In Brown, K. (ed.) *The encyclopedia of language and linguistics*. 2nd edn. 14 vols. New York: Elsevier Science. Vol. 11: 656–66.

HUANG, YAN (2006b). Neo-Gricean pragmatics. In Brown, K. (ed.) *The encyclopedia of language and linguistics*. 2nd edn. 14 vols. New York: Elsevier Science. Vol. 8: 586–90.

HUANG, YAN (2006c). Anaphora, cataphora, exophora, logophoricity. In Brown, K. (ed.) *The encyclopedia of language and linguistics*. 2nd edn. 14 vols. New York: Elsevier Science. Vol. 1: 231–8.

HUANG, YAN (2006d). Coreference: identity and similarity. In Brown, K. (ed.) *The encyclopedia of languages and linguistics*. 2nd edn. 14 vols. New York: Elsevier Science. Vol. 3: 203–5.

HUDSON, JOYCE (1985). Selected speech act verbs in Walmutjari. In Hutter, G. and Gregerson, K. (eds.) *Pragmatics in non-western practice*. Dallas: Summer Institute of Linguistics. 63–83.

HURFORD, JAMES R. and HEASLEY, BRENDAN (1983). *Semantics: a course book*. Cambridge: Cambridge University Press.

HWANG, J. (1990). 'Deference' versus 'politeness' in Korean speech. *International Journal of the Sociology of Language* 82: 41–55.

HYMAN, LARRY and COMRIE, BERNARD (1981). Logophoric reference in Gokana. *Journal of African Languages and Linguistics* 3: 19–37.

HYSLOP, CATRIONA (1993). Towards a typology of spatial deixis. Honours thesis. The Australian National University.

IDE, SACHIKO (1989). Formal forms and discernment: two neglected aspects of universals of linguistic politeness. *Multilingua* 8: 223–48.

IMAI, SHINGO (2003). Spatial deixis. PhD dissertation. State University of New York at Buffalo.

INGRAM, D. (1978). Typology and universals of personal pronouns. In Greenberg et al. (ed.) 213–47.

JACKENDOFF, RAY (1983). *Semantics and cognition*. Cambridge, MA: MIT Press.

JACKENDOFF, RAY (1990). *Semantic structure*. Cambridge, MA: MIT Press.

JACKENDOFF, RAY (1992). *Languages of the mind*. Cambridge, MA: MIT Press.

JACKENDOFF, RAY (1997). *The architecture of the language faculty*. Cambridge, MA: MIT Press.

JAGGAR, PHILIP J. and BUBA, MALAMI (1994). The space and time adverbials NAN/ CAN in Hausa: cracking the deictic code. *Language Sciences* 16: 387–421.

JANSSEN, THEO (1997). Compositionality. In van Benthem, J. and ter Meulen, A. (eds.) *Handbook of logic and language*. Amsterdam: North-Holland. 417–73.

JARVELLA, ROBERT and KLEIN, WOLFGANG (eds.) (1982). *Speech, place and action: studies in deixis and related topics*. Chichester: John Wiley and Sons.

JASZCZOLT, K. M. (2002). *Semantics and pragmatics: meaning in language and discourse*. London: Pearson Education.

JASZCZOLT, K. M. (2005). Default semantics: foundations of a compositional theory of acts of communication. Oxford: Oxford University Press.

JASZCZOLT, K. M. and TURNER, K. (eds.) (1996). *Contrastive semantics and pragmatics*. New York: Elsevier Science.

JOHNSON, MARK (1992). Philosophical implications of cognitive semantics. *Cognitive Linguistics* 3: 345–66.

JUNGBLUTH, KONSTANZE (2003). Deictics in the conversational dyad: finding in Spanish and some cross-linguistic outlines. In Lenz, F. (ed.) 13–40.

JURAFSKY, DANIEL (2004). Pragmatics and computational linguistics. In Horn, L. R. and Ward, G. (eds.) 578–604.

KADMON, NIRIT (2001). *Formal pragmatics: semantics, pragmatics, presupposition, and focus*. Oxford: Blackwell.

KAMP, HANS and REYLE, UWE (1993). *From discourse to logic: introduction to model theoretic semantics of natural languages, formal logic and Discourse Representation Theory*. Dordrecht: Kluwer.

KAPLAN, DAVID (1989). Demonstratives: an essay on the semantics, logic, metaphysics, and epistemology of demonstratives and other indexicals. In Almog, J. et al. (eds.) *Themes from Kaplan*. Oxford: Oxford University Press. 481–563.

KARTTUNEN, LAURI (1973). Presuppositions of compound sentences. *Linguistic Inquiry* 4: 169–93.

KARTTUNEN, LAURI (1974). Presupposition and linguistic context. *Theoretical Linguistics* 1: 182–94.

KARTTUNEN, LAURI and PETERS, STANLEY (1979). Conventional implicature. In Oh, C.-K. and Dineen, A. D. (eds.) *Syntax and semantics 11: presupposition*. London: Academic Press. 1–56.

KASHER, ASA (1976). Conversational maxims and rationality. In Kasher, A. (ed.) *Language in focus: foundations, methods and systems*. Dordrecht: Reidel. 197–216.

KASHER, ASA (ed.) (1998). *Pragmatics: critical concepts*. 6 vols. London: Routledge.

KASPER, GABRIELE and BLUM-KULKA, SHOSHANA (eds.) (1993). *Interlanguage pragmatics*. Oxford: Oxford University Press.

KATZ, JERROLD J. (1977). *Propositional structure and illocutionary force*. New York: Crowell.

KAY, PAUL (1990). *Even. Linguistics and Philosophy* 13: 59–111.

KAY, PAUL (2004). Pragmatic aspects of grammatical constructions. In Horn, L. R. and Ward, G. (eds.) 675–700.

KEATING, ELIZABETH (1998). Honor and stratification in Pohnpei, Micronesia. *American Ethnologist* 25: 399–411.

KEENAN, ELINOR OCHS (1976). The universality of conversational implicature. *Language in Society* 5: 67–80.

KEMPSON, RUTH (1975). *Presupposition and the delimitation of semantics*. Cambridge: Cambridge University Press.

KIM, SUN-HEE (1993). Division of labor between grammar and pragmatics: the distribution and interpretation of anaphora. Ph.D. dissertation. Yale University.

KING, JEFFREY and STANLEY, JASON (2005). Semantics, pragmatics, and the role of semantic content. In Szabó, Z. G. (ed.) 111–64.

KÖNIG, EKKEHARD and SIEMUND, PETER (2000). Intensifiers and reflexives: a typological perspective. In Frajzyngier, Z. and Curl, T. S. (eds.) 41–74.

KOUTLAKI, SOPHIA A. (2002). Offers and expressions of thanks as face enhancing acts: *tæ'arof* in Persian. *Journal of Pragmatics* 34: 1733–56.

KRAHMER, EMIEL (1998). *Presupposition and anaphora*. Stanford: CSLI.

KRIPKE, SAUL (1977). Speaker's reference and semantic reference. *Midwest Studies in Philosophy* 2: 255–76.

KUNO, SUSUMU (2004). Empathy and direct discourse perspectives. In Horn, L. R. and Ward, G. (eds.) 315–43.

LAKOFF, GEORGE (1972). Hedges: a study in meaning criteria and the logic of fuzzi concepts. *Papers from the Regional Meeting of the Chicago Linguistics Society* 8: 183–228.

LAKOFF, GEORGE (1987). *Women, fire, and dangerous things: what categories reveal about the mind*. Chicago: University of Chicago Press.

LAKOFF, GEORGE and JOHNSON, MARK (1999). *Philosophy in the flesh: the embodied mind and its challenge to western thought*. New York: Basic Books.

LALITHA MURTHY, B. and SUBBARAO, K. V. (2000). Lexical anaphors and pronominals in Mizo. In Lust, B. et al. (eds.) 777–840.

LANDMAN, FRED (1986). Conflicting presuppositions and modal subordination. *Papers from the Regional Meeting of the Chicago Linguistics Society* 22: 105–207.

LANGACKER, RONALD (1987). *Foundations of cognitive grammar*, vol. 1. Stanford: Stanford University Press.

LANGENDOEN, D. TERENCE and SAVIN, HARRIS (1971). The projection problem for presuppositions. In Fillmore, C. and Langendoen, D. T. (eds.) *Studies in linguistic semantics*. New York: Holt, Reinhardt and Winston. 373–88.

LAPPIN, SHALOM (ed.) (1996). *The handbook of contemporary semantic theory*. Oxford: Blackwell.

LASNIK, HOWARD (1989). *Essays on anaphora*. Dordrecht: Kluwer.

LE PAIR, R. (1996). Spanish request strategies: a cross-cultural analysis from an intercultural perspective. In Jaszczolt, K. M. and Turner, K. (eds.) 651–70.

LEECH, GEOFFREY N. (1983). *Principles of pragmatics*. London: Longman.

LEECH, GEOFFREY N. (2003). Towards an anatomy of politeness in communication. *International Journal of Pragmatics* 13: 101–23.

LEE-WONG, SONG MEI (2000). *Politeness and face in Chinese culture*. Frankfurt am Main: Peter Lang.

LEGENDRE, GÉRALDINE, GRIMSHAW, JANE, and VIKNER, STEN (2001). Optimality-theoretic syntax. Cambridge, MA: MIT Press.

LENZ, FRIEDRICH (ed.) (2003). *Deictic conceptualisation of space, time and person*. Amsterdam: John Benjamins.

LEVINSON, STEPHEN C. (1983). *Pragmatics*. Cambridge: Cambridge University Press.

LEVINSON, STEPHEN C. (1987a). Minimization and conversational inference. In Verschueren, J. and Bertuccelli-Papi, M. (eds.) 61–129.

LEVINSON, STEPHEN C. (1987b). Pragmatics and the grammar of anaphora. *Journal of Linguistics* 23: 379–434.

LEVINSON, STEPHEN C. (1988). Putting linguistics on a proper footing: explorations in Goffman's concepts of participation. In Drew, P. and Wooton, A. (eds.) 161–293.

LEVINSON, STEPHEN C. (1989). A review of *Relevance. Journal of Linguistics* 25: 455–472.

LEVINSON, STEPHEN C. (1991). Pragmatic reduction of the binding conditions revisited. *Journal of Linguistics* 27: 107–61.

LEVINSON, STEPHEN C. (1995). Three levels of meaning. In Palmer, F. (ed.) 90–115.

LEVINSON, STEPHEN C. (1996). Frames of reference and Molyneux's question: cross-linguistic evidence. In Bloom, P. et al. (eds.) *Language and space*. Cambridge, MA: MIT Press. 109–69.

LEVINSON, STEPHEN C. (2000). *Presumptive meanings: the theory of generalized conversational implicature*. Cambridge, MA: MIT Press.

LEVINSON, STEPHEN C. (2003). *Space in language and cognition: explorations in cognitive diversity*. Cambridge: Cambridge University Press.

LEVINSON, STEPHEN C. (2004). Deixis and pragmatics. In Horn, L. R. and Ward, G. (eds.) 97–121.

LEWIS, DAVID (1979). Scorekeeping in a language game. *Journal of Philosophical Logic* 8: 339–59.

LI, CHARLES N. (ed.) (1976). *Subject and topic*. London: Academic Press.

LI, CHARLES N. and THOMPSON, SANDRA A. (1976). Subject and topic: a new typology of language. In Li, C. N. (ed.) 457–98.

LOCHER, MIRIAM A. (2004). *Power and politeness in action: disagreements in oral communication*. Berlin: Mouton de Gruyter.

LUST, BARBARA, WALI, K., GAIR, JAMES, and SUBBARAO, K. V. (eds.) (2000). *Lexical anaphors and pronouns in selected South Asian languages*. Berlin: Mouton de Gruyter.

LYCAN, WILLIAM G. (1991). *Even* and *even if. Linguistics and Philosophy* 14: 115–50.

LYONS, JOHN (1977). *Semantics*. 2 vols. Cambridge: Cambridge University Press.

LYONS, JOHN (1982). Deixis and subjectivity: loquor, ergo sum? In Jarvella, R. and Klein, W. (eds.) 101–24.

LYONS, JOHN (1987). Semantics. In Lyons, J. et al. (eds.) *New horizons in linguistics* 2. London: Penguin. 152–78.

LYONS, JOHN (1995). *Linguistic semantics*. Cambridge: Cambridge University Press.

MACDONALD, L. (1990). *A grammar of Tauya*. Berlin: Mouton de Gruyter.

MAJID, A., BOWERMAN, M., KITA, S., HAUN, D., and LEVINSON, STEPHEN C. (2004). Can language restructure cognition? The case for space. *Trends in Cognitive Sciences* 8: 108–14.

MALOTKI, ECKEHART (1982). Hopi person deixis. In Weissenborn, J. and Klein, W. (eds.) 223–52.

MANNING, H. PAUL (2001). On social deixis. *Anthropological Linguistics* 43: 54–100.

MAO, LUMING ROBERT (1994). Beyond politeness theory: 'face' revisited and renewed. *Journal of Pragmatics* 21: 451–86.

MARCU, DANIEL (1994). A formalisation and an algorithm for computing pragmatic inferences and detecting infelicities. PhD dissertation. University of Toronto.

MÁRQUEZ-REITER, ROSINA (2000). *Linguistic politeness in Britain and Uruguay: a contrastive study of requests and apologies*. Amsterdam: John Benjamins.

MARMARIDOU, SOPHIA S. A. (2000). *Pragmatic meaning and cognition*. Amsterdam: John Benjamins.

MARTINET, A. (1962). *A functional view of language*. Oxford: Clarendon Press.

MARTINICH, A. P. (1984). *Communication and reference*. Berlin: Walter de Gruyter.

MATSUI, TOMOKO (2000). *Bridging and relevance*. Amsterdam: John Benjamins.

MATSUMOTO, YO (1995). The conversational condition on Horn scales. *Linguistics and Philosophy* 18: 21–60.

MATSUMOTO, YOSHIKO (1988). Reexamination of the universality of face: politeness phenomena in Japanese. *Journal of Pragmatics* 12: 403–26.

MATSUMOTO, YOSHIKO (1989). Politeness and conversational universals: observations from Japanese. *Multilingua* 8: 207–21.

MATTAUSCH, JASON (2004). Optimality Theory Pragmatics and binding phenomena. In Blutner, R. and Zeevat, H. (eds) 63–90.

MATTHEWS, PETER H. (1995). Syntax, semantics, and pragmatics. In Palmer, F. (ed.) 48–60.

MEIRA, SÉRGIO (2003). 'Addressee effects' in demonstrative systems: the cases of Tiriyó and Brazilian Portuguese. In Lenz, F. (ed.) 3–11.

MERCER, ROBERT (1992). Default logic: towards a common logical semantics for presupposition and entailment. *Journal of Semantics* 9: 223–50.

MERIN, ARTHUR (1994). Algebra of elementary social acts. In Tsohatzidis, S. (ed.) 234–66.

MERIN, ARTHUR (1999). Information, relevance, and social decision making: some principles and results of decision-theoretic semantics. In Moss, L. S.,

Ginzburg, J., and de Rijke, M. (eds.) *Logic, language, and computation*, vol. 2. Stanford: CSLI. 179–221.

MERIN, ARTHUR (2003). Probabilistic and deterministic presuppositions. In Bauerle, R. et al. (eds.).

MEY, JOCOB L. (2001). *Pragmatics: an introduction*. 2nd edn. Oxford: Blackwell.

MILLER, ROY A. (1967). *The Japanese language*. Chicago: University of Chicago Press.

MILNER, G. B. (1961). The Samoan vocabulary of respect. *Journal of the Royal Anthropological Institute* 91.

MITHUN, MARIANNE (1999). *The languages of native north America*. Cambridge: Cambridge University Press.

MIZUTANI, OSAMU and MIZUTANI, NOBUKO (1987). *How to be polite in Japanese*. Tokyo: Japan Times.

MONTALBETTI, MARIO (2003). Reference transfers and the Giorgione problem. In Barss, A. (ed.) *Anaphora: a reference guide*. Oxford: Blackwell.

MORGAN, JERRY L. (1978). Two types of convention in indirect speech acts. In Cole, P. (ed.) 261–80.

MORRIS, CHARLES (1938). *Foundations of the theory of signs*. Chicago: University of Chicago Press.

MÜHLHÄUSLER, PETER and HARRÉ, ROM (1990). *Pronouns and people*. Oxford: Blackwell.

NEALE, STEPHEN (1992). Paul Grice and the philosophy of language. *Linguistics and Philosophy* 15: 509–59.

NEMO, FRANÇOIS (1999). The pragmatics of signs, the semantics of relevance, and the semantics–pragmatics interface. In Turner, K. (ed.) 343–417.

NEMO, FRANÇOIS and CADIOT, P. (1997). Un problème insoluble? *Revue de sémantique et pragmatique* 1: 15–22, 2: 9–40.

NICOLLE, STEVE and CLARK, BILLY (1999). Experimental pragmatics and what is said: a response to Gibbs and Moise. *Cognition* 69: 337–54.

NOVECK, IRA A. (2001). When children are more logical than adults: experimental investigations of scalar implicature. *Cognition* 78: 165–88.

NOVECK, IRA A. and SPERBER, DAN (eds.) (2004). *Experimental pragmatics*. New York: Palgrave Macmillan.

NUNBERG, GEOFFREY (1979). The non-uniqueness of semantic solutions: polysemy. *Linguistics and Philosophy* 3: 143–84.

NUNBERG, GEOFFREY (1993). Indexicality and deixis. *Linguistics and Philosophy* 16: 1–44.

NUNBERG, GEOFFREY (1995). Transfers of meaning. *Journal of Semantics* 12: 109–32.

NUNBERG, GEOFFREY (2004). The pragmatics of deferred interpretation. In Horn, L. R. and Ward, G. (eds.) 344–64.

NWOYE, ONUIGBO (1989). Linguistic politeness in Igbo. *Multilingua* 8: 259–75.

NWOYE, ONUIGBO (1992). Linguistic politeness and socio-cultural variations of the notion of face. *Journal of Pragmatics* 18: 309–28.

OLSHTAIN, ELITE and WEINBACH, LIORA (1993). Interlanguage features of the speech act of complaining. In Kasper, G. and Blum-Kulka, S. (eds.) 108–22.

PALMER, FRANK (ed.) (1995). *Grammar and meaning: essays in honour of Sir John Lyons.* Cambridge: Cambridge University Press.

PAPAFRAGOU, ANNA and MUSOLINO, JULIEN (2003). Scalar implicatures: experiments at the semantics–pragmatics interface. *Cognition* 86: 253–82.

PARKER, E. (1986). Mundani pronouns. In Wiesemann, U. (ed.) 131–66.

PECCEI, JEAN STILWELL (1999). *Pragmatics.* London: Routledge.

PERRAULT, C. RAYMOND (1990). An application of default logic to speech act theory. In Cohen, P. (eds) *Intentions in communication.* Cambridge, MA: MIT Press. 161–86.

PERRY, JOHN (1993). The problem of the essential indexical and other essays. Oxford: Oxford University Press.

PERRY, JOHN (1998). Indexicals, contexts and unarticulated constituents. In Aliseda-Llera et al. (eds.).

POPPER, KARL (1973). *Objective knowledge.* Oxford: Oxford University Press.

POSNER, R. (1980). Semantics and pragmatics of sentence connectives in natural language. In Searle, J. R., Kiefer, F., and Bierwisch, M. (eds.) *Speech act theory and pragmatics.* Dordrecht: Reidel. 169–203.

POTTS, CHRISTOPHER (2005). *The logic of conventional implicatures.* Oxford: Oxford University Press.

PRINCE, ALAN and SMOLENSKY, PAUL (1993). Optimality Theory: constraint interaction in generative grammar. Ms.

PRINCE, ALAN and SMOLENSKY, PAUL (2004). *Optimality Theory: constraint interaction in generative grammar.* Oxford: Blackwell.

PRUCHA, J. (1983). *Pragmalinguistics: East European tradition.* Amsterdam: John Benjamins.

PUSTEJOVSKY, JAMES (1995). *The generative lexicon.* Cambridge, MA: MIT Press.

RAY, TAPAS S. (2000). Lexical anaphors and pronouns in Oriy. In Lust, B. et al. (eds.) 575–636.

REBOUL, ANNE (2004). Conversational implicatures: nonce or generalized? In Noveck, I. and Sperber, D. (eds.) 322–32.

RECANATI, FRANÇOIS (1989). The pragmatics of what is said. *Mind and Language* 4: 295–329.

RECANATI, FRANÇOIS (1993). *Direct reference: from language to thought.* Oxford: Blackwell.

RECANATI, FRANÇOIS (1994). Contextualism and anti-contextualism in the philosophy of language. In Tsohatzidis, S. (ed.) 156–66.

RECANATI, FRANÇOIS (2000). *Oratio obliqua, oratio recta: the semantics of metarepresentations.* Cambridge, MA: MIT Press.

RECANATI, FRANÇOIS (2001). What is said. *Synthèse* 125: 75–91.

RECANATI, FRANÇOIS (2002). Does linguistic communication rest on inference? *Mind and Language* 17: 105–26.

RECANATI, FRANÇOIS (2004a). *Literal meaning*. Cambridge: Cambridge University Press.

RECANATI, FRANÇOIS (2004b). Pragmatics and semantics. In Horn, L. R. and Ward, G. (eds.) 442–62.

RECANATI, FRANÇOIS (2005). 'What is said' and the semantics/pragmatics distinction. In Bianchi, C. (ed.) 45–64.

REESINK, G. P. (1987). *Structures and their function in Usan: a Papuan language of Papua New Guinea*. Amsterdam: John Benjamins.

RICHARD, M. (1990). *Propositional attitudes: an essay on thoughts and how we ascribe them*. Cambridge: Cambridge University Press.

RIEBER, STEPHEN (1997). Conventional implicatures as tacit performatives. *Linguistics and Philosophy* 20: 51–72.

REINHART, TANYA and REULAND, ERIC (1993). Reflexivity. *Linguistic Inquiry* 24: 657–720.

ROBERTS, CRAIGE (1996). Anaphora in intensional contexts. In Lappin, S. (ed.) 215–46.

ROBERTS, CRAIGE (2004) Context in dynamic interpretation. In Horn, L. and Ward, G. (eds.) 197–220.

ROSALDO, MICHELLE Z. (1982). The things we do with words: Ilongot speech acts and speech act theory in philosophy. *Language in Society* 11: 203–37.

ROSS, JOHN ROBERT (1970). On declarative sentences. In Jacobs, R. and Rosenbaum, P. S. (eds.) *Readings in English transformational grammar*. Waltham: Ginn. 222–72.

RUNDQUIST, SUELLEN (1992). Indirectness: a gender study of flouting Grice's maxims. *Journal of Pragmatics* 18: 431–49.

RUSSELL, BERTRAND (1905). On denoting. *Mind* 14: 479–93.

RYLE, GILBERT (1954). *Dilemmas*. Cambridge: Cambridge University Press.

SADOCK, JERROLD M. (1974). *Toward a linguistic theory of speech acts*. New York: Academic Press.

SADOCK, JERROLD M. (1978). On testing for conversational implicature. In Cole, P. (ed.) 281–98.

SADOCK, JERROLD M. (1994). Toward a grammatically realistic typology of speech acts. In Tsohatzidis, S. (ed.) 394–406.

SADOCK, JERROLD M. (2004). Speech acts. In Horn, L. R. and Ward, G. (eds.) 53–73.

SADOCK, JERROLD M. and ZWICKY, ARNOLD M. (1985). Speech act distinctions in syntax. In Shopen, T. (ed.) vol. 1: 155–96.

SAEED, JOHN I. (2003). *Semantics*. 2nd edn. Oxford: Blackwell.

SALMON, NATHAN (1991). The pragmatic fallacy. *Philosophical Studies* 63: 83–97.

SARANGI, SRIKANT K. and SLEMBROUCK, STEFAAN (1992). Non-cooperation in communication: a reassessment of Gricean pragmatics. *Journal of Pragmatics* 17: 117–54.

SAUL, JENNIFER (2002). What is said and psychological reality: Grice's project and relevance theorists' criticisms. *Linguistics and Philosophy* 25: 347–72.

SCHLADT, M. (2000). The typology and grammaticalization of reflexives. In Frajzyngier, Z. and Curl, T. S. (eds.) 103–24.

SCHÖTER, ANDREAS (1995). The computational application of bilattice logic to natural reasoning. PhD dissertation. University of Edinburgh.

SCHUTZ, ALFRED (1970). *Reflections on the problems of relevance*. New Haven: Yale University Press.

SCOLLON, RONALD and SCOLLON, SUZANNE WONG (1995). *Intercultural communication: a discourse approach*. Oxford: Blackwell.

SEARLE, JOHN R. (1969). *Speech acts: an essay in the philosophy of language*. Cambridge: Cambridge University Press.

SEARLE, JOHN R. (1975a). A taxonomy of speech acts. In Gunderson, K. (ed.) *Minnesota studies in the philosophy of science 9: language, mind and knowledge*. 344–69.

SEARLE, JOHN R. (1975b). Indirect speech acts. In Cole, P. and Morgan, J. L. (eds.) 59–82.

SEARLE, JOHN R. (1979). *Expression and meaning: studies in the theory of speech acts*. Cambridge: Cambridge University Press.

SEARLE, JOHN R. (1980). The background of meaning. In Searle, J., Klifer, F., and Bierwisch, M. (eds.) *Speech act theory and pragmatics*. Dordrecht: Reidel. 221–32.

SEARLE, JOHN R. (1983). *Intentionality: an essay in the philosophy of mind*. Cambridge: Cambridge University Press.

SEARLE, JOHN R. (1992). *The rediscovery of the mind*. Cambridge, MA: MIT Press.

SEARLE, JOHN R. (1996). *The construction of social reality*. Oxford: Blackwell.

SEARLE, JOHN R. (2002). *Consciousness and language*. Cambridge: Cambridge University Press.

SEARLE, JOHN R. and VANDERVEKEN, DANIEL (1985). *Foundations of illocutionary logic*. Cambridge: Cambridge University Press.

SELLS, PETER (1987). Aspects of logophoricity. *Linguistic Inquiry* 18: 445–79.

SEUREN, PETER (2000). Presupposition, negation and trivalence. *Journal of Linguistics* 36: 1–37.

SEUREN, PETER (2004). *Chomsky's minimalism*. Oxford: Oxford University Press.

SHIBATANI, MASAYOSHI (1990). *The Languages of Japan*. Cambridge: Cambridge University Press.

SHIBATANI, MASAYOSHI (1999). Honorifics. In Brown, K. and Miller, J. (eds.) *Concise encyclopedia of grammatical categories*. New York: Elsevier Science. 192–201.

SHOPEN, TIM (ed.) (1985). *Language typology and syntactic description.* 3 vols. Cambridge: Cambridge University Press.

SIEWIERSKA, ANNA (2004). *Person.* Cambridge: Cambridge University Press.

SIFIANOU, MARIA (1992). *Politeness phenomena in England and Greece: a cross-cultural perspective.* Oxford: Clarendon Press.

SIMON, HORST J. and WIESE, HEIKE (eds.) (2002). *Pronouns: grammar and representation.* Amsterdam: John Benjamins.

SINHA, ANJANI KUMAR (1972). On the deictic uses of 'coming' and 'going' in Hindi. *Papers from the Regional Meeting of the Chicago Linguistic Society* 8: 351–58.

SMITH, BARRY. (1990). Towards a history of speech act theory. In Burkhardt, A. (ed.) *Speech acts, meaning and interactions: critical approaches to the philosophy of John R. Searle.* Berlin: W. de Gruyter. 29–61.

SMITH, NEIL (2004). *Chomsky: ideas and ideals.* 2nd edn. Cambridge: Cambridge University Press.

SOAMES, SCOTT (1979). A projection problem for speaker presuppositions. *Linguistic Inquiry* 10: 623–66.

SOAMES, SCOTT (1982). How presuppositions are inherited: a solution to the projection problem. *Linguistic Inquiry* 13: 483–545.

SOAMES, SCOTT (1989). Presupposition. In Gabbay, D. and Guenthner, F. (eds.) *Handbook of philosophical logic.* Vol. 4. Dordrecht: Reidel. 553–616.

SPERBER, DAN and WILSON, DEIRDRE (1986). *Relevance: communication and cognition.* Oxford: Blackwell.

SPERBER, DAN and WILSON, DEIRDRE (1987). Précis of *Relevance. Behavioral and Brain Sciences* 10: 697–710.

SPERBER, DAN and WILSON, DEIRDRE (1995). *Relevance: communication and cognition.* 2nd edn. Oxford: Blackwell.

SPERBER, DAN and WILSON, DEIRDRE (2002). Pragmatics, modularity and mind-reading. *Mind and Language* 17: 3–23.

STALNAKER, ROBERT C. (1972). Pragmatics. In Davidson, D. and Harman, G. (eds.) *Semantics of natural language.* Dordrecht: Reidel. 380–97.

STALNAKER, ROBERT C. (1973). Presuppositions. *Journal of Philosophical Logic* 2: 447–57.

STALNAKER, ROBERT C. (1974). Pragmatic presupposition. In Munitz, M. and Unger, P. (eds.) *Semantics and philosophy.* New York: New York University Press. 197–214.

STALNAKER, ROBERT C. (1978). Assertation. In Cole, P. (ed.) 315–22.

STALNAKER, ROBERT C. (1999). *Context and content.* Oxford: Oxford University Press.

STANLEY, JASON (2000). Context and logical form. *Linguistics and Philosophy* 23: 391–434.

STANLEY, JASON and SZABÓ, ZOLTÁN G. (2000a). On quantifier domain restriction. *Mind and Language* 15: 219–61.

STANLEY, JASON and SZABÓ, ZOLTÁN G. (2000b). Reply to Bach and Neale. *Mind and Language* 15: 295–8.

STIRLING, LESLEY (1993). *Switch-reference and discourse representation*. Cambridge: Cambridge University Press.

STRAWSON, PETER F. (1950). On referring. *Mind* 59: 320–44.

STRAWSON, PETER F. (1952). *Introduction to logical theory*. London: Methuen.

STRAWSON, PETER F. (1964). Intention and convention in speech acts. *Philosophical Review* 73: 290–302.

STRECKER, IVO (1993). Cultural variations in the notion of 'face'. *Multilingua* 12: 119–41.

SUBBARAO, K. V. and LALITHA MURTHY, B. (2000). Lexical anaphors and pronouns in Telugu. In Lust, B. et al. (eds.) 217–76.

SWEETSER, EVE (1990). *From etymology to pragmatics: metaphorical and cultural aspects of semantic structure*. Cambridge: Cambridge University Press.

SZABÓ, ZOLTÁN G. (2005a). Introduction. In Szabó, Z. G. (ed.) 1–14.

SZABÓ, ZOLTÁN G. (ed.) (2005b). *Semantics versus pragmatics*. Oxford: Clarendon Press.

TAAVITSAINEN, IRMA and JUCKER, ANDREAS H. (2003). *Diachronic perspectives on address term systems*. Amsterdam: John Benjamins.

TAKAHASHI, TOMOKO and BEEBE, LESLIE M. (1987). The development of pragmatic competence in Japanese learners of English. *JALT Journal* 8: 131–55.

TAKAHASHI, TOMOKO and BEEBE, LESLIE M. (1993). Cross-linguistic influence in the speech act of correction. In Kasper, G. and Blum-Kulka, S. (eds.).

TAYLOR, KENNETH (2001). Sex, breakfast, and descriptus interruptus. *Synthèse* 128: 45–61.

THOMAS, JENNY (1995). *Meaning in interaction: an introduction to pragmatics*. London: Longman.

THOMASON, RICHMOND H. (1990). Accommodation, meaning, and implicature: interdisciplinary foundations for pragmatics. In Cohen, P. R., Morgan, J., and Pollack, M. E. (eds.) *Intentions in communication*. Cambridge, MA: MIT Press. 325–64.

TOMASELLO, MICHAEL (2003). *Constructing a language: a usage-based theory of language acquisition*. Cambridge, MA: Harvard University Press.

TRAUGOTT, ELIZABETH CLOSS (2004). Historical pragmatics. In Horn, L. R. and Ward, G. (eds.) 538–61.

TRAUGOTT, ELIZABETH CLOSS and DASHER, RICHARD D. (2001). *Regularity in semantic change*. Cambridge: Cambridge University Press.

TRAVIS, CHARLES (1981). *The true and the false: the domain of the pragmatic*. Amsterdam: John Benjamins.

TRAVIS, CHARLES (1985). On what is strictly speaking true. *Canadian Journal of Philosophy* 15: 187–229.

Travis, Charles (1991). Annals of analysis: *Studies in the Way of Words*, by H. P. Grice. *Mind* 100: 237–64.

Travis, Charles (1997). Pragmatics. In Hale, B. and Wright, C. (eds.) *A companion to the philosophy of language*. Oxford: Blackwell 87–107.

Travis, Charles (2001). *Unshadowed thought. representation in thought and language*. Cambridge, MA: Harvard University Press.

Trosborg, Anna (1995). *Interlanguage pragmatics: requests, complaints, and apologies*. Berlin: Mouton de Gruyter.

Trudgill, Peter (2000). *Sociolinguistics: an introduction to language and society*. 4th edn. London: Penguin.

Tsohatzidis, Savas L. (ed.) (1994). *Foundations of speech act theory: philosophical and linguistic perspectives*. London: Routledge.

Turner, Ken (1997). Semantics vs. pragmatics. In Verschueren, J. et al. (eds.) *Handbook of pragmatics*. Amsterdam: John Benjamins. 1–23.

Turner, Ken (ed.) (1999). *The semantics–pragmatics interface from different points of view*. New York: Elsevier Science.

Ueda, K. (1974). Sixteen ways to avoid saying 'no' in Japanese. In Condon, J. C. and Saito, M. (eds.) *Intercultural encounters with Japan: communication, contact and conflict*. Tokyo: Simul Press.

Urmson, J. O. (1956). *Philosophical analysis: its development between the two wars*. Oxford: Clarendon Press.

van der Sandt, Rob (1988). *Context and presupposition*. London: Croom Helm.

van der Sandt, Rob (1992). Presupposition projection as anaphora resolution. *Journal of Semantics* 9: 333–77.

Vanderveken, Daniel (1990). *Meaning and speech acts vol. 1: principles of language use*. Cambridge: Cambridge University Press.

Vanderveken, Daniel (1991). *Meaning and speech acts vol. 2: formal semantics of success and satisfaction*. Cambridge: Cambridge University Press.

Vanderveken, Daniel (1994). A complete formulation of a simple logic of elementary illocutionary acts. In Tsohatzidis, S. (ed.) 99–131.

Vanderveken, Daniel (2002). Universal grammar and speech act theory. In Vanderveken, D. and Kubo, S. (eds.) 25–62.

Vanderveken, Daniel and Kubo, Susumu (eds.) (2002). *Essays in speech act theory*. Amsterdam: John Benjamins.

van Eijk, Jan (1997). *The Lillooet language: phonology, morphology, syntax*. Vancouver: University of British Columbia Press.

van Kuppevelt, J. (1996). Inferring from topics: scalar implicatures as topic-dependent inferences. Linguistics and Philosophy 19: 393–443.

van Mulken, D. (1996). Politeness markers in French and Dutch requests. In Jaszczolt, K. M. and Turner, K. (eds.) 689–702.

van Rooy, Robert (2004). Relevance in bidirectional Optimality Theory. In Blutner, R. and Zeevat, H. (eds.) 173–210.

VAN ROOY, ROBERT (forthcoming). Signalling games select Horn strategies. *Linguistics and Philosophy*.

VERSCHUEREN, JEF (1985). *What people say they do with words*. Norwood, NJ: Ablex.

VERSCHUEREN, JEF (1999). *Understanding pragmatics*. London: Arnold.

VERSCHUEREN, JEF and BERTUCCELLI-PAPI, MARIA (eds.). (1987). *The pragmatics perspective*. Amsterdam: John Benjamins.

VINCENTE, BEGOÑA (2002). What pragmatics can tell us about (literal) meaning: a critical note on Bach's theory of impliciture. *Journal of Pragmatics* 32: 403–21.

VOORHOEVE, C. L. (1975). Central and western trans New Guinea Phylum languages. In Wurm, S. A. (ed.) *New Guinea area languages and language study 1*. Canberra: Pacific Linguistics C-38. 345–459.

WALI, KASHI and SUBBARAO, K. V. (1991). On pronominal classification: evidence from Marathi and Telugu. *Linguistics* 29: 1093–110.

WARD, GREGORY L. and HIRSCHBERG, JULIA (1991). A pragmatic analysis of tautological utterances. *Journal of Pragmatics* 15: 507–20.

WATKINS, L. J. (1984). *A grammar of Kiowa*. Lincoln: University of Nebraska Press.

WATTS, RICHARD J. (2003). *Politeness*. Cambridge: Cambridge University Press.

WEBBER, BONNIE LYNN (1991). Structure and ostension in the interpretation of discourse deixis. *Language and Cognitive Processes* 6: 107–35.

WEISSENBORN, JÜRGEN and KLEIN, WOLFGANG (eds.) (1982). *Here and there: crosslinguistic studies on deixis and demonstration*. Amsterdam: John Benjamins.

WEIZMAN, ELDA (1993). Interlanguage requestive hints. In Kasper, G. and Blum-Kulka, S. (eds.) 123–37.

WELKER, KATHERINE (1994). Plans in the common ground: toward a generative account of conversational implicature. PhD dissertation. Ohio State University.

WIERZBICKA, ANNA (1987). Boys will be boys. *Language* 63: 95–114.

WIERZBICKA, ANNA (1991). *Cross-cultural pragmatics: the semantics of human interaction*. Berlin: Mouton de Gruyter.

WIESEMANN, URSULA (ed.) (1986). *Pronominal systems*. Tübingen, Narr.

WILKINS, DAVID and HILL, DEBORAH (1995). When 'GO' means 'COME': questioning the basicness of basic motion verbs. *Cognitive Linguistics* 6: 209–59.

WILSON, DEIRDRE (1975). *Presupposition and non-truth-conditional semantics*. New York: Academic Press.

WILSON, DEIRDRE and SPERBER, DAN (1986). Pragmatics and modularity. *Papers from the Regional Meeting of the Chicago Linguistic Society* 22.2: 68–74.

WILSON, DEIRDRE and SPERBER, DAN (1993). Linguistic form and relevance. *Lingua* 90: 1–25.

WILSON, DEIRDRE and SPERBER, DAN (2004). Relevance theory. In Horn, L. R. and Ward, G. (eds.) 607–32.

WITTGENSTEIN, LUDWIG (1953). *Philosophical investigations*. Oxford: Blackwell.

YULE, GEORGE (1996). *Pragmatics*. Oxford: Oxford University Press.

ZEITOUN, ELIZABETH (1997). The pronominal system of Mantauran (Rukai). *Oceanic Linguistics* 36: 114–48.

ZEYREK, DENIZ (2001). Politeness in Turkish and its linguistic manifestations: a socio-cultural perspective. In Bayraktaroglu, A. and Sifianou, M. (eds.) 43–74.

ZHU, HUA, LI, WEI, and QIAN, YUAN (2000). The sequential organisation of gift offering and acceptance in Chinese. *Journal of Pragmatics* 32: 81–103.

ZIFF, P. (1960). *Semantic analysis.* Ithaca, NY: Cornell University Press.

ZIPF, GEORGE K. (1949). *Human behavior and the principle of least effort: an introduction to human ecology.* Cambridge, MA: Addison-Wesley.

ZRIBI-HERTZ, ANNE (1989). Anaphor binding and narrative point of view: English reflexive pronouns in sentence and discourse. *Language* 65: 695–727.

ZRIBI-HERTZ, ANNE (1995). Emphatic or reflexive? On the endophoric character of French *lui-même* and similar complex pronouns. *Journal of Linguistics* 31: 333–74.

ZWICKY, ARNOLD M. (1974). Hey, whatsyaname! *Papers from the Regional Meeting of the Chicago Linguistic Society* 10: 787–801.

Suggested solutions
to exercises

Chapter 1

1. The propositional content of (i)–(viii) is THE SHOPKEEPER HAD REDUCED THE PRICES.
2. Entailment
   - (i) Yes
   - (ii) No
   - (iii) No
   - (iv) Yes
   - (v) Yes
   - (vi) No
   - (vii) Yes
   - (viii) No

Chapter 2

1. Violated maxim is the maxim of Relation.
2. Opted-out maxims
   - (i) Quality
   - (ii) Quantity
   - (iii) Relation
   - (iv) Manner
   - (v) Manner
   - (vi) Relation
   - (vii) Quantity
   - (viii) Quality
3. The conversational implicature Joe failed to work out is that there might be some honey in the beehive in the oak tree. It is a conversational implicature$_o$.
4. The conversational implicature of Mary's reply is that what John said is absurdly incorrect. This is a conversational implicature$_F$. The maxims of Quality and Relation are flouted. The conversational implicature of the clergyman's response is that he did not think that the person who spoke to him (i.e., Lord

Rutherford) was Lord Rutherford. This is also a conversational implicature$_F$. The maxims of Quality and Relation are also flouted.

5. The conversational implicature in question is that President Kennedy would stand by the people of West Berlin. The maxim of Quality is flouted.

6. Generalized versus particularized conversational implicature
   (a) is the generalized conversational implicature
   (b) is the particularized conversational implicature.

7. It is because of the Navajo taboo of not speaking the names of the dead, as pointed out by the author of the novel. The example is not a real counter example to Grice's first submaxim of Quality; what it shows is that this sub-maxim can be overridden by a sociolinguistic rule.

8. Q-implicatures and their types
   (i) The man Mary is chatting with is not her husband; Q-scalar implicature
   (ii) Baird might or might not invent television—the speaker doesn't know which; Q-clausal implicature
   (iii) They don't teach, for example, Chinese and English here as well; Q-unordered alternate implicature
   (iv) John does not love/adore Mary; Q-scalar implicature
   (v) Her uncle is not the president; Q-ordered alternate implicature
   (vi) The Smiths have not divorced; Q-ordered alternate implicature
   (vii) John will send it perhaps as an e-mail, or perhaps not as an e-mail; perhaps as an attachment, or perhaps not as an attachment; Q-clausal implicature
   (viii) Not most/all people enjoy a cappuccino with breakfast; Q-scalar implicature
   (ix) It isn't the case that none of her colleagues can speak Italian; some of them can; Q-scalar implicature

9. Q-implicatures
   (i) <... 9.6, 9.7, 9.8, 9.9>
       He can't run 100 m in less than 9.9 seconds
   (ii) <...8, 9, 10>
       He hasn't cut down his smoking to less than ten cigarettes a day

10. One or two Q- or Horn-scales
    No, it does not. In fact, the seven lexical items under consideration form two Q- or Horn-temperature scales: (i) <boiling, hot, warm> and (ii) <freezing, cold, cool, lukewarm>. Given that the *Concise Oxford Dictionary of Current English* defines *lukewarm* as 'moderately warm, tepid; not zealous, indifferent', why is it put in (ii) rather than (i)? The reason is that as pointed out in Horn (1989) and by Larry Horn (personal communication), *lukewarm* functions as a weaker version of *cool/cold/freezing* rather than of *warm/hot/boiling*. This can be shown by the contrastive behaviours of *lukewarm* using the following diagnostic tests.
    (i) a. The tea is not just lukewarm, but downright cool!
        b. Her greeting was lukewarm, if not downright chilly!
        c. The prime minister's reception was lukewarm, verging on cool.
    (ii) a. ?The tea is not just lukewarm, but downright warm!

b. ?Her greeting was lukewarm, if not downright friendly!

c. ?The prime minister's reception was lukewarm, verging on warm.

The reason why the seven lexical items do not form one Q- or Horn-scale is that they have two opposite orientations. The same is true of quantifiers such as *all, most, many, some, none, few,* and *not all.*

11. Metalinguistic versus descriptive negation
   (i)   Descriptive negation
   (ii) Metalinguistic negation
   (iii) Descriptive negation
   (iv) Metalinguistic negation
   (v)   Metalinguistic negation
   (vi) Descriptive negation
   (vii) Descriptive negation
   (viii) Metalinguistic negation
   (ix) Metalinguistic negation
   (x)   Metalinguistic negation
   (xi) Metalinguistic negation
   (xii) Metalinguistic negation

12. I-implicatures
   (i)   John is reading two modern European languages other than modern English at Oxford
   (ii) If and only if you let me see the manuscript will I make a donation to the library
   (iii) Mary ate the whole cake after dinner
   (iv) His female secretary talked learnedly about the internet
   (v)   The police first moved in and then the suspects were arrested, or
         The police moved in and thereby caused the suspects to be arrested, or
         The police moved in in order to arrest the suspects
   (vi) John and Mary scrubbed the carpet afresh together
   (vii) The speaker has no idea if John is in a sexual relationship

13. M-implicatures
   (i)   John went to a particular university or a particular university campus without doing the things (such as studying for a degree) that are socially stereotypically associated with the institution, as conventionally I-implicated by its corresponding (a) utterance. The same is true of *John went to church/the church, jail/the jail,* and *school/the school.*
   (ii) John didn't stop the alarm in the normal way
   (iii) Mary has a dress whose colour can't be described exactly as pink
   (iv) John had the ability to swim the English Channel, but he didn't, cf. the I-implicature of the (a) utterance, namely, John could swim the English Channel, and he did

(v) Their new boss is less friendly than what the uttering of the (a) sentence would suggest

(vi) That may not be his father; he could be his stepfather

14. Conventional implicatures

(i) John is going to finish his thesis

(ii) Although it is hard to believe, the two families live opposite each other

(iii) Others, besides his sister, belly-danced in a Lebanese restaurant two nights a week; and of those under consideration, his sister was among the least likely to do so, or

His sister is the least likely (in a contextually invoked set) to belly-dance in a Lebanese restaurant two nights a week

(iv) Someone other than Mike forgot to ring the client

(v) The VIPs' arrival is expected

(vi) Mary was born in London. By contrast, her husband was from Pakistan

(vii) It was difficult for John to complete his thesis on virtual reality technology

(viii) The addressee is socially superior to or distant from the speaker

Chapter 3

1. Presuppositions

(i) The burglar had been filmed on closed circuit television

(ii) John ought to have done, or intended to do, the washing up

(iii) John had an accident

(iv) Professor Huang had solved one of the evolution's great mysteries

(v) John was off cigarettes before

(vi) Someone moved to Spain

(vii) Susan's husband was having an affair

(viii) Mary wasn't emptying the shopping bags before

(ix) John doesn't know how to telnet

(x) Jane married before

(xi) John missed the interview

(xii) John's brother used all the printer paper

2. Presuppositions

(i) John wasn't a professional footballer

(ii) John read mathematics at Harvard

(iii) There are rabbits

(iv) John hadn't had a bath for more than three weeks

(v) Susan was wearing a fur coat

3. Presuppositions or not

(i) No. It is a conversational implicature.

(ii) Yes

(iii) Yes

(iv) No. It is a conventional implicature.

(v) No

(vi) No. It is an entailment.

(vii) No. It is a conventional implicature.

(viii) No. It is a conventional implicature.

4. Putative presuppositions and their cancellations

(i) Manchester United lost the game, cancelled by overt denial

(ii) Dr Smith was promoted to an associate professor, cancelled by real-world knowledge, namely that universities normally do not promote a person after he or she has left them. (Needless to say, what we are talking about here is a promotion within the same university where Dr Smith had been working for some time.)

(iii) Someone fancies Henry, cancelled by reduction arguments

(iv) Neil Armstrong was the first man to travel in space, cancelled by real-world knowledge, namely that Yuri Gagarin was the first man to travel in space

(v) The news was announced, cancelled by explicit suspension

(vi) He is the tsar of Russia, cancelled by overt denial

(vii) Cambridge wins the boat race, cancelled by the Q-clausal conversational implicature that Cambridge may not win the boat race

5. Entailment versus presuppositions under negation and in model contexts

If (i) is negated, as in (ii), or put in model contexts, as in (iii) and (iv), its entailment will not survive. (I use '$\sim \|$-' to stand for 'does not entail'.)

(i) The nursery teacher sold nine Christmas raffle tickets.

$\|$- The nursery teacher sold eight Christmas raffle tickets

(ii) The nursery teacher didn't sell nine Christmas raffle tickets.

$\sim \|$- The nursery teacher sold eight Christmas raffle tickets

(iii) It's possible/there's a chance that the nursery teacher sold nine Christmas raffle tickets.

$\sim \|$- The nursery teacher sold eight Christmas raffle tickets

(iv) The nursery teacher could/should/ought to sell nine Christmas raffle tickets

$\sim\|$- The nursery teacher sold eight Christmas raffle tickets

On the other hand, the presupposition will get through under the same circumstances. This is shown by (v) below and (3.33) and (3.34) in the text.

(v) The nursery teacher didn't sell nine Christmas raffle tickets.

>> There is a nursery teacher

On the basis of the above comparison, the conclusion we can draw is that there are at least some linguistic contexts in which entailments cannot survive but presuppositions can.

Chapter 4

1. Performatives versus constatives
    (i) constative
    (ii) performative
    (iii) constative
    (iv) performative
    (v) performative
    (vi) constative
    (vii) performative
2. Explicit versus implicit performatives
    (i) implicit
    (ii) implicit
    (iii) explicit
    (iv) implicit
    (v) implicit
    (vi) explicit
3. Performative verbs
    (i) Yes
    (ii) Yes
    (iii) Yes
    (iv) No
    (v) No
    (v) Yes
4. Performatively versus non-performatively
    (i) non-performatively
    (ii) performatively
    (iii) performatively
    (iv) non-performatively
    (v) performatively
    (vi) non-performatively
5. The Austinian felicity condition Diana violated is B (i). It is a misfire.
6. Locutionary, illocutionary, and perlocutionary acts
    (i) Locution: The mother uttered the words 'Give me that *Playboy* magazine' to her son, meaning 'Hand that *Playboy* magazine over to me', with *me* referring to the mother.
    Illocution: The mother requested (or ordered) her son to give her the *Playboy* magazine. Or the mother performed the speech act of requesting (or ordering) her son to give her the *Playboy* magazine.
    Perlocution: The mother persuaded her son to give her the *playboy* magazine. Or the son refused to give her mother the *Playboy* magazine.
    (ii) Locution: The dean's secretary uttered the word 'Coffee?' to the professor, meaning 'Would you like a coffee?'

Illocution: The dean's secretary offered a coffee to the Professor. Or the dean's secretary performed the speech act of offering a coffee to the professor.

Perlocution: The professor accepted the coffee from the dean's secretary with thanks. Or the professor declined the coffee from the dean's secretary with thanks.

7. Searlean felicity conditions
   (i) Questioning
      (i) Propositional content: any proposition or propositional function
      (ii) Preparatory: (a) S does not know the answer, i.e., for a yes/no question, he does not know whether p is true or false; for a WH-question, he does not know the missing information. (b) It is not obvious to both S and H that H will provide the information at that time without being asked
      (iii) Sincerity: S wants this information
      (iv) Essential: the utterance of e counts as an attempt to elicit this information from H

      where p stands for the proposition expressed in the speech act
   (ii) Thanking
      (i) Propositional content: past act A done by H
      (ii) Preparatory: S believes that A benefits S
      (iii) Sincerity: S feels grateful or appreciative for A
      (iv) Essential: the utterance of e counts as an expression of gratitude or appreciation
   (iii) Warning
      (i) Propositional content: future event or state, etc. E
      (ii) Preparatory: S has reason to believe that E will occur and that it is not in H's interest
      (iii) Sincerity: S believes that E is not in H's best interest
      (iv) Essential: the utterance of e counts as an undertaking that E is not in H's best interest

      where E stands for event.
8. Classification of speech acts
   (i) directive
   (ii) expressive
   (iii) directive
   (iv) commissive
   (v) declaration
   (vi) declaration
   (vii) representative
   (viii) expressive
9. Direct versus indirect speech acts
   (i) indirect
   (ii) direct
   (iii) indirect (No one cares!)
   (iv) indirect

(v) indirect

(vi) direct

10. FTA-avoiding strategies

    (i) Don't perform the FTA

    (ii) On record, with negative politeness redress

    (iii) Off record

    (iv) On record, without redress

    (v) On record, with positive politeness redress

Order of politeness, starting with the most polite: (i), (iii), (ii), (v), (iv)

11. Interlanguage compliment response

The main pragmatic error here is that the Chinese L2 learner of English uses self-denigration as the response to the foreign visitor's compliment. The typical response by a native speaker of English here would be acceptance/thanking. The error is largely the result of the influence of the typical compliment response formula in Chinese, as pointed out in the text.

Chapter 5

1. Used deictically, and if so, gesturally or symbolically?

    (i) Yes, symbolically

    (ii) Yes, gesturally

    (iii) Normally, no. *You* is used as impersonal here.

    (iv) Yes, gesturally

    (v) No. *He* is used anaphorically here.

    (vi) *There* is used both anaphorically and deictically in a symbolic way. *His* is used anaphorically.

2. Yiddish joke

The Hebrew teacher should have used 'my slippers' rather than 'your slippers'. He forgot the fact that in deixis, my 'I' is your 'you', my 'here' is your 'there', and my 'this' is your 'that'. This is also true of 'my', that is, his 'my slippers' is his wife's 'your slippers'.

3. Deictic projection

    (i) No

    (ii) Yes, the deictic centre has been projected to the next station.

    (iii) No

    (iv) Yes, the deictic centre has been shifted to New Zealand. So *next summer* is not next British summer but next New Zealand summer.

    (v) No

    (vi) Yes, the deictic centre has been projected on to the addressee.

4. Why (ii) is anomalous?

The *us* in *let's* has to be understood inclusively. This explains why (i) is OK but (ii) is anomalous. In (i), the speaker and the addressee can both go to the airport to collect a third person, whereas in (ii), the speaker and the addressee normally cannot both go to the airport where one of them already is.

5. Why is *we* used?
   (i) *We* is used here to show that the doctor has taken the perspective of the patient or identified him or her with the patient.
   (ii) This is known as the 'business' *we*. *We* is used here to indicate 'I + powerful', expressing both the *we* as office and the *we* of the group.
   (iii) *We* is used here to diminish the face-threatening act of ticket-inspecting, and thereby satisfy the face needs of the passenger.

6. Use of *here*
   (i) The region referred to is restricted to the speaker's place and excludes that of the addressee.
   (ii) The region referred to is of broad extent and includes both the speaker and the addressee(s).
   (iii) The place referred to is a small segment of the body of the speaker.
   (iv) The region referred to is a deferred place using a map in the common perceptual field of the interlocutors.

7. Deictically versus non-deictically
   (i) (a) Deictically
   (i) (b) Non-deictically
   (ii) (a) Non-deictically
   (ii) (b) Deictically

8. *Come* versus *go*
   (i) Since *go* designates movement away from the speaker's location at the time of speaking, and the use of *there* indicates that the location it encodes will be away from the speaker, both readings of *we* are possible.
   (ii) Given that one of the conditions for the use of *come* is movement towards the addressee's location at arrival time, and *there* establishes that one of the interlocutors, namely, the addressee will be away from the speaker at arrival time, the addressee is excluded from *we*.

9. Deictic expressions and their types
   (i) I (person), here (space), there (space)
   (ii) Good morning (time), ladies and gentlemen (person, social), this (space)
   (iii) We (person), this year (time), that (discourse)
   (iv) I (person), came (space), you (person), last week (time), there (space)
   (v) Good afternoon (time), Sir (person, social), I (person), you (person)

Chapter 6

1. Explicatures
   (i) The speaker has visited the Great Wall in China at some point in his life
   (ii) The thieves have stolen everything that is valuable

(iii) Much of the Walled Garden at the Botanic Garden is made up of approximately rectangular botanical family borders

(iv) e.g., The oven is hot enough for cooking the lamb moussaka

(v) e.g., Jane has found a small burrowing insectivore

(vi) e.g., Nobody in our class understood the professor's talk on genetic engineering

(vii) The building collapsed a relatively long time after the bomb went off

(viii) The explicature of this sentence uttered is that the lexical concept, encoded by *heart* underwent an *ad hoc* adjustment involving both broadening (i.e., to include 'heart' that is made of chocolate) and narrowing (i.e., to exclude 'heart' that is a human or animal organ).

(ix) e.g., John told Steve that John had won the prize

(x) The speaker hasn't shaved this morning

(xi) There was an Italian waiter in the pizza restaurant they went to

(xii) e.g., The children are coming from a small town in Russia

2. Higher-order explicatures

(i) The speaker tells (the addressee) frankly that she doesn't fancy him (who is not the addressee)

(ii) a. The father is telling his son to pick up the books which are on the floor

b. It is moderately desirable to the father (and achievable) that his son pick up the books which are on the floor

c. The father is requesting his son to pick up the books which are on the floor

(iii) a. The speaker believes that their European patent has been granted

b. The speaker is glad that their European patent has been granted

(iv) a. John is telling his wife that he will not drink heavily any more

b. John's wife prefers his not drinking heavily any more

c. John is promising his wife that he will not drink heavily any more

3. Implicated premises and conclusions

(i) Implicated premise

The Last Emperor directed by Bernardo Bertolucci is a period epic

Implicated conclusion

Mary does not want to go and watch *The Last Emperor*

(ii) Implicated premise

If the kitchen is closed, dinner will not be served

Implicated conclusion

The guest is too late for dinner

(iii) Implicated premise

If one's paper is one of the best submitted to a conference, it will be accepted for presentation at that conference

Implicated conclusion

Steve's paper has been accepted for presentation at the conference

(iv) Implicated premise

If Lucy has been paying a lot of visits to London lately, she may have a boyfriend there

Implicated conclusion
Lucy may have a boyfriend in London these days
(v) Implicated premise
If it's snowing heavily outside, it's not possible to play football
Implicated conclusion
John (and Mary) can't play football outside
(vi) Implicated premise
Chinese supermarkets normally sell soy sauce
Implicated conclusion
John can buy soy sauce in the small Chinese supermarket just around the corner

4. Strong and weak implicatures
Strong implicatures:
Implicated premise
A vegetarian does not eat any beef or pork
Implicated conclusion
Mary will not have any beef or pork
Weak implicatures: e.g.,
Implicated premise
A vegetarian does not eat any lamb
Implicated conclusion
Mary will not have any lamb
Implicated premise
People who are vegetarians are also environmentalists
Implicated conclusion
Mary is an environmentalist

Chapter 7

1. Saturation/completion, free enrichment/expansion, semantic transfer, loosening
   (i) I haven't been to Australia before (free enrichment/expansion)
   (ii) Christmas is a considerable time away (free enrichment)
   (iii) Mary isn't slim enough to be a model (saturation/completion)
   (iv) Roughly speaking, the tram is full (loosening, expansion)
   (v) In all probability John is going to marry the woman who has a pretty face (semantic transfer)
   (vi) The university campus is a considerable distance from the rail station (free enrichment)
   (vii) Peter and Susan drove to LA together (expansion). Their car broke down roughly half way (expansion)
   (viii) This laptop is cheaper than that one (saturation/completion)

(ix) A book written by Confucius is on the top shelf. It is bound in leather (semantic transfer)

(x) She's a real beauty with high-functioning brains (free enrichment)

(xi) The children stood in an approximate circle around the Christmas tree (loosening, expansion)

(xii) The semantics/pragmatics conference starts at nine or a few minutes later (expansion)

(xiii) Susan lost everything that is valuable (free enrichment/expansion)

(xiv) People say that he owns a painting by van Gogh (semantic transfer)

2. Pragmatic intrusion and type of conversational implicature

(i) Yes. M-implicature

(ii) Yes. Q-$_{scalar}$ implicature

(iii) Yes. I-implicature

(iv) Yes. M-implicature

(v) Yes. I-implicature

(vi) yes. M-implicature

(vii) Yes. Q-$_{scalar}$ implicature

Chapter 8

1. Binding condition A pattern

(i) Yes

(ii) No. *Seg* in Norwegian is an anaphor in the Chomskyan sense. As such, it should be able to be bound within its local domain, given binding condition A. But this is not the case.

(iii) Yes

(iv) No. *Aaplyaa-laa* in Marathi is bound in a long-distance way outside its local domain, which is the embedded clause.

(v) Yes

(vi) No. *Sig* in Icelandic is bound in a long-distance way outside its local domain, which is the embedded clause.

2. Binding condition A pattern (c-command)

(i) Yes

(ii) Yes

(iii) No. Here *Xiaoming* does not c-command *ziji* (self).

(iv) No. The same is true of *John* and *himself*.

(v) Yes

(vi) No. In this Icelandic example, *Siggu* does not c-command *sig* (self).

3. Binding condition C_1 or C_2 pattern

(i) Yes

(ii) Yes

(iii) Yes, if binding condition C_1 is allowed to be subject to parametric variation with regard to Vietnamese; otherwise, no.

(iv) Yes

(v) No. Given Lasnik's binding condition C_2, *he* and *David* must be free. But they are bound or co-indexed.

(vi) Yes

4. Predicate meaning/reflexivizing strategy correlation

   (i) In the (a) sentence, since 'wash' is used here as a reflexive- or self-directed predicate, the use of the morphologically simplex *zich* (self) is enough. By contrast, in the (b) sentence, 'admire' is an other-directed predicate. Consequently, the more marked, morphologically complex *zichzelf* (self self) has to be used.

   (ii) 'Wash' is a reflexive- or self-directed predicate in Turkish. When it is reflexive-marked, a simple emphatic marker is used, as in (a'). By comparison, 'beat' is an other-directed predicate. When it is reflexive-marked, the more complex 'self self' has to be employed, as in (b').

5. Possessive anaphora

   (i) This is a case of 'pronoun only' possessive anaphora. The preferred coreferential interpretation between 'Asad' and 'his' is due to the I-principle.

   (ii) This is a case of 'reflexive only' possessive anaphora. The coreferential interpretation between 'Roja' and 'self's' is due to the I-principle. The disjoint in reference reading is due to the Q-principle (<self's, his>).

   (iii) This is a case of 'both reflexive and pronoun' possessive anaphora. The coreferential interpretation between 'Rama' and 'self's' and the preferred coreferential interpretation between 'Rama' and 'his' are due to the I-principle. The emphatic reading arising from the use of 'self's' is due to the M-principle ({his, self's}).

6. Neo-Gricean pragmatic analyses of anaphoric patterns

   (i) The coreferential interpretation is due to the I-principle. A less radical alternative is to say that this interpretation is due to binding condition A.

   (ii) The disjoint in reference interpretation is due to the Q-principle (<himself, him>) and the RDRP.

   (iii) The same as in (ii). (<herself, Kylie>)

   (iv) The disjoint in reference interpretation between *Kylie* and *her* is due to the Q-principle (<herself, her>), as is the disjoint in reference reading between *she* and *her* (<herself, her>). The preferred coreferential interpretation between *Kylie* and *she* is due to the I-principle.

   (v) The same as in (iv), except that the disjoint in reference interpretation between *Kylie* and *the woman* is due to the M-principle ({she, the woman}).

   (vi) The coreferential interpretation is due to the I-principle.

   (vii) The same as in (vi). In addition, the use of *the president* is subject to the M-principle ({he, the president}), which engenders the M-implicated difference between a man and his office.

(viii) The coreferential interpretation between *Lee* and *caki* (self) is due to the I-principle, as is the preferred coreferential interpretation between *Lee* and *ku*. The use of the marked *caki* is subject to the M-principle ({ku, caki}), which gives rise to the logophoricity reading.

Index of names

Index of languages, language families, and language areas

This index includes all the individual languages, larger genetic groupings of languages, and larger non-genetic, geographic groupings of languages referred to in the book.

Index of subjects